INTERNATIONAL ORDER AND ECONOMIC INTEGRATION

WILHELM RÖPKE

INTERNATIONAL ORDER AND
ECONOMIC INTEGRATION

D. REIDEL PUBLISHING COMPANY / DORDRECHT-HOLLAND

INTERNATIONALE ORDNUNG – HEUTE

First published by Eugen Rentsch Verlag AG
Erlenbach – Zürich, Switzerland

Translated by Gwen E. Trinks, Joyce Taylor and Cicely Käufer

Printed in the Netherlands by D. Reidel, Dordrecht

TABLE OF CONTENTS

PREFACE TO THE ENGLISH LANGUAGE EDITION

The present book which has now the honour of being published in an English translation has been written almost six years ago. It would be futile to hope that, in a time of rapid change like ours, it would still correspond to actual conditions in every detail. Since, however, it is meant to be a book whose principal aim it is to draw attention to the essential problems of international order and the fundamentals involved and since those can hardly be said to have seriously changed within the last years, I venture to submit that it may still be useful as a guide through the maze of questions in the field of international economic relations. This, I hope, will prove particularly true with regard to the special problems which have been raised by the recent important events in Europe, i.e. by the organization of the European Economic Community and the European Free Trade Association and by the new system of convertible currencies which has taken the place of the European Payments Union since the beginning of 1959. The reader will have little difficulty to understand the critical attitude which I have taken *vis-à-vis* the European Economic Community and which I have explained at greater length in some recent publications (a.o. *Gemeinsamer Markt und Freihandelszone*, Ordo Jahrbuch für die Ordnung von Wirtschaft und Gesellschaft vol. X, 1958, pp. 31–62; *Zwischenbilanz der europäischen Wirtschaftsintegration*, ibidem, vol. XI, 1959, pp. 69–94). One of these articles, entitled '*European Free Trade – the Great Divide* and published in the September 1958 issue of 'The Banker' has been inserted in this book as an epilogue.

There is another event which has occurred since the German publication of this book and which also is of primary importance on the international scene. I refer to the dramatic change of the USA balance of payments from a surplus to a deficit which is tantamount to a change from a 'dollar shortage' to a 'dollar abundance'. But here again the reader will understand why the author has not precisely taken by surprise, and he will find, after having read this book, no difficulty to understand what has happened and why it has happened. Since the author has never believed in the 'dollar scarcity' as an Act of God he has nothing to retract from what he has said six years ago on this subject – as on many others.

WILHELM RÖPKE

Graduate Institute of International Studies
Geneva

February 1960

PART ONE

A SURVEY OF THE PROBLEM

I

THE INTERNATIONAL CRISIS

NATURE OF THE INTERNATIONAL CRISIS

The author of this book belongs to the generation which in its youth saw the sunset glow of that long and glorious sunny day of the western world, which lasted from the Congress of Vienna until August 1914, and of which those who have only lived in the present arctic night of history can have no adequate conception. His experience has therefore been similar to that of so many of his contemporaries in all those countries which were drawn into the whirlpool of the first world war. Like other Germans, Englishmen, Frenchmen and Belgians he knew as a young man the horrors of the gigantic battles on the plains of France. This experience became a determinant factor for the rest of his life as it did for his contemporaries. At the most impressionable age for such influences, he received a shock which suddenly caused him to see many things which his upbringing had up to then kept hidden from him. Never again were the pictures of those days to forsake him, nor the ideas which from that time on made him a fervent hater of war, of brutal and stupid national pride, of the greed for domination and of every collective outrage against ethics. He made a solemn promise, that if he should escape from that inferno, the main purpose of his life from then on could only consist in his devoting himself to the task of helping to prevent a recurrence of this disaster, and in reaching out beyond the narrow confines of his own nation to join forces with all other fellow-workers in the same cause. Thousands and thousands of his contemporaries and fellow-sufferers within and beyond the frontiers of his country had come to the same conclusion.

At the time, therefore, when he was growing out of childhood into maturity, the author came face to face with that terrible crisis in the history of human society which the first world war signified. This it was that determined him to take up the study of economics and sociology, in order to be able to understand the causes of this crisis and then to help to overcome them. When he looks back today over the twenty-five years which have passed since then, twenty-five years in which he has lived through two revolutions, the greatest inflation of all times, the mental ferment and social upheaval of his country, and finally the exile which took him, the scholar, to many universities of the old world and the new, he realizes that, consciously or unconsciously, he has always been pursued by the battlefields of Picardy. The crisis of international relationships and the necessity of sorting them out have, first and foremost, always been the primary motives of his studies and the incentive to his work.

The author knows that for many of his friends, who at that time faced each other in opposite camps under the obligation to kill, the shock was equally great, and the effect the same as that which continues to move him today. We also resemble one another in that since then our thoughts have gone through the same phases of development. Under the impact of the first shock our impressions were stronger than our reason. We contented ourselves with the argument that a society which was capable of such hideous deterioration must be rotten through and through, and since what we had learnt sufficed for us to give this society the name of 'Capitalism', and to understand by this term all that we rightly considered worthy of damnation, we became Socialists.

For a young German of that time this was a very obvious step, since all the political groups, with the single exception of the Socialists, had become supporters of the political system represented by Prussia. If one wished to give a radical form to the protest against this system, which we in our youthful enthusiasm felt challenged to make, then the natural course was to become a Socialist. Probably modern Socialism as a mass movement can never be completely understood unless one considers that it is to a very large extent the product of the particular political development which took place in Germany during the 19th century, after the genuine liberal and democratic forces which came to the surface for the last time in the ill-fated revolution of 1848 had been throttled by Bismarck. The more the German bourgeoisie accepted Bismarck and his State, the more did Social Democracy become the only collecting ground, not for the social revolutionaries alone, but also for those to whom the social revolution was entirely secondary in importance, and the political revolution the main object. Only very few people actually had any idea how much Prussianism lay hidden in this very Socialism, since as long as it

4

was only a persecuted opposition party far removed from all responsibility, the Socialist leaders succeeded in concealing the hopeless inner contradictions of their doctrine from the mass of the people.

The train of reasoning which we formulated in the trenches of the first world war was, as I have said, very simple. This war, we said to ourselves, is a declaration of bankruptcy on the part of the entire 'system'. Protest against Imperialism, Militarism and Nationalism was for us synonymous with the protest against the ruling political and economic system, that is, against Feudalism and Capitalism. Once this Negative was established, the Positive likewise emerged under the name of Socialism. We were, it is true, not quite clear as to how we pictured this in detail, and those from whom clarity was to be expected did not really seem to know either. But this did not deter us, it only spurred us on to search for ourselves.

And search we did. But what we found after years of confusion was something quite different. We discovered that our premises had been entirely false and had led us astray. This realization came bit by bit, for one in the shape of scientific study, while for another it emerged at the same time through practical experience of every kind. Since our unchangeable premise had been the protest against war and nationalism, it was for us as economists a matter of course that we should profess Liberalism with regard to international trade and become Free-Traders. On this point we were determined not to yield and we have kept this promise. No unusual perception was necessary, however, to make us realize that on this question an unbridgeable gulf yawned between Socialism and international economic Liberalism, which could not be done away with simply by mere professions of Free Trade from certain Socialists. Nobody believed in World Socialism. If, however, Socialism was only going to be achieved on a national scale, did not this imply that the national frontiers would then acquire a quite new and specifically economic significance? Was it not a question of simple logic, that a Socialist state, which controlled the economic life of the nation at home, could not even concede the same freedom to foreign trade it had still retained under the previous régime of mere tariff protection, which we had attacked. This argument was then everywhere confirmed where the Socialists were to be seen in power. Our conclusion was that there could only be one single form of Socialism, namely the national form. But with this we refused to have anything to do.

5

Other considerations were added. After we had reflected on the causes of the world war and had recognized the extent to which our own government had been guilty, we realized with horror the paramount force of the modern state and also the influence of single pressure groups within the nation. Both had exposed themselves ostensibly during the war. The passionate conclusion which we drew from this was that the power of the State must be limited and influential power groups must be suppressed. At first it seemed that these were also essential points of a Socialist party programme. Only gradually, and not without the help of the great liberal thinkers, did we realise that the ideas involved here are essentially liberal ones which we in our inexperience had held to be Socialist, because as long as they themselves were not in power the Socialists could afford to go on making use of them. Does not Socialism mean increasing the power of the State to the utmost? And was there the slightest guarantee that this power would come into the hands of the wisest and most suitable persons, even supposing we were prepared to tolerate the best and most enlightened form of despotism? To combat irresponsible pressure groups, monopolies and cliques representing private interests also seemed to be the genuine solution offered by the Socialists. But had it not become evident after the war that everywhere where Socialism had gained an influence on the government, what was termed 'nationalisation' or 'planned economy' had really only proved to be a strengthening of these pressure groups? Should Socialism acquire sole power after the pattern of Russia, would not the concentration of power in one single hand be a thousand times worse than the former coexistence of numerous individual, albeit intolerable, constellations of power?

As soldiers too we had learnt what it meant to be crammed for years into a machine in which the individual had no other life than that of the mass, a life determined by force, unconditional obedience and constraint. Even outside the army the war brought with it a hitherto unknown degree of restriction upon elementary freedoms. Waging war did not only mean killing and being killed, inconceivable hardships, mud, vermin, hunger, thirst and disease, destroying, lying and hating; it also meant militarism, giving and obeying orders, the unchaining of brutal thirst for power, the triumph of unbridled ambition, the exploitation of uncontrollable positions of power, the degradation of the human being, mass existence, by day and night, mass feeding, spiritual stagnation, restriction of the

6

most primary freedoms. It meant never being alone, never being one's own master, never to think or to question. Only when we look back today are we able to recollect that this life also had its compensations. The idea that prevailed with us at that time, however, was that such an existence was unworthy of a human being and could only be tolerated in the light of higher aims and the feeling of fulfillment of duty. We might safely have been termed anti-militarists, we were seized with an indescribable craving for the simple human quality of civilian life, a craving which made every leave a foretaste of Paradise. The fact that in all these matters no difference existed between us and our workingclass comrades refutes the cheap suggestion that then as now we were lamenting the loss of a liberty of which the working-class had long been deprived. Leave – that is to say a temporary return to the elementary freedom of civilian life – meant just as much to the worker as to the student, so that we are speaking today not only for ourselves, but also in the name of the working-class, when we denounce the slavery of a collectivist, i.e. a militarised, economic and social system.

It was the war, therefore, that taught us the meaning of freedom in the most elementary sense of the word, and so made anti-militarists of us. Here too it was in keeping with our general thoughtlessness when we gave expression to our protest by adopting Socialism. Only gradually did the realization mature in us that we had chosen a social ideal whose very existence must consist in perpetuating militarisation.

If we examined ourselves rightly, our revolt against war amounted actually to a passionate protest against the intolerable domination of the State. This was the sinister, intangible authority, impervious to ethical standards, which had led us into war, and which now continued to cause us suffering by cowing us and lying to us at the same time. War was simply the State run riot, collectivity let loose. It was what happened when the few had too much power over others and were able to make them dance like puppets. Was it therefore not absurd to clothe this protest against the domination of man over man in the shape of a profession of collectivism? Be they ever so honest, what can all the professions of pacifism, antimilitarism, humanism, or demands for freedom on the part of the Socialists avail against the fact that Socialism, if it is to have any meaning at all, must make a leviathan of the State, not only for the emergency times of war, but for an incalculable period? Would that not

7

mean increasing the abuse of political power both at home and abroad to an infinite degree? And was it not making an unreasonable demand upon our credulity to expect that just such a State should free us from militarism, imperialism, war, thirst for power and authority, mass existence, command and slavery? Would not all that become worse? Or did the Socialists not really mean it seriously with their collectivism? In that case they ought to be told that they were playing with fire, in trying to swell their ranks with a propaganda that proclaimed aims which only the most radical were prepared to carry into effect, but which in principle were rejected by the more prudent.

This marked out for us the path to be taken, and for over twenty-five years we have followed it stage by stage. Often enough have we gone astray and had difficulty in finding our direction again. The path led us first and foremost into a bitter struggle against war-mindedness, nationalism, machiavellism and international anarchy, and consequently against all groups, powers and influences which opposed us in this struggle. In economic policy it implied combatting the irresponsible pressure groups of the monopolies, heavy industry and the big landowners, as well as the inexcusable inflation, obscured by those responsible with untenable theories, against every firm of economic nationalism, against the errors of tariff protection, and finally against the absolute madness of self-sufficiency. We fought in favour of a reuniting the broken links of international trade and for a normalisation of international monetary and credit relationships, and charged ourselves with reducing certain speciously expedient theories as to the effects of German Reparations to their right proportions, without caring very much whether we would be called unpatriotic for doing so. We were on the side of those whose aim was to achieve the peaceful re-integration of the conquered countries in a democratic and liberal world, and when the great world depression developed in 1929, we did all we could to advise the governments against an economic policy which ended in a cul-de-sac of deflation and autarchy, instead of seeking by international co-operation to restore confidence and revive the stagnating circulation. With horror, and without any illusions as to the terrible danger which was gathering, we observed the rising tide of political radicalism and nihilism, and to the very last sought to uphold reason against hysteria. When the dam broke we did not hesitate to sacrifice our homes, our positions and our security to our unshakeable convictions, and, despite all enticements, to accept the bitter fate of the emigrant.

Such has been the life of those among whom the author of this book counts himself, and it may be said that this path has been the thorniest and most difficult imaginable. From time to time the changing circumstances resulted in temporary alliances with certain large groups, but in the long run it was our fate to be really understood by only very few, until the world catastrophe brought us at least the one hope that we should all at once gain a hearing.

From the very beginning the difficulty was – to express it in sharp paradox – that we agreed with the Socialists in rejecting Capitalism and with the followers of Capitalism in rejecting Socialism. We began with the first rejection in the trenches, where we learnt to hate every form of repression, abasement and exploitation of mankind; we learnt the second form of rejection later, when experience and reflection taught us the true nature of Socialism. It seemed to us that Capitalism and Socialism were each right in a certain way and wrong in another way. Everything depended upon discovering in what way to achieve the best combination of what was right on both sides. The natural result was that we continually sought for the solution which later, as its outlines became more clearly defined, came to be known as 'the third way' or 'economic humanism'.

The beginning of this mental evolution therefore was the psychological shock to my generation from the catastrophe which afflicted the nations of the world in the first war. It was the international character of this which opened our eyes for the first time to the general crisis in our society. The line which finally led to the 'third way' and the 'civitas humana' had its starting point in the shell holes of the battlefields, then took its course through the monstrous upheavals of the revolution, the inflation, deceptive prosperity, mass unemployment, civil war, exile and finally the second world war, which the author was able to spend upon an island in the midst of the European tornado, which, although constantly threatened, was constantly spared. It was therefore possible for him, in the midst of the general agitation, to collect and formulate his ideas. The path has meant living and experiencing and not, as the literary disposed critic whose life has been less disturbed might imagine, a retreat to books and learned hair-splitting.

If then the international aspect of the crisis in human society of today has played such a dominant part in the life and thoughts of the author, and is of greater importance to him than anything else, how is it that the account of it forms the end rather than the beginning, and that this book on 'International Order' comes after the others on 'Die Gesellschafts-krisis der Gegenwart' and 'Civitas humana?' The answer is not a matter of chance, but is more deep-seated. This apparent contradiction in the order in which these books have appeared reflects a particular conception of the actual nature of the international crisis, it implies a distinct theory regarding the causes of the same, and regarding the ways which point to a new international order. This theory is at heart nothing but a new variation of the proverb 'charity begins at home'. Let me try to explain in a few words what is meant by this.

The international aspect of the social crisis attracts attention to itself to a specially high degree. It constitutes a particular danger and challenge, and since international relationships are always the most susceptible spot of human society as a whole, any disintegration here becomes apparent not only very early on, but also in its most aggravated form. International relationships are a screen upon which the evidences of internal social dissolution are magnified and thus become visible, long before they come to the surface inside the countries themselves. Reckless-ness, lack of chivalry, departure from standards, despotism and social disruption here find their first and easiest victims, and, as is shown by the example of the totalitarian states, it is even possible to postpone for a while the entire break-down of the nation, by diverting the forces of destruction to outward agression.

Under these conditions the temptation at the beginning was great to consider and to fight the international crisis as an isolated factor, as a regrettable aberration among a community of nations which in other respects was fairly healthy. The causes of the political and economic disintegration of the nations were sought for in the narrow field of inter-national relationships alone, in the failure of international organizations, in unsolved diplomatic problems, in the lack of mutual understanding, in the effects of international indebtedness, or simply in exaggerated protectionism or the mistakes of national monetary policies. The cure for the evil was consequently conceived to be the combatting of these supposed causes: by amending the Statute of the League of Nations, by holding disarmament and world economic conferences, by revising debts, by 'peaceful change', by co-operation between the central banks, by all kinds of pacts and conventions, by repetition of the incontrovertible arguments in favour of free trade, by projects for economic unions and federations of all kinds.

Each of us knows this phase very well because each has gone through it himself. Sooner or later, however, came the inevitable conclusion that we had only been applying symptomatic therapy. We had been behaving like a doctor who had diagnosed as a whitlow what in reality was a syphilitic ulcer. This discovery was not only a terrible one, but also made us impatient towards those who cling to the old diagnosis and its corresponding therapy, and who would not grasp how deep and organic the cause of the evil was. For a decade we fought in vain to arouse people's imagination and to make the knowledge common property that the international crisis is only a part of the general social crisis, and must be understood from within and from beneath. The uselessness of these efforts in the small field of learning and science only reflects the general fateful course of events into which we were allowed to drift up to August 1939. As we shall presently see, we are today still very far from drawing all the conclusions from the realization although today no one can any longer turn a blind eye to it.

An economist, who since his youth has held the international crisis which for the second time has culminated in a ghastly world war and threatens to rush into a still more ghastly third one, as the most serious evil of his age, and who has devoted the greater part of his studies to international questions, must of necessity make a wide detour if he can hope at all to attain his goal. Once it was clear that the international crisis was only one large abcess on the entirely decayed body of society, it could only be properly assessed if the social crisis itself had been understood beforehand and traced back to its deepest causes. And only from this point of view could a cure be undertaken which really gave promise of success. Still better, only then could inner and outer crises be grasped and combatted as a single unit. That was the conclusion which had been forcing itself upon us for a long time and which today has become plainly evident. Whatever reform is to be applied it must everywhere take into consideration the comprehensive and fundamental character of the social crisis.

FALSE AND TRUE INTERNATIONALISM

The nature of the international crisis does not only explain the fact that this treatise forms the last instead of the first of the trilogy, but also something else which is not just to be taken for granted. Questions of international political organization which are being discussed everywhere today will not be given the same place in these chapters which many others would accord to them. Actually very little will be said about the constitution to be given to the international system of states after this war, or how the various states are to be grouped and what powers should be accorded to the new international organization. I hope it is not necessary expressly to assure any man of good will that this is not due to a disparagement of these equally difficult and important questions. There are other reasons for this, the mention of which introduces us at once to the real character of the international problems.

In spite of the overall nature of the world crisis it is unavoidable that each should approach it in the light of his own particular profession or temperament. The economist will emphasize other aspects than the lawyer, the theologian or the philosopher. No one need hold this against another, rather should each regard himself as a lowly worker at a gigantic task which surpasses the power of the individual: and should take care to avoid any doctrinaire exclusiveness. The more our ideas allow room for those of others the better it is, provided that this does not involve an unbridgeable difference in basic principles which it would be dishonest to disguise. Each should approach the common task from the side with which he himself is most familiar. This is the first reason why in this book less space has been given to questions of international law and international political organization than to those of sociology and economy, and why no new plan for a community of nations is to be found here.

The second reason lies deeper and brings us back to the nature of the international crisis as we see it. It is nothing less than the conviction that a one-sided emphasis upon the legal and organizational side of international inter-relations fails to do justice to the deep and comprehensive nature of the international crisis, and involves serious dangers, including the most serious of all, namely that by a mere symptomatic treatment the actual evil can be still more aggravated. In order to avoid any confusion let the following be said: there is no debating the fact that a new and

12

strong international organization must be created which must learn from the mistakes of the old League of Nations; that all countries, or at least those primarily concerned, must always be determined and able to curb disturbers of the peace and aggressors; that not enough legal acumen and political good will can be applied to improving the constitutional framework of international interrelations; that everything possible must be done to cultivate a satisfactory international code of ethics, to develop among the civilized nations a genuine public opinion capable of standing up to the pernicious philosophies of Machiavellism and imperialism; that a will to peace and a horror of war must be as firmly planted in the mind of civilized man from his childhood as is the love of his own country and the determination to defend it against every aggressor; that Europe in particular must evolve a form of federal union which shall not only put an end to the internecine wars of this old continent, but which shall above all make it capable of holding its own against the assault of the Communist Russian imperium. All these are urgent necessities. And all the same we have the impression that this alone will not suffice, indeed it is perhaps not even the most essential.

What can all these things avail, what can the finest plans for an international order avail if the soul of each individual is disordered, if the political, economic and social structure of the individual nations does not fulfill the pre-requisites for an international order, in short, if the moral, intellectual, political, economic and social disorder in our society is not righted throughout its entire structure, beginning with the individual, and including the family, our fellow-workers, the local community and the whole nation? Is it not starting to build the house with the roof if we subscribe to a falsely understood 'internationalism', and should not the foundations come first? What can be expected from international conferences and conventions under such circumstances? Is it not the same old paper-rustling and clap-trap that the world has grown sick of during the last two decades? Is there not a chance of international conferences and organizations only developing into new sources of dissension instead of harmony for the nations as long as the latter are not sound within, and before their ethical and mental state, as well as their political and economic constitutions, have become mature enough for a far-sighted and generous universalism? What can all the disarmament conferences avail – whether political, military, intellectual or

13

economic – if everything else is not prepared for such disarmament? If this preparedness does not exist, however, what in the world can be hoped for from a conference?

As is so often the case, the most direct way here is the longest one, and the patient approach by a long detour the shortest. Like Edith Cavell, the English heroine of the first world war, who spoke the noble words, 'Patriotism is not enough', we are entitled to say, 'Internationalism is not enough'. Indeed we may further assert that a fundamental error exists which may be termed *false internationalism*, which term refers to the wrong tendencies which we have censured.

It would be well to illustrate this by a concrete example. One of the most important demands upon an international order today is that a genuine world economic system should exist, which would meet with as little obstruction as possible from the economic policies of the individual states. The closest approach to this ideal was made at the time when people really believed in it and tried to carry it out in their separate countries by means of a liberal economic policy. They have increasingly distanced themselves from this ideal, as those responsible for economic policy in the individual countries have turned from the principles of economic liberalism and adopted the philosophy of economic stateism and collectivism, as selfish pressure groups have, in the course of this changeover, gained the upper hand and allied themselves with economic nationalism, as monopolies made headway and the increase of state intervention in the economy deprived the individual countries of the adaptability which is a prerequisite for a genuine economic community of nations, as the most elementary precepts of economy were set aside as out-of-date or were just forgotten, and a very noxious and short-sighted national egoism led to lack of consideration, narrow-mindedness and disregard of the rules of civilized intercourse. All these forces resulted in the complete breakdown of the world economic system in the period between the two world wars. But the same period introduced the phenomenon that one international economic conference followed the other and that more oratory than seldom before was devoted to the necessity of international economic co-operation. It is no exaggeration to say that the era of decay of the world economy was at the same time the era of international economic conferences. Their minutes and documents fill the archives while the practical results amount to nothing. This failure

14

was just as unavoidable as that of the disarmament conferences, as long as the conditions for success were not fulfilled on the national level. Had they been fulfilled, however, it is questionable whether an international conference would have been necessary at all. This conferencitis, with its inaction and illusions, its waste of time, money and talent, is, however, more rampant than ever today.

There is yet another particular reason why the efforts to arrest the decay of the world economy by means of international negotiations and conventions failed miserably at that time. Since it had become customary to despise the basic precepts of economics, delegates met at the conference tables with the pernicious idea that the import of goods was to be compared with a flood or an invasion. Slogans from the world of military thought, with which the advocates of economic nationalism have always sought to boom their dubious doctrines, had brought confusion everywhere. The primitive notion was far too prevalent, that in foreign trade the interests of the individual national economies stood opposed to each other like two enemy armies, and that every trade concession was a sacrifice to foreigners at the expense of the entire national economy, a sacrifice which one was only prepared to make under extreme pressure and for equivalent returns. It had been forgotten that in reality the opposing fronts run in a quite different direction and that in a question of trade policy the interests of the home producers who are in favour of a protective tariff are opposed to the joint interests both of the consumers and of all the other producers of every nation. The alleged international front is thus in reality a home front and every trade concession is not a sacrifice which the entire nation is forced to make in favour of the foreigner, but one which the special group of protection seekers is forced to concede to the rest of the nation. That this actual conflict of interests which cuts through the middle of the nation is disguised as a conflict between home and abroad is only a superficial phenomenon which accounts for the fact that the naive identification of protectionist group interests with the interests of the nation as a whole by means of an appeal to patriotism succeeds with the broad mass of the people. If one realizes that the international division of labour works exactly like a machine in raising the productivity of human labour, then one cannot fail to perceive the true state of affairs.

The case of world economy, therefore, demonstrates very impressively that *a good order on the national level is required to assure a working order also on the international level.* The same applies to a smoothly working system of international payments, without which it is impossible to conceive of a real world economy. Here too in the much-abused age of Liberalism the civilized world set up a truly international monetary system, without requiring a single conference or convention for the purpose. The gold standard – which is what I am referring to – seems, at a superficial glance, to be based upon a certain technique, but its real basis is the readiness of each single government, following deeply-rooted economic, political and moral convictions, conscientiously to obey the rules which this international standard imposes upon every single country. These rules are fundamentally the same as demanded by every international monetary system, whatever its nature be; their essential point is that each country should behave in matters of monetary policy as if a universal monetary standard really existed. The gold standard broke down because the readiness to observe its rules disappeared, and a generally-accepted monetary internationalism gave place to a very deliberate and inconsiderate monetary nationalism. What opinion is one to have of the efforts made at conferences of all kinds to establish an international monetary system on the basis of an agreement to be concluded by the countries participating, but not, like the gold standard, on the basis of harmonious interplay of the national currency systems. An international monetary system which is worthy of the name can only be successful if the same conditions are fulfilled upon which the gold standard is dependent: national order in the fields of public money and credit, flexibility of prices and costs, a minimum of freedom in foreign trade and a solid body of convictions and opinions by which it is backed. If these conditions are not fulfilled an international monetary union will be in vain. Should they be fulfilled, however, it is open to question whether the machinery of an international monetary organization would be at all necessary, and whether a new gold standard, with certain improvements which will be discussed later, would not function at least equally well.

If we go one step further we touch upon a point of general significance, which is important for the entire reorganization of world economy. We anticipate thereby an extremely important point which will be dealt with in more detail at a later stage in this book. It may be asked namely, whether the gold standard presents not merely just as good a solution,

but indeed a far better one than the best international monetary organization can offer. In addition to its other good qualities, does not the gold
standard above all possess the great advantage that it removed, as far
as possible, the national and international monetary systems from the
realm of politics and therefore of arbitrariness, emotions and rivalries?
Is it not a great asset that the gold standard, more than any other
monetary system, preserves the management of money from political
direction with all its inherent dangers, not only in the home sphere, but
also in international relations? Is it not very much better for an international monetary system to be established by every separate country
co-operating according to simple but strict rules, namely by behaving in a
way best conducive to both the national and international interests?
And is it not very much more dangerous, if instead of this international
monetary arrangements rest in the hands of an international body, where
disputes inevitably arise concerning relative power positions, and where
the settlement of international payment transactions becomes a matter
of politics, in which quotas, executive positions and the pressure exerted
by the strong upon the weak all play a leading part? And since this is
obvious in the case of international monetary organizations does not the
same apply equally to all other international planning schemes, which are
also schemes for the political direction of international economic activities? In an age when international politics are supposed to be governed
by ideals of freedom, harmony, justice and equality, does not this represent a dangerous retrograde step compared with the former liberal
international economic system?

This faulty method which we term false internationalism is frequently
the outcome of an impatience which although honourable in its motives,
is misguided. The opinion exists that decisive results must emerge when
the representatives of the nations meet round a table to discuss and pass
resolutions. Today we know only too well the disappointments which
are to be expected here. Just as frequently, however, internationalism
springs from more dubious motives, such as faulty thinking, inability to
comprehend the problems, or, what is worse, the aversion to tackling the
real tasks involved in a radical reform of society, and finally the endeavour
to meet the desire of the peoples for smoothly-functioning international
interrelations by means of sham solutions on the principle of 'ut aliquid
fieri videatur'. Nowhere is there so great a temptation to try to make an

omelette without breaking eggs as in the sphere of international politics, indeed if we may be frank, the term international cant may be used. There seems today to be an irradicable tendency to use the expression 'international co-operation' as a sort of deus ex machina when no other solution presents itself, thereby acquiring the semblance of constructive thinking and particularly go-ahead views, although it is putting the cart before the horse to begin by drawing up an ambitious programme of international tasks instead of with the *structure* and the *spirit* of international order, which for its part must rest upon a national order. This tendency is all the more remarkable since all the disappointments of the past twenty-five years should have sufficed to check it, and even today examples are not wanting to show how infinitely arduous or indeed impassable is the path to the successful fulfilment of a programme of international co-operation which does not rest upon national order. Often enough does the verse of Horace apply here, 'Parturiunt montes, nascetur ridiculus mus'.

It may perhaps help to make things clear if I try to illustrate this tendency of 'detached' internationalism by means of something which happened to me. As I was still very young and inexperienced, I once discussed the narrow-minded immigration policy pursued by the Australian Government after the first world war with one of the most outstanding representatives of international law, a man who had always inspired me with the highest respect through his courageous struggle against war and imperialism. He agreed with my condemnation of this policy and then remarked with emphasis that he had always been of the opinion that it was one of the chief duties of the League of Nations to abolish such a misuse of national sovereignty. This reply gave me so much food for thought that it has remained imprinted on my mind, although more than a quarter of a century has passed since then. Even at that time I could not suppress the heretical thought that in its struggle with the monopolist policy of the Australian trade unions, who were in reality responsible for the immigration restrictions, the League of Nations would get the worst of it, and an improvement could only be expected from a change of heart within Australia itself, a change which does indeed seem to have taken place today, after the bitter lesson of the last war.

If such internationalism places too optimistic hopes upon international institutions, it is again liable to unjustified pessimism as soon as these hopes are inevitably disappointed. It is then very ready to put the blame

18

upon the international institutions as such instead of upon the lack of preparedness on the part of nations and governments to use such institutions and keep them going. This abrupt change of opinion from optimism to pessimism was experienced by the League of Nations, although its Statute would probably have sufficed to achieve a complete success, if the national prerequisites upon which it depended had given it sufficient support.

The logical consequence is that this sort of internationalism, while unjustly condemning the old international institution, proceeds to concentrate all its expectations upon the new one, without asking itself how far the failure of the old was due to the deep-seated conditions under which it had to operate.

The purpose of our criticism of such false internationalism will not, I hope be misunderstood. When we say that international and national order are inextricably interwoven and the first cannot be attained without the second, we have nothing in common with any form of nationalism which understands national order only as a programme of ruthlessness and narrow-mindedness. What we envisage is the exact opposite of this; not a national order which is an end in itself and which in the event of a conflict sacrifices the international order, but one whose line of conduct is fixed upon the principles of international order and whose whole social organization is fundamentally directed towards building up and supporting it. We are not complaining of too much, but on the contrary of too little internationalism, and we demand that – like charity in the proverb quoted earlier on – it should begin at home. There's wisdom in another English saying, 'Every tub must stand on its own bottom'.

It is a fact that the actual cause of the international crisis is not to be sought for at the international top level, but deep down at the national, or even the individual level, so that the attempt to overcome the crisis must begin at this point. An internationalism such as we consider genuine is not narrower, but wider and deeper than the one we consider false, and the one therefore contains the other. We say that direct efforts towards an international order without striving at the same time for a national order lack the prerequisite for complete and lasting success, but we do not say that these efforts should not be undertaken with all possible energy and all the ingenuity and good will available. We recommend that both should be regarded as a duty and their close connexion be kept in mind.

The outlook is bad, however, if the nations strive after international order while at home they continue to pursue a policy contrary to what is required for it. The close connexion between the two duties also works in the opposite direction, since the national order depends upon the international. If it is true that international order presupposes, among other things, freedom among the nations and an outlook which is not conditioned by a state of permanent and acute military preparedness, the opposite is also true; the more reason the nations have to feel themselves in danger of attack from outside, the more unfavourable are the conditions for the development of liberal ideas and institutions. Just as it is true to say that free trade is an incalculable contribution to international order, it is equally true that it can only thrive in an atmosphere of peace.

THE LESSON OF THE ATOM BOMB

A few weeks after the first German edition of this book appeared, an event took place which shook the world, and which threw a new and very disturbing light upon the above considerations, namely, the invention of the atom bomb, the first victim of which was the Japanese town of Hiroshima. It might be imagined that the fixed stars which twinkle incandescently in the sky owe their origin to a fate which has also come horifyingly close to us. They too might have been worlds inhabited by people where it was not just a matter of chance that the highly-specialized scientific-technical brainpower, which on our earth is usually honoured with the Nobel Prize, happened to discover the secret of nuclear energy just at a time when the inhabitants of that star were least prepared to prevent this discovery being used for the purpose of general destruction, because over their mathematical formulae, microscopes and cyclotrones, this brainpower had forgotten the meaning of justice, truth, freedom, political wisdom and love.

Since Hiroshima it is a generally known fact that this play of the imagination is very gravely significant. Although we may not like to think about it anymore than about our own death, we still know what it means that in the course of that steady progress, which ominously enough is peculiar to scientific technical thinking, mankind had come into possession of cosmic powers of destruction, while its political discernment and moral fortitude, far removed from any progress, has dropped alarmingly below the level of an earlier age which was unenlightened by technical science. On the one side we are worse than barbarians, who, as a rule, do behave according to definite, immovable, if perhaps non-understandable beliefs and principles, while on the other hand we are in possession of forces which in olden days were attributed to the Gods alone, and with the aid of which we can blow up the world. That is the terrible position in which mankind finds itself after Hiroshima, and it knows it.

The unleashing of atomic energy, which was to be expected almost according to schedule, only made glaringly evident what must have been clear beforehand to every thoughtful person. After our planet has been in existence for millions of years we have now for the first time reached the point when political, technical and economic developments, combined with the gigantic increase in the population which has taken place during the last century, have made the political and economic unity of mankind a question of its further existence. But in the spiritual and moral realm, and that of the natural conditions of human existence, the same development has brought about changes which make the solution of the problem of the political and economic unity of mankind more difficult than ever before. And everything depends upon this solution being found.

That the juridical structure of a new league of nations merely provides a shell without a core, as long as the moral, political and economic prerequisites of international unity are not fulfilled, is clear to everyone who does not suffer from self-deception. Here too the discovery of nuclear energy has merely had a revealing effect. It has forced the great powers to acknowledge openly that the new international organization had failed to supply a basis upon which one would dare to share such an important military secret, while at the same time the existence of such a secret is bound to destroy any hope that such confidence might develop.

The idea of a general control of armaments, to which recourse has been had in this dilemma, also provides only a sham solution, as long as liberal countries with a constantly wakeful and free public opinion and all those liberties which make it very difficult to preserve secrets, stand opposed to other, collectivist and totalitarian countries, of which exactly the opposite is true. It is the existence of the latter – to be exact, of the Communist imperium – which does not even permit of confidence being placed in the workings of a system of international armaments control, which is itself the outcome of mistrust.

21

That in this apparently hopeless state of affairs people turn to the very radical solution of a genuine world state, which would put an end to the sovereignty of the separate countries and therefore of their foreign policies, is understandable and in the first exuberance may seem to provide a remedy. Unfortunately this must soon be followed by the sober realisation that setting up such a goal does no more than establish a general orientation, as long as we are unable to discover the way to attain it. The question has quite rightly been put, as to what the West imagines a world parliament would be like, in which non-European nations would hold an overwhelming majority. Of far greater weight, however, is the fact that such a world state – always supposing that it is to be a democratic one – would only be possible at all if individual countries, namely the collectivist totalitarian ones, were prepared to relinquish not only their sovereignty but also the political and economic pattern of their Society. Since this is of course impossible, the result is either that the world state will fail owing to the existence of the totalitarian countries, or that it would only be possible as a totalitarian state, which would surrender to the direction of the Communist imperium. Since, however, the free world can no more be expected to commit suicide than can the potentates of the Kremlin, the idea of a world government, above all in respect of the actual source of the danger of war (to be looked for in the antagonism between the free world and the Communist imperium), proves to be nothing but an ignis fatuus, and indeed a very dangerous one, since it might tempt naive persons, who never cease to exist, in the name of the ideal of the world state, to become accomplices of Moscow in establishing a world despotism of Communism.

But the plan of a world state is not merely a Utopia, nor even a harmless one at that, it also contains some false reasoning. It derives from the over-simplified idea that the degree of political and economic unity mankind needs is entirely incompatible with national sovereignty. That is certainly true with regard to the average present-day degree of this sovereignty. But just as there are various degrees of nationalism, so are there various degrees of sovereignty, ranging from the relative, which imposes such restrictions upon itself as are required for the peaceful co-existence of nations and free economic relations between them, to the absolute type, which ignores these restrictions. The whole difference between peace and well-being on the one hand, and war and poverty on the other, lies in the fact of whether or not the states observe certain standards of political and economic behaviour on the grounds of deep conviction; whether or not they proclaim themselves to be the final and absolute power to which their subjects must submit; whether or not they allow of free public opinion and an unhindered Opposition; whether or not by permitting free markets at home they create a prerequisite which is indispensable for free international trade; whether or not, failing a true and universal religious faith, nationalism is made into a substitute religion for the masses; and whether the children are drilled by the authorities or brought up as free persons, for whom justice and truth are of more importance than the 'Fatherland'. In other words, everything depends on whether we are dealing with states which are not merely 'democratized' but with liberal states where the constitution guarantees justice to the individual, where the government is kept within rigid and narrow limits, and where by means of federalism, economic freedom, the prevention of the amassing of gigantic fortunes and of monopolies, by free intellectual life and a division of power, the supreme power has been so decentralized as to make it innoxious both at home and abroad. This division of powers has always been the real and enduring programme of Liberalism.

This programme of the *decentralization of power* derives from a deep insight into the nature of man, confirmed in the course of thousands of years, which teaches us that there is no concentration of power which is not abused. We know that every accumulation of power deserves to be regarded with extreme mistrust and considered as a menace. This political wisdom applies to conditions inside a country, but also to the relations between one state and another. There is always an instinctive feeling which tells people from which states they may expect a breach of the peace, and if they attempt to reason out this feeling they find that these are states in which the concentration of power has reached a dangerous degree, because the supremacy of the government is in no way checked by supranational convictions, free public opinion, good political sense on the part of the citizens, freedom of markets at home and abroad, an unhindered Opposition and legal standards which exclude the possibility of arbitrariness. In 1914 the world knew that peace was threatened by the semi-absolute military monarchies of Germany, Austria-Hungary and Russia, and not by France where Jaurès fell a victim to the bullet of a chauvinist, and not by England, where members of the Cabinet gave free expression to their opposition to war. The same world knew after 1933 from which state alone an attack upon peace was to be expected, and today it knows it again. It is not a democratic constitution alone which makes a country peaceful, but the liberal character of its national and social order in the sense of decentralizing and limiting the power of the state, – not the fact that there are majorities whose unbounded power is just as much to be feared as that of tyrants, but that, on the other hand, there are minorities which check the power of the majorities.

The problem today is not that there are sovereign states. The problem is rather to be sought in the fact that the degree of sovereignty is becoming constantly intensified by a growing process in which nationalism, state-control and political direction acquire such power over the people as to burst all bounds and become 'total'. The promotion of this process – as I have discussed in detail in my book 'Mass und Mitte', – has meanwhile become the essence of all such efforts as are summarized by expressions such as 'Socialism', 'Collectivism' or 'Stateism'. Our problem therefore is supra-nationalism and the supra-sovereignty which corresponds to it. It is obvious, however, that both of these would be impossible in a democratic age unless they found support among the mass of the population and no amount of goodwill for many of the motives, representatives and aims of Socialism can do away with the fact that this commitment of the population to the nation and the state takes place predominantly in the name of Socialism and is pursued daily in its name. That is the disturbing nature of the problem. Although it is easy and popular to denounce imperial trusts and war-happy aristocrats, no one who values his peace, his career, his honour and the part he plays in public life would be well-advised to stigmatize popular movements as dangerous to the common weal. He may consider himself lucky if nothing more than his intelligence is doubted.

Imperialism begins at home. Everything is included in this sentence. A threat to peace only ever comes from states in which beforehand an extraordinary accumulation of power has taken place which shuts out the forces which act counter to the intemperance to which a state constantly tends. The absolute sovereignty which overrides the rights and the peace of other nations must, to use the words of Friedrich Wilhelm I,

24

the real creator of the Prussian war machine, first of all be stabilized at home as a 'rocher de bronze'.

There is every justification for pointing to this increasingly absolute sovereignty of the states as the actual cause of the present world chaos, but it is wrong and quixotic to denounce sovereignty as such and only to leave us the choice between a world state and apocalyptic destruction. Such a charge sounds particularly strange from the mouths of Socialists, whose programme envisages raising the power of the state to the nth degree.

Anyone who considers that sovereignty as such is the villain of the piece, no matter of what degree or no matter whether it is that of the small countries, whose naturally limited sovereignty has the very useful function of being troublesome to the too powerful sovereignty of the larger countries, or that of the highly-centralized mammoth states, is treading a path which can only lead to complete despair, since no one can seriously advocate melting down the sovereign national states into a universal state. Whoever is able to see the difference and to realize that the present day world crisis is the final stage along a path which has led to the constant increase and finally to the absolutism of national sovereignty, holds a point of view which alone can bring hope. Although the abolition of national sovereignty appears impossible, it is very possible to place the controls upon it which will curb the Leviathan of the modern state and thus realize the condition demanded by universalist social philosophy in which the individual state shall so conduct itself as if a world state existed, and this because it is the will of the peoples. This path too is a difficult one – not because, like the utopia of the world state it demands something which is contrary to the nature of the matter, but because it demands the strict renunciation of popular ideologies.

THE SOCIOLOGY OF WAR

That the various factors are interwoven with extraordinary intricacy becomes particularly evident in the dramatic catastrophe of international interrelations which we call war [1]). One of the moral perversities with which our age is afflicted was to deny at times the supremely catastrophic character of war, until two world wars brought disillusionment – let us hope for ever. For centuries the time-honoured belief existed that war was, as a rule, one of the incomprehensible evils of the world system, which – like the other Horsemen of the Apocalypse – Pestilence, Hunger and Death – had to be borne with resignation. Pacifism, in the sense of a mass movement directed towards the abolition of war, only became possible after the beginning of the modern age, when war, like all other things alleged to be the Will of God, came to be regarded in the light of critical and ameliorative reason, and, together with other social institutions, as a work of man which it would be quite possible to alter. Thus instead of being a subject of theology, war became a subject of sociology.

Has it in this way become entirely comprehensible? To be honest we must admit that we are still very far from understanding it. Although men have at all times pondered over the phenomenon of war, and although recent generations especially have amassed a gigantic literature on the sociology of war, all that progress adds up to is that we possess a fairly complete list of the possible causes of war and that we realize the extraordinary intricacy which links these causes and which excludes any monistic theory of war sociology. Only a separate and comprehensive volume could do justice to the epistemology which results.

There is now a serious danger of our losing ourselves in the jungle of sociological and psychological argument, and failing to see the practical problem of how to prevent war in the right light. All these involved theories do nothing to alter the fact that wars would be impossible if international interrelations were subject to an effective judicial system which would curb the arbitrary use of force between the nations in exactly the same way as does a national judicial system between individuals. All efforts directed towards an international order must therefore in the long run be directed towards reaching the same stage of development in international interrelations as has been taken for granted in civilised countries ever since the law of the jungle has been supplanted by public peace. This comparison must indeed not blind us to the fact that the task of establishing an international peace based on justice will be infinitely more difficult than that of a national peace based on justice, because the citizens of one nation have always tended to integrate particularly strongly owing, not least, to the constant danger from without. The task of accomplishing a world wide peace based on justice is so great that it can certainly only be achieved in stages, always with the provision that the peoples shall have become sufficiently mature for such an international judicial system. All the foregoing considerations of a sociological nature apply also to the achievement of such maturity.

In order to understand in detail what an international peace based on justice must accomplish, the various categories of war must be distinguished. Above all a difference must be made between two types of war, the importance of which is not lessened by the fact that they have often been combined with each other in the course of history and that there are borderline cases in which it is not easy to say whether the one or the other type predominates. A war may arise either through a conflict over concrete claims, which may be compared with a case under civil law *(war of conflict)*, or through an act of violence which corresponds to a breach of the peace under criminal law *(war of aggression)* [2]). Whereas individual legal disputes arising from contentions of personal honour or material claims are finally settled by judicial decision, international conflicts of this kind may easily lead to war, as long as a decision by force of arms, which corresponds to the ordeal of the Middle Ages, is not abolished through obligatory international legal procedure, and before this is the case we shall continue to regard war rather as a tragic chain of events than as a vicious action. From their very nature such wars of conflict make it difficult to clarify the question of guilt, provided one of the warring parties – as is however often enough the case – does not misuse the conflict as an excuse for a war of aggression, or does not oppose the readiness of the antagonist to come to an understanding with inexcusable intransigence. This last applies on the whole to the case of the first world war, whereas we should not hesitate to characterize the second in its origin and in all its phases purely as a war of aggression, after it had already been preceded by the wars of aggression in China and Abyssinia.

Whereas it is not easy to find examples in history of pure wars of conflict, there is no difficulty at all as regards examples of pure wars of aggression. Since we may assume in addition that a war of conflict would seldom develop if there did not exist, at least upon one side, a mentality which, given favourable circumstances, would be quite likely to wage also a war of aggression, we realize that it is the last-named type of war which presents the real problem of war-prevention. Whereas a war of conflict is, by its very nature, a war with limited aims which can easily be terminated by a permanent settlement, the war of aggression always contains

27

at the same time the germ of the worst possible type of war, *the war of destruction and supremacy*, which is limited neither by set and unchangeable concrete aims, nor by the number of the original antagonists, and which therefore degenerates into a general international war. Such were the Napoleonic wars and the world wars of our century (the first in its later stages, the second from the very beginning). One of the characteristics of this devastating type of war, which compared with the localised war of conflict is as the typhoon to the breeze, is that during its course the warring parties are constantly engaged in re-formulating their 'war aims', and that it becomes exceedingly difficult to terminate it by a permanent settlement, unless the peacemakers happen to possess the wisdom of the Congress of Vienna.

The preventive measures are in accordance with the two main types of war – the war of conflict on the one hand and the war of aggression on the other. The answer to the question of how wars of conflict can be done away with is an international judicial system, which, after the pattern of national judicial systems, shall compel the individual nations to submit every conflict – whether it be of a strictly judicial nature or of a political nature – to an international court of law or of arbitration, and which shall proclaim a resort to arms to settle the conflict a criminal breach of international peace. As regards the far more dangerous case of the war of aggression, the effective solution is that all nations should possess the undubitable will and the well-organized means to use their combined economic and military power against the aggressor. An aggressor would implicitly mean any nation which either did not refer a claim to the decision of the international court of law or arbitration, or which did not submit to the verdict or award of the same.

The terrible lessons which the two world wars have taught us confirm the very important fact that, as a rule, war will only break out if the aggressor considers that the risk involved is a slight one. Every disagreement among the peace-loving nations, every inclination to weakness, every marked difference in the degree of armament are therefore factors which favour the outbreak of war, whereas the danger is lessened by everything which induces even the most determined aggressor to reflect upon the enormous risk he would be taking in defying the organized defensive forces – of which, in tones of persecuted innocence, he may perhaps complain of as 'encirclement'. Now there are two conditions which act in favour of an aggressively disposed country and which are therefore fostered by it with all possible means of propaganda, hypocrisy and diplomacy. In the first place, namely, the danger to peace is enhanced the more the will to war on the side grows in inverse proportion to pacificism on the other. Since however in our day the aggressively disposed country will always be a collectivistic-totalitarian one, whose allmighty dictatorship always suppresses any expression of opinion which does not suit the government and whose all-encompassing propaganda shapes the opinion of the masses in the way the government desires, the tension between the unrestrained military preparedness, both actual and psychological, of the aggressor, and the defensive power of his victim, weakened by pacifism, will be very great and very dangerous.

This is the real source of the policy of Appeasement, which contributed so fatefully to the outbreak of the second world war, and which since the end of the war has once again created a highly dangerous situation with regard to the totalitarian imperium of Communism with Russia at its head. All the more since after the overthrow of Germany, Japan and Italy there remained in the world only one totalitarian great power with its cynical lust for conquest, which, no longer held in check by the rivalries of the totalitarian powers among themselves, has long enough made the most unscrupulous, skilful and successful use of the loathing of the world for its defeated rivals and the fear of their renaissance, and has behind this smoke screen prepared its advance to world mastery. And so once more the world looks on at the repulsive and lying drama in which the totalitarian centre of aggression in the world raises its own war potential to the maximum, and by means of an unscrupulous propaganda of hate, fear and ideology develops a condition of war-preparedness in the minds of its own population, while at the same time abusing as warmongers all those in the West who admonish resistance, and putting the whole machinery of its psychological warfare into operation in order to cripple resistance by a campaign for pacifism and in order to deceive simple souls with the fata morgana of neutralism. It has up to now succeeded to a disastrous degree.

This experience brings us to the distressing conclusion that pacifism, merely as an attitude of mind which rejects war, is not only sterile but indeed dangerous to a tragic degree, since at the very moment when the danger of war is greatest it further increases that danger immeasurably

29

degree by encouraging the attacker, thereby merely becoming a weapon in the hand of the aggressively-disposed country. Pacifism has a real significance only in the case of a war of conflict, in which it may be assumed that the active desire for war is lacking on both sides. In the case of a war of aggression, however, that is to say in practically all cases today, it not only fails but actually becomes one of the fatal links in the chain of causes which trigger off the war and possibly effects the triumph of the aggressor. It is the fate of pacifism today, therefore, to be restricted to the lamb of the fable, and not, as we might wish, to the wolf.

The second condition by which the danger of war is seriously enhanced owing to the overgreat difference between the forces of attack and defence is to be found in the fact that almost everywhere military organization tends to be extremely conservative, as illustrated by the classic maxim of the Duke of Cumberland, Commander-in-Chief of the British army in Gladstone's days, who said 'The right time for a change is when you can't help it'. In the absence of a strong impulse from without, the military power of a country, as history has shown and as simple pyschology goes to explain, easily succumbs to the superannuation of the General Staff, to bureaucracy and to the numbing influence of that feudal character which is peculiar to all standing armies. In the midst of such conservative military systems a country which has utilized unusual political conditions to revolutionize its army always has a good start. The three main cases in modern history of such a constellation disastrous to peace are the wars of Napoleon, Bismarck and finally Hitler.

The conclusion to be drawn from all this is that the chief task of war-prevention is to make it plain to every potential aggressor, beforehand and in a completely indubitable way, that the risk is overwhelming. This aim is achieved in an imperfect and constantly endangered form by the establishment of a balance of power in the international grouping of states. Since experience has shown, however, that the balance established in such cases is always of an unstable nature, it must in future be supplanted by the stable balance of an international organization of justice and peace.

Is not then the solution of the war problem in reality very simple and only dependent upon the firm determination of the governments and the peoples? If this were our opinion we should be contradicting ourselves, since earlier on we termed just such thinking 'internationalism' and warned our readers against it. In actual fact this contradiction is only an apparent one. To explain it we should consider that the problem can be regarded from various angles. In formulating the solution of the war problem so sharply and smoothly above, we were regarding it from the juridical angle. Here in fact everything appears much simpler than it actually is. To be content with such considerations is to lapse into that monistic way of thinking which may be termed legalism and which is no better than economism or any other one-sided outlook. In indicating the legal solution the question has still not been answered as to the conditions under which the peoples and governments would be prepared to accept it firmly and undeviatingly. This question however brings us back to the higher level of the sociological, ethical and political considerations with which we started [3]).

NOTES

1. (p. 25) The Sociology of War:

The vast literature has been clearly and very learnedly summarized in: 'A Study of War', by QUINCEY WRIGHT, Cambridge University Press, 1942. One of the best and shortest explanations, which also deals with the latest ethnographical and prehistoric research is: 'Zur soziologischen Ortsbestimmung des Krieges', by ALEXANDER RÜSTOW, 'Friedenswarte', 1939, Vol. 39, No. 3. The point of view expounded there coincides almost completely with that stated here (cf. 'Krieg und Demokratie', by W. RÖPKE, Friedenswarte, 1939, Vol. 39, No. 2). From among the older literature on the sociology of war, 'La Guerre et la Paix', by P. J. PROUDHON, Paris 1861, deserves to be read, despite all its absurdities. Very important aspects are dealt with in the exciting and to a great extent prophetic book of GUGLIELMO FERRERO, 'La Fin des Aventures, Guerre et Paix', Paris 1931.

2. (p. 27) War of Conflict and War of Aggression:

The difference between the limited and the unlimited war (war of destruction and supremacy) is specially discussed by G. FERRERO, (see above) and G. FERRERO, 'Les Formes de la Guerre et l'Anarchie Internationale', and in the collected works of the Institut Universitaire de Hautes Etudes Internationales 'La Crise Mondiale', Zürich 1938, pp. 90 foll. WALTER LIPPMANN, in 'The Good Society', Boston 1937, pp. 131 foll., treats the same subject in a way which is entirely in harmony with the present book.

3. (p. 31) The inadmissable over-simplification of the peace problem:

A good example of such inadmissible over-simplification of the peace problem, which hides the actual difficulties under alluring statements, is 'The Anatomy of Peace', EMERY REEVES (1945), which created a great stir immediately after the war. In spite of a wealth of ideas it is a model example of sterile tautological argument. War is defined as a conflict between sovereign states, and it is a fact that a definition of war necessarily contains the idea of sovereignty – and contrariwise the absence of an international government. Although this is correct, little is to be gained by demanding that sovereignty be abolished, as though it were a question of a button, as it were, which everyone else had failed to see, and which only needed to be pressed. This would only be presenting the problem anew, which is certainly not without merit, but a definition of peace is not a solution. If we had a world government we should certainly have no more wars, since there would be no more sovereign states, a conflict between which is defined as war. But such a conclusion avails little, since there always remains the possibility of a 'civil war'. Cf. pp. 35– 42.

II

THE NATION AND THE COMMUNITY OF NATIONS

MACHIAVELLISM AND REALISM

In actual fact what can all the international treaties and all the appeals
to the nations to restrict their sovereignties in the higher interests
of an international order avail if the conviction prevails that treaties
need only be adhered to as long as appears profitable? That states can
live according to their own code of laws, which is beyond good and evil?
That politics turn only on the conception of friend and foe and are
subject to a different set of morals than obtain between individuals?
That the sacrosanct egoism of the nation justifies falsehood, breach of
contract and force.

These are the convictions which are meant in speaking of Machiavellism,
leaving aside the question of whether this is not being unjust to the great
Florentine [1]). Four hundred years of criticism have, however, so brought
this term into disrepute that only the opponents of the theory of unscrupulous statecraft make use of it, while the disciples of such prefer other
expressions. Power-politics, reasons of state, realist politics – all these
expressions need not necessarily involve Machiavellism in its most absolute
and brutal form, but even in weak dilutions the pungent essence can still
be distinguished. Even when the doctrine of Machiavellism confronts us
under the cloak of scientific positivism and tries to prove to us that the
behaviour of states is determined by objective factors, such as 'constant
historical values', 'lines of geographical force' or 'economic laws', we must
not let that deter us. And the real geographical romanticism which becomes
inebriated over an atlas in the same way as historical romanticism over a
mediaeval chronicle, exudes the same strong odour of Machiavellism,
mingles with the perfume of scientific positivism.

Europe would not have become a charnel house and a heap of smoking
ruins if these doctrines had not during the last century gained an ever
stronger hold over people's minds and an increasingly unrestrained influence over foreign politics. The history of this development of modern

Machiavellism has still to be written. This is not the place for it, but a few remarks are unavoidable.

As apparent to all today as is the destruction which this doctrine of a double-barrelled morality has brought about, so indubitable is it that no international order of any kind will be possible in the future unless the confusion of moral ideas is abolished which this doctrine has created. Just as any human relations are impossible if falsehood, force and breach of contract are made maxims of conduct, so must a policy which undermines confidence between governments by such maxims make any international understanding or agreement worthless, and inevitably lead to war. It replaces international law by the law of the jungle.

Machiavellism like every other form of cynicism is presented to us with an expression of pitying superiority for those who have still retained their childish faith and who in their innocence do not yet know what is going on behind the scenes, whereas this alleged superiority is in reality nothing but callowness and superficiality. Because the expression 'realist politics' is used we are given to understand that in regarding it as dangerous we are shutting our eyes to reality. The grim humour of this is not recognized, namely that these realist politicians reveal their lack of reality, before their fatal results even become apparent, by ignoring the decisive reality of moral forces. The advocates of this doctrine also have another trait in common with all cynical disillusioners in that they regard all statesmen who declare themselves their opponents as hypocrites who are only out to deceive others.

Alone the fact that the relationship of politics to morals is one of the oldest problems of civilized man gives some idea of the extent and difficulty of the questions to be discussed here. It is all the more important that we should not lose our way among them, but pick out certain decisive points.

In the *first* place it may be said that modern Machiavellism cannot lay claim to the fact that it is only recommending a practice which is as old as political history itself. It is true that we meet with Machiavellism in practice on almost every page of world history, but that this practice should be recommended is something new. Falsehood, force and breach of contract have always existed, but one should realize very clearly the mighty difference it makes whether this happens with a bad conscience and while basically acknowledging the moral principles which are being abused, or with an impudent grin. When occasional practice is converted into a

34

philosophy the axe is indeed laid to the root of any international community, and this is the novelty which the last centuries have introduced. It should be said further that were Machiavellism as old a doctrine as it is a practice it might still be asked whether there were no hope of ever conquering it, and whether humanity today had not reached a degree of mutual dependence which for the first time in history makes this conquest an absolute necessity.

The *second* essential point is that Machiavellism is not only bad morals but even bad politics. The famous comment of Boulay (wrongly ascribed to Talleyrand) on the execution of the Duc d'Enghien (1804), also applies here, 'C'est pire qu'un crime, c'est une faute'. The only thing which is supposed to justify it is just that which is denied to it in the long run, namely success. In the end it leaves behind it a heap of ruins which makes one want to shout 'to be thieves and murderers for this!' If all the same it is always tried out by political adventurers this is because final failure is always preceded by brillant success at the beginning. To be a machiavellist is to bet against time, and this is a bet which is certain to incite gamblers, just as certain as that they must lose in the end. It is the pact with the devil as described in the legend: Satan, after giving him all the splendours of the world, comes in the end to fetch the soul destined for damnation. It may not happen for a long time, but what is left of the great kingdoms which were built up by force and falsehood? One might well advise machiavellists to recollect the saying of an eminent and noble thinker of pre-Bismarkian Germany, 'The realist in politics is right for a moment, ideas are a matter of eras' (F. A. Lange in 'Die Arbeitsfrage', which appeared in 1865). Even if one is less confident about the final victory of ideas there can be no doubt about the other, the realist in politics is wrong in the end. If he were not, human society would have been impossible from the beginning.

This links up with the *third* point, that Machiavellism is one of those things which have a meaning only as long as they enjoy the monopoly of the trade secret of their origin, which monopoly they are bound to lose sooner or later. Falsehood and force can only succeed as long as there are enough people who assume that truth and a peaceable disposition are the maxims of human relations. As soon as the machiavellist is seen through no one believes a word he says, be it true or untrue. He therefore must wish that all the other people should embrace collectively a code of morals directly the opposite of his own, which therefore proves that his are

35

completely unsuitable as a *principle* of statecraft. But the very fact that he pursues a machiavellist policy makes the fulfillment of his wishes impossible. The others have no need to become machiavellists, they only need be on their guard against Machiavellism to deprive him of his success. If everyone became a machiavellist, however, we should find ourselves in a state of war of all against all, which would be the end of both human society and all social philosophy. Voltaire probably had something similar in mind when, referring to the royal author of 'Antimachiavellism', he said, 'Il crache au plat pour en dégoûter les autres'.

Machiavellism – and here we come to the last and decisive point – proves its unsuccessfulness on a higher plane when we seek to discover the political aims that it is to promote. Machiavellism thinks only of wealth, power or fame, and forgets that the intrinsic value of justice is higher than these external gains. A state which squanders this treasure misses its highest aim; in the words of St. Augustine it is nothing more than a great band of robbers (magnum latrocinium). A policy which makes the abuse of justice a basic principle is irreconcilably opposed to the common weal in the highest and final sense. This is, however, true of all degrees of Machiavellism.

This by no means covers everything of importance which is to be said on this difficult subject. Above all one aspect remains to be considered, which after the end of the second world war became increasingly significant. To put it shortly it is a question of confronting Machiavellism as a philosophy of political amorality with another set of ideas which in their upshot are possibly no less pernicious: with moralistic illusionism, easily kindled idealism and impracticable optimism, which fail to recognize the tough game of international politics. Since a policy which permits itself to be overinfluenced by such optimistic and illusionist ideas generally meets with cruel disappointments, there is a danger that those who find themselves fooled in this way, wrathfully determined not to be tricked a second time and fall victim to their own high-flown ideas, may fly to the other extreme and join the ranks of the 'realists' and machiavellists.

The history of international politics since the end of the first world war does indeed justify our decrying dillettant 'idealism', impracticable optimism and moralistic doctrinarianism in this field. They have resulted in modern wars becoming passionate crusades and stern punitive expeditions; conclusions of peace deteriorating into moral judgements, and, in the name of justice and democracy, highflown principles (such, for example, as 'the right of self-determination of the peoples'), resulting in so upsetting the sensitive political equilibrium that bad has turned to worse. Those were not far wrong who contrasted the wisdom of the Congress of Vienna with the madness of modern peace conferences, the benefits of a compromise with the disasters of inflexible doctrinarianism (as expressed, for example, in the demand for 'unconditional surrender' of the Axis powers); the discretion of secret diplomacy with its sober negotiations which are free from the pressure exerted by whipped up mass emotions with the 'open diplomacy' of conferences which turn to demagogic displays. Not without reason has sharp criticism been expressed that the principle of the balance of power, which is no longer understood today, has been all too quickly sacrificed in favour of the all too legalist set-up of universal organizations. The truth of the saying has been experienced that the wars of the peoples are worse than the wars of the kings. We have learnt that the international 'anarchy' of the past, which has been rightly condemned, did all the same have its limits in the prevailing system of international justice, in an unwritten code of behaviour and in a chivalry which perished in the hecatombs of the first world war. Today we make the depressing discovery that not only has the anarchy remained, but that it is worse than before, while international justice, manners and chivalry have disappeared.

It is understandable that the horrors of the last war, for which a daemonic political dilettante, eaten up with fanaticism, together with his accomplices and by means of the flood of ideology which he released, alone bore the responsibility as seldom before any individual in history, evoked the desire to punish all 'war criminals' in the name of outraged morals. People sobered down, however, when it became evident that the definition of a 'war criminal' includes being defeated, and that only the victors ever take their place on the judgement seat, not omitting the representatives of a victorious power which is well able to hold its own with the conquered as regards cruelty and ruthlessness. And a generation which has discovered what questionable things can take place even in the name of a crusade for humanity, international morals and democracy, may be excused if in future it mistrusts all the big talk, if behind every appeal to the ideals of international politics it suspects hidden intentions and propaganda and if it reflects before accepting as adequate an unequivocal distinction between absolute bad and absolute good in this field. Everything absolute, doctrinaire and emotional then becomes suspect, and accordingly every belief in the possibility of complete and comprehensive solutions, in the dawn of a 'new age', in big programmes and projects.

The present generation cannot be blamed for being extremely susceptible on this and similar subjects, in fact almost all over the western world today young people above all are moved by a spirit of chilly disillusionment. Who would deny that this is not only understandable but that it has its uses? It is by no means undesirable that people should become more sober and reserved, and, in the light of our merciless age, learn to consider and weigh with new understanding the methods, principles and results, as well as the leaders of international politics of the past. It is to be hoped that the reader of this book will also discover in it no small measure of this spirit of reserved and sober retrospection; illusionism has been sufficiently criticised in the foregoing pages. A dash of conservative thinking on this subject is a good counterweight to the dangerous overstatements of dilettantish or even doublefaced 'idealism' or 'progressivism', and a better knowledge of history never did any harm.

But it would be fatal to go from one extreme to the other. In making due concessions to a new realism in international politics, we should bear in mind that these must stop where a re-estimation of the past tends to relapse into the 'realist politics' of a machiavellian nature against which we have warned our readers. Sobriety, honesty, avoidance of phrase-making, a sense of reality, understanding of 'politics' as the sphere of compromise, a delicate investigation of the possibilities of a situation which should as far as possible be kept free from passion and vague emotions; respect for the lessons of history and the laws of organic growth; a serious endeavour to come to terms with the extraordinary complications of international life and a distrust of oversimplification, disassociation from every form of dilettantism with its good intentions and bad results – all this is excellent. Talleyrand, one of those masters of old diplomacy who cut such a poor figure in the text books, but who in our times has been justly recognized as a classical model of international politics, had just this in mind when he advised young diplomats, 'Surtout, pas trop de zèle'. And Proudhon later expressed it more strongly, 'Je ne connais pas de mouvement qui, né dans l'enthousiasme, ne se toit terminé dans l'imbécillité'. But from realism of this kind it is only a short step to cynicism, opportunism, nihilism and Machiavellism. And we should beware of this step, once again having in mind the master Talleyrand, who professed his faith in the classical principle of Montesquieu, 'Le droit des gens est naturellement fondé sur ce principe, que les diverses nations doivent se faire dans la paix le plus de bien, et dans la guerre le moins de mal qu'il est possible'.

We should eschew empty phrases as we do impudent grins. In international politics there are final values and principles which to ignore would be to commit a betrayal which turns all so-called political success to dust – namely the precepts of humanity, truth and justice. We must drop phrases and, in a sober and humble spirit, honour these sovereign precepts with more honesty and conviction.

This attitude of mind will also help to preserve us from the error into which we might be tempted to fall if in disillusionment we turn back to the old style of international politics with its realism, its alliances, its compromises and makeshifts and its appeal to the stronger battalions, on whose side, according to the cynical words of Frederick the Great, God is to be found. Although we are not wrong in thinking that this old style was not quite so bad as we had assumed after 1914, after Wilson and the League of Nations, we should not forget that it did indeed end in the terrible catastrophe which divided two eras of world history.

With all due respect to Metternich and the Congress of Vienna, world history has, in the meantime, owing to the enormous development of the technique of destruction and the inalterable material interdependence of all nations, reached a point where the methods of the old international order no longer suffice and new and more comprehensive forms of international order must be found. This task is not so simple as was assumed in the days of jubilant enthusiasm and we have learnt how wrong we were to forget or to despise the experience of the past and much of the wisdom of the old diplomacy. But it is in the interests of the task with which we are faced today if, in a modest and openminded spirit, we compare our mistakes and failures with the honourable achievements of the past.

This leads to another consideration which recent developments make particularly appropriate. While, despite the revival of realism we definitely reject Machiavellism in every shape and form, we must, under present-day conditions, be particularly on our guard against an optimism, an illusionism and a moral simplicity which can only be of benefit to the threat to world peace presented by the extreme Machiavellism of the communist imperium of Russia. This brings us back to the remarks made earlier on a pacifism, which, preached today at the wrong time and in the wrong place, is only qualified to further the plans for war and conquest of the new aggressor.

It has always been difficult to understand how it was possible during the last decade that the slogan of 'one world' which is so at defiance with reality could take such hold of the popular mind, and, in view of the manifest incompatibility of the western and the communist worlds, a world government and the like could ever have been dreamt of, how the Statute of the United Nations could ever have been based on this fiction, and how, relying on the disarming effect of a genuine will to peace, the communist imperium could ever have been granted a position of power which has made a third world war a horrifying possibility. Today it sounds like a bad joke when one remembers how in 1942 one of the architects of this policy of illusion, Henry Wallace, who at that time was Vice-President of the United States, with unbounded guilelessness explained in a public speech that he had told the Russians, 'The object of this war is to make sure that everybody in the world has the privilege of drinking a quart of milk a day'. The decent honest fool and the most cunning machiavellists in history – the historians of our times could wish for no more cruel contrast to prove that, to reverse the words of Mephistopheles, the pure and open heart is just 'part of the power that would, still do good but still does evil' (Faust I).

Not all such fools are so open and honest as this American in penitently acknowledging their mistakes today, and it would seem that even he does not recognize that the actual cause of his error was 'social progressivism', which I think I have discussed adequately in my book 'Maß und Mitte'. When such fools – who in Europe display terrifying obstinacy – appeal in their inexcusable guilelessness to Christianity, they should recall Martin Luther, who in the ninety-second of his famous Theses declares, 'Away with all the prophets who say to the people of Christ 'peace, peace', and there is no peace'.

The debt which communistic Machiavellism owes to this foolish illusionism is in truth enormous and unfortunately is growing from day to day. This innocence in the face of the blackest cunning is the most alarming example of the fact that there is a moralizing way of judging international politics, a way which is neither moral nor intelligent, the fateful upshot of which is that it furthers Machiavellism and its threats to peace. Such unenlightened

40

innocence, in which reason is choked by emotion, such irresponsible ingenuousness, is a mere unsuspecting willingness to become a pawn in the game of an unscrupulous reckoner. The admonition that we are all sinners, otherwise so worthy of observance, becomes here, in the face of open evil, nothing but condemnable tepidity. Our rejection of Machiavellism must not be mislead us into evading the brave and honourable decision, which a sense of responsibility imposes upon us, to oppose a satanic policy with all our force and to expose its deceit and inhumanity. Not to do this would be immoral and unchristian.

We cannot dismiss this subject without, in conclusion, saying a few words about the Great Men of history [2]). Who are they? In what way were they great? Where does the dangerous idolatry begin which the nations and the ages carry on with these figures? By what methods is the popular vote cast over the centuries which awards the title of 'Great?' How is it that to some it sticks so closely, so that we cannot imagine an Alexander or a Charlemagne without this title, whereas with others we hesitate as to whether or not they deserve this lasting reverence, and in the case of others again find the title presumptious? A list of figures in world history who have been awarded the title of 'great', and an examination of the circumstances which in each individual case contributed to the bestowal of this temporal canonisation, would be interesting. Among other things it would reveal that only one scholar (Albertus Magnus) and only one hierarch (Gregory I) is to be found among them, and not a single discoverer or artist, while for the most part the list consists of famous rulers, always to be imagined as mounted on horseback with the haughty look of a Colleoni. And perhaps it is worth while reflecting that no new awards have been made for the last century and a half. The last one to succeed in carrying off the title of 'Great' was King Frederick II of Prussia.

Can it be that the popular idea of the Great Men of history contains a goodly portion of masochistic adoration of power, perhaps indeed a slight disturbing readiness to convert the shivers of horror and fear of the scourge of a national leader into feelings of worshipful submission and pleasureable admiration, and to enjoy the Great Men as heroic figures in the panorama of world history? Does not the danger increase the more the figures are recast by popular imagination into mythical characters – Barbarossa, Henry V of England (who, in spite of Shakespeare, was a cruel executioner), or Fredericus, so that they become part of the pattern of the brightly-coloured carpet which every nation tries to weave out of its own history? Although such queries are healthy and useful, and the suggested suspicions are justified, there is no doubt on the other hand that the political power which arouses our suspicions of the Great Men of history is that which made them characters of outstanding quality and force, to deny or belittle the importance of which would be to disembowel history of its meaning. There is a particular and deep-seated reason for the fact that history is to a large extent the history of international conflicts, in which the conception of power is a force which cannot be ignored. We do not doubt that Alexander and Charlemagne will always be termed Great because in their case the will of a single man was able to seize upon the right moment to divert the course of history with such immeasureable results that they continue to affect us all down to the present day, without, as we see it, there being any reason to consider their greatness seriously overshadowed by reprehensible actions.

Certain it is that among the Great Men in political history there are few rulers who, like Louis IX, also deserve the title of Saint. But even in this field, where it is almost impossible to be a saint, it is at least possible to be a really great man. If only it were not so difficult, more difficult than in any other sphere of human activity, to distinguish the great men of history from the false or the dubious ones, the nobility from the crook, the criminal on a colossal scale from the political master-builder, legitimate quality from 'The abuse of greatness ... when it disjoins remorse from power'. Above, lonely as the stars and of such mysterious rareness as the prime numbers of higher arithmetical quantities, stand the few saints and sages among the mighty ones, Asoka, Trajan, Marcus Aurelius, Louis, perhaps Alfred. But below these, on the level of earthly passions, the real great names of history deserve to be differentiated from the bringers of ruin, the self-idolatrists, the madmen, the Scourges of God and daemons of the nations. What the title is worth – whether clean or stained, whether convincing or dubious – is a question which can be debated the longer and the more indecisively the smaller the human figure is who has emerged as an instrument in history and the further away the century is which separates us from him.

This discussion will never end. But just as history as a whole appears in a different light in different ages, so are there certain periods when there is a particular reason or urge to re-examine the historical lists of honour. As in the 18th century, we are disposed to extreme scepticism and not inclined to look favourably upon what we consider an uncritical cult of greatness. The decisive factor here is probably the experience we have had with power in its most terrible form. We who know what tyrants and despots are, and what lies behind the glory of their 'historical missions', are bitterly determined to test the diplomas issued by historians or tradition with the accuracy of a criminal investigator, and are only prepared to accord reluctant recognition in exceptional cases.

We should however recognize that we are in danger of going too far and of regarding almost all the great figures of the past as no better than a Hitler or a Stalin. More urgently than ever before are we faced today with the task of defining and limiting historical greatness, perhaps most urgently in a country like Germany, which has produced a Hitler. In the midst of the terrible catastrophe which he has left behind him, a new outlook upon history must be found which, while condemning this man and his machiavellist policy, and criticising the historical stages which led up to it, loyally acclaims the more noble aspects of national tradition, to which a nation whose self-confidence has been so shaken will cling all the more closely.

NATION, SOVEREIGNTY AND A COMMUNITY OF NATIONS

After these necessary reflections on the final ethical questions of international order, we may sum up all the foregoing considerations by saying that humanity has now finally reached the point where unless future development succeeds in extending beyond the conception of the nation which has been regarded up to now as the final and highest form of social organization, the resulting punishment will be the downfall of our civilization [3]). What shape this organization must take if it is to be healthy, permanent and conformable to the principles of our civilization, will be primarily determined by its relation to national organization. Is this to disappear altogether? If not, to what extent should national sovereignty be limited, and how should an international community of nations be constructed which is to take the lead over nations restricted in their sovereignty? What kind of national consciousness – one of the strongest collective feelings which the 19th century taught us to take into account – will be considered possible as a prerequisite?

It is obvious that these questions all circle round the final point as to the place the nation and the national state are to occupy in the feelings and in

43

the political organization of mankind in the future, and this suggests to us to examine without prejudice conceptions which have become second nature with us. The very fact, however, that only in the course of the last century have the nation and the national state become so important – taking due account of the differences between one country and another, above all between large and small states, – should make such a radical revision easier for us, and raises the question whether something which is of such recent origin could not make room for new formative forces. Surely the catastrophe of thirty years of world warfare which this paroxysm of national collective feeling brought upon us is the strongest proof we could have of the total madness in which this highly unhealthy trend has ended.

In order to clarify the task we have to fulfil it would be well first of all to formulate the dilemma in which we find ourselves. On the one hand we are all agreed that a supra-national organization is a necessity. On the other hand most of us would agree that the idea of an international organization which would degrade the individual nations to mere administrative areas is still more insufferable than the previous side-by-side existence of sovereign nations. We want neither latent or open anarchy of nations which are not subject to any binding and incontestable law, nor a Civitas Maxima of a continental or global nature. What we obviously wish is that due consideration should be given both to the individual life of the nation as well as to an international community. Neither should proliferate at the expense of the other; there should be a balance between them.

The same dilemma recurs at the next lowest level, however, when we consider the relations between the nation and its geographical sub-divisions. Here too neither the one nor the other is desirable, neither a centralized national state which degrades the smaller units to mere administrative districts, nor a luxuriating local egoism which we call Particularism. The ideal condition appears to us to be a balance between the dividing and the uniting forces. The growing clarity with which the people of today view this problem – especially in the highly centralized states – runs parallel with a corresponding realization in the international field. In both cases we are entirely in agreement that immeasurable damage results when one form of organization overbears another. Whether we are discussing the reform of the individual state or that of international interrelations, in both cases an overgrowth of the nation must be viewed with dismay, the only dif-

44

ference being that in the first case we deplore the detriment to the super-ordinate community and in the second to the subordinate one. Criticism in both cases concentrates upon the *hypertrophy of nationalism*, attacked in the one case from below, in the other from above.

The same ideas may be expressed by saying that the nation in its political organization is partly too large and partly too small. Too large for the evolution of genuinely free and neighbourly communal life and for true and permanent integration, which is able to exist without degenerating into nationalistic self-intoxication of mass-consciousness. Too small for those intellectual, political and economic relations which today can only flourish satisfactorily in an international community.

All that this amounts to is that nationalism (especially in the large central-ized states), considered the greatest and most triumphant achievement of the 19th century, has reached a crisis which today affects us very deeply indeed. This is what we are discussing whether we speak of a new national or a new international order. In both cases there is only one solution we can suggest: *Federalism*. A federal structure permits of the weight of political power being so split up between the smaller and larger units within the state and in the relations between the states, that in each case only such tasks fall to the larger units as have proved too universal for the smaller. This structure preserves the individual rights of each member unit, without endangering the necessary combination in the respective overall associations.

This solution is so convincing that nothing remains to be added here to all that has been said about it from various sides in recent years. But the enormous difficulties should not be overlooked which stand in its way. Both in the case of national as well as of international federation these difficulties arise from the fact that it is the ascendancy of the national state which has to be reduced. We should realize the very great strength of the forces which impel the national state to hold its ground both against local autonomy within the country itself, as well as against a supra-national unification over its head, in the one case by means of the appeal to central-ization, in the other to separation. What the national state is unwilling to grant to its member units, namely the autonomy which is their due, does it strive all the more obstinately to fight for on its own account. We should not be federalists if we did not accord our fullest sympathy to the last-named efforts, but at the same time we should not be champions of

45

international federalism if our sympathy did not draw the line before the necessity of a supra-national community. Our ideal is that of a constant state of balance, in which the relations of the member units to the nation as a whole are similar to those of the nation to the supra-national organization.

A centrally-organized large state, however intense its internal crisis may be and however strong the forces of opposition within itself are, still presents a counterweight to all efforts towards international federation which will certainly not be easy to remove. The task is therefore a difficult one. It could probably be tackled more easily if international federation were undertaken at the same time as a reorganization of the centralized states on a federal basis, just as, vice versa, the second process would be helped by the first. The education in mutual respect for individual rights within the state which federalism effects would also have beneficent results in international relations and would further the same liberal outlook as we find today in the few really federal states such as Switzerland.

It is very certain that so close a union as international federation constitutes will require such a high degree of mental and moral integration between the nations that it would be an empty ambition to begin with too vast plans. The impatient motto of all or nothing might jeopardize the whole business. We must also consider between which states an adequate degree of integration might already be expected. The question of concrete geographical groupings which might be taken into account can not be discussed in detail here.

In what follows we shall concentrate upon the main task: the setting up of a European community.

EUROPE AS A COMMUNITY

We shall begin with a general consideration. Every age is dominated by certain slogans which sway discussion and also influence thought, even when they are not directly expressed. They characterize the ideals of a generation, which possess such directive force for the very reason that they are nourished from deep-seated sources of devotion, feeling and political intent which can neither be explained nor destroyed by reason. Their domination is as inescapable as is the fashion in clothes or the way of life which modern engineering has created. It will always be a moot point whether it is men who make history or anonymous forces of the masses, but one thing is certain, whoever makes history does it *through* the leading ideas of the time – *with* them and not *against* them. The mysterious course of history can only be really understood if the coming and going of these main leading ideas is followed.

Even the analyst, who, like the author, feels mainly qualified to examine economic questions and, equipped with this legitimation, embarks on a sober and critical investigation of the possibilities of an *economic* union of Europe (as will be given in the course of this book), will first reconnoitre the wide field he then enters and with certain hesitation will ask himself whether 'Europe' is so indubitably one of the great leading ideas of our age, as the noisy and confusing activity in this field appears to prove. Before speaking as an economist he will wish to prove to his own satisfaction how strong the magnetic forces are which operate here and what intrinsic worth he himself is prepared to accord them. He will begin by acknowledging that the economic unity of Europe can only exist as a part of general unity and that this general unity of Europe is more important than the specifically economic one. He will wish to protect himself from being suspected of blindness to a greater ideal, which perhaps cannot be restrained by any fetters of economic reason, and which his age passionately affirms.

We must therefore begin by asking whether 'Europe' is in sober truth one of the greatest and truest leading motives of our age. The mightly display of rhetoric and literature will make us as sceptic on this point as the succession of conferences, commissions and proclamations which claim to further the idea, but which up to now have brought its achievement scarcely one single step nearer. It is difficult to discover a genuine and strong historical force in a movement in which such readiness to self-deceit, wordiness and disregard both of political realities and logical ideas are to be found. If we recollect the saying of Talleyrand already quoted – a very European saying – and because we have learnt to mistrust deeply any effusiveness in politics, we shall be inclined to doubt whether an idea which suffers from such an obvious prevalence of overheated emotions over cool reason can ever prove to have any staying power. We might perhaps have less scruples if, in addition, it were not very often a question of feelings which are by no means of an elemental and original nature, such as love of one's country and the brotherliness which springs from true fellowship, but rather one of lifeless conceptions drawn from literature and rhetoric, such as thrive best in the conditioned air of conferences. The fact, moreover, that so many politicians and intellectuals maintain themselves spiritually and materially in this way, does not dispose us more favourably towards it.

After saying all this with blunt honesty, however, the same honesty forces us to admit that even the worst we can say about the slogan of 'Europe' and the movement which rallies under this flag, cannot destroy the conviction that it is indeed one of the leading ideas of our age and one of historical force and urgency. 'Europe' is more than literature, catchwords, rhetoric and an empty excuse for congresses. Not unlike the national unity of the 19th century, continental unity has become a longing which must find fulfilment in a suitable and reasonable form, and perhaps its greatest significance is in overcoming the tendency towards national centralization which is so characteristic for the past. The centralized state has, indeed, doubly proved its insufficiency as already stated: being too large and amorphous to permit the growth of such true fellowship as can only thrive in smaller political units, and being too small and narrow for the great tasks of our age, which can no longer be solved even on the national level. We know already that the only answer to this problem of finding a form of organization which can at one and the same time do justice to two such contrary needs is federalism. This is the keynote we must always strike in discussing the economic problems of the European community.

If we examine the idea of 'Europe' more closely we see that there are two main qualities which give it vital force. The first may be described rather vaguely as '*Europeanism*'. By this is meant the urge, which can no longer be denied or suppressed, to take into account what Europe has in common, to emerge from the narrow confinements of national singleness, to offer a neighbourly hand to the other nations of Europe, to make our common spiritual heritage a living factor, and, with a sort of European patriotism, to hold our own in this field against what is not European, in short, a desire for spiritual and moral integration . . . We are becoming increasingly conscious of the need for Europeans to assert themselves with all their power and in all fields against the other continents, but they can only hope to do this in unison, not as a great cock-pit upon which the others look down, half in pity and half in contempt, and in which they stage their struggles for power. Since no great power is left in Europe which can match up to the great powers outside Europe, even a partial union of Europe would basically alter the set-up in its favour.

The more the non-European great powers emerge, and the civilizations of other continents begin to regard us with condescending self-confidence, the more it becomes both natural and necessary for the feeling of spiritual and moral homogeneousness among Europeans to increase powerfully. The more, thanks to modern improvements in transport, distances dwindle and Europeans come into closer contact both with one another and with the rest of the world, the more must the demarcation lines of national frontiers, language and religion, the dissimilarities between differing groups and national idiosyncrasies give place to internal unity on this continent, as the womb of the world-wide civilization of today. Its inhabitants should become all the more conscious of their common share in the same spiritual heritage, and the experience shared in common of the great phases of European history; from its origins in Greek culture, through the birth of Christianity and the Roman Empire, the interpenetration and final fusing of the Romanic and Germanic peoples and their cultures, the Crusades, the Age of Chivalry, the spread of the monasteries, the Papacy, the mediaeval Holy Roman Empire, Scholasticism, the foundation of the Universities, the heyday of the independent cities, the Renaissance, the Reformation and Counter-Reformation, up to the latest stages of development, the dissolution of Feudalism, the Age of Enlightment, the French Revolution, the Napoleonic Wars, the Romantic Age, the Industrial and Agrarian Revolutions, the evolution of national consciousness and the struggles for Liberalism, Democracy and Socialism.

We Europeans, conscious of our individuality, our common history and standard of values cling with a deep emotion of our own to the spots in our landscape with which our history is particularly associated. Whether we gaze from the Parthenon on to the deep blue Bay of Salamis, where two and a half thousand years ago the fate of Europe was decided for the first time; whether, standing on the lonely castled hilltop of Carthage, we wonder what would have become of Europe if Carthage and not Rome had been victorious; whether we stand on the Kahlenberg with Vienna at our feet, where, thanks to the bravery of the Poles, the fate of Europe in the face of assault from Asia was decided on another occasion; whether we bend over the venerable document in the Federal Archives in Switzerland in which the original Swiss Cantons confirmed their confederacy against the spirit of tyranny; whether, on the dyke at West Kapelle, the strongest human bulwark on the coast of Europe against the inroads of the sea, we look across the broad landscapes of the Dutch painters; whether we reverently enter the room in Weimar in which Goethe died – wherever it may be, we are always overcome by the same consciousness of the deep ties of our common and unspeakably precious heritage. It is the same feeling which during the last war caused us to tremble for the fate of Rome, Athens, Florence, Paris, Cologne or Munich as for the issue of a decisive battle, and to mourn equally for all historic buildings which were destroyed as for something irreplaceable.

And as Europeans do we not know that in spite of all our differences we share in common with all others on our continent a certain way of living and thinking. However much of this we may have handed on to other continents, our way is a western way, which today more than ever must hold its own against every other. This European way of life is, however, only legitimate if it can assert itself out of self-loyalty and not in enmity and self-glorification and can face everything strange and new with an open mind and that reason which has been given to all men alike. The destruction of mediaeval cathedrals is a terrible disaster, particularly when it is not due to the chances of war or to unavoidable strategic necessity, but to wanton indifference, but Europe itself stands unshaken as long as it remains the home of humanity, tolerance, reason and religious veneration.

Many possibilities both good and bad are contained in this Europeanism. As long as it is restrained by moderation and humanity, it represents healthy European self-confidence, a proud but also a tolerant profession of its individual creed and the indispensable sense of separation which is unquestionably essential to the political and economic integration of Europe. No human community – from the smallest to the greatest – can exist without such feelings, and when we see today the readiness with which Europeans seem to be prepared to abdicate inwardly before the non-European world, it would seem that the danger of too little European self-confidence is greater than the opposite danger of too much. Europeanism can, however, also mean the dangerous tendency to exclusive continentalism which transfers the arrogance, impatience and enmity of nationalism on to a higher geographical level. This degeneration would, as we shall see, find its economic expression in a tendency to form autarkic blocs on a continental basis and to create new areas of self-sufficiency, the fatal effects of which we know only too well.

However ambiguous and indefinite the first of the three motives of Europeanism may be, there is no doubting the grim and unyielding inevitability of the *second*: the necessity of uniting all political and spiritual forces in Europe in elementary defence against the imperialism of world Communism as organized and directed by Russia. The spiritual and economic integration of Europe may be aims which admit of various interpretations, just as the ways by which they are to be attained may be seriously disputed. The *political integration* of Europe, however, is an aim which not only can be unequivocally defined, but which is also generally acclaimed in spite of differences of religion, philosophy and economic convictions, always excepting the Communists and their conscious or unconscious fellow-travellers. Irrespective of the degree to which this union of the spiritual and political forces in Europe takes place in this hour of acute danger, or of the form it assumes, the motto is, really and truly, 's'unir ou périr'. This inexorable decision, which mortal danger from without forces upon Europe in a manner unknown since the time of Ogdai Khan, embodies the strongest historical force which gives the idea of European union the character of a genuine and inescapable leading idea of the time, as to unite has become a vital commandment upon which the existence and the civilization of the West depends. This is where phrase-making at last stops and the matter becomes deadly serious. Here we face the direct, simple and vital aim which can no longer be disputed with more or less ingenious theories. Hannibal ante portas, this is the common ground for all those who do not stand in the camp of the Punicians of today, and this is the situation which compels us to take it as a measure of all things and to relate everything to it. It is obviously difficult to separate this political integration of Europe from spiritual integration. All the more so since the main weapon of the new world conqueror is mental confusion which he tries to evoke by means of undermining psychological tactics, until the resistance of the West has become paralysed by a process of mental and moral softening – by the untimely pacificism which we have already condemned, by 'Neutralism', by illusions regarding possibilities of a compromise, by having public attention side-tracked to alleged neo-fascist dangers, by the cat-and-mouse game of notes and conferences – until the final military decision is only the finishing stroke.

51

The will to united self-assertion is given its real strength and deep significance through the spiritual tradition which for us is linked with the idea of 'Europe', and through the forms and values of a civilization which is characterized by its irreconcilable opposition to every kind of mass-despotism and by the consequent determination to resist it. Political self-assertion, therefore, presupposes that this tradition is indeed regarded as a common and inestimable spiritual and moral heritage, which is not to be sold for a mess of pottage. In the conviction, however, that the 'open society' of Bergson, i.e. the community of free human beings, is the main object of defence for the West, this consciousness – and here we strike another keynote of our later economic considerations – must also recognize that the economic system must be in accordance with this system of society if we are not to sacrifice the aim to the means, or, according to Juvenal's saying, propter vitam perdere causas vitae.

To make this clear, certain *precise statements* need to be made.

Firstly: it would be entirely illogical, as we have already said, were one to challenge Europe to combine its forces in self-defence and at the same time grudge Europeans the indispenable minimum of 'European patriotism' necessary for it, instead of actually welcoming the same. It would be equally irrealistic were we to expect that in the near future anything like such a degree of pan-European community spirit will develop as would entitle us to speak of a European nation in the precise way that we speak of a French or a German nation. As we shall see later, many ideas of European economic integration come to grief over the fundamental error of assuming that such a degree of spiritual and political integration exists, and of trying to apply the experience gained in economic planning inside a nation on the European level, without asking whether this experience does not rather rely upon the spiritual and political set-up of the national state, and whether it can, without a with-your-leave-or-by-your-leave, be transferred onto a pan-European scale.

Even while sharing Montesquieu's view of Europe as a 'nation de nations', and counting upon a growing European consciousness, it would be pure illusionism to build any plans on the expectation that this continental community consciousness will in general and in the long run become stronger than the national one or even be able to counterbalance it, whenever and wherever the two come into serious conflict with each other. The integrating effect of a common peril is once again likely to show also in the case of Europe, that great political amalgamations usually come about through pressure from without and not through a free decision from within – in defiance of something and not in favour of something. But anyone who knows the special character of Europe and who avoids any hide-bound rationalism can have no doubt that, despite the pressure from without, national consciousness and the self-will of the national states will continue to exist to a degree which will necessitate extreme tact and caution. To brush this aside and to complain would be the very opposite of a constructive policy.

It is indeed possible that the suppression of national consciousness in favour of a continental consciousness might constitute a serious danger to the resistance power of Europe, namely when the strivings for European integration dull the sense of responsibility which rests upon every nation to defend itself against Communist-Russian aggression, and instead becomes a screen behind which inactivity and indecision hide under the motto 'ut aliquid fieri videatur'. What we said earlier on about false internationalism should be taken to heart, and it should be considered that the will to defence in Europe cannot be stronger than that of each individual nation. How do matters stand here?

In a famous debate in the English House of Commons just before the outbreak of the first world war, the Irish leader Tim Healy defined the nation as 'a thing for which people are ready to lay down their lives'. This is obviously inadequate as a definition but it does undoubtedly stress a necessary aspect of the nation. It is a disquieting question whether we may assume without further ado that all European nations are prepared to make this extreme sacrifice in view of the Communist Russian danger, disquieting not because they are permeated with Communism, since (in contrast to France and Italy) this does not apply to Germany, one of the countries in greatest danger, but above all for the reason that their will to self-defence has been weakened by illusions, fear and hopelessness. The justification for this question is demonstrated by the apparently insuperable disinclination of most European nations today to consider military defence as an obvious duty which primarily concerns them and for which it is unavoidable that sacrifices must be made. Instead of this they show a regrettable tendency to push this duty on to the United States and to play the part of the tired onlooker.

Under these circumstances is the possibility to be entirely rejected that the present efforts towards the political integration of Europe may just become an excuse for avoiding national action and the growth in conferences, European plans and organizations may just correspond to a shrinkage in natural self-assertion on the part of the individual nations. And is it only fear of a bogy to think that perhaps nothing decisive will take place either on a national or on a continental plane in the time that is still left to us? That Europe will try to lean upon the individual nations and the individual nations upon Europe? That national patriotism *no longer* suffices and continental patriotism *does not yet* suffice for the maximum resistance which is necessary? Only if in the eagerness to attain a European community it is not forgotten that this can only be built upon the foundations of strong nations, do these anxious questions become unnecessary.

We see therefore that the degree of European patriotism must be carefully weighed both with regard to its possibility and its desirability. On the other hand a warning must be uttered against the tendency to drive this community consciousness so far that Europe becomes detached from the cultural and political union of the West, and the higher level is ignored at which Europe links up especially with the United States of America in a union which today has become a matter of life and death. To those fools who may still think that Washington is spiritually and politically scarcely less far removed from us than Moscow, James Burnham, a clever American, has recently given the right answer when he said with grim humour, 'Coca-cola may be a horrible drink, but it is not nearly so horrible as a Russian concentration camp'.

This leads to a *second* important realization. It is that not only would any idea of European neutralism be suicidal today, but that it has also become increasingly evident that the spiritual and political integration of Europe – i.e. the combination of its forces and the expansion of its powers of resistance – only makes sense as part and parcel of a higher combination and organization of the resistance potential of the *entire* western world on both sides of the Atlantic. Anyone who reflects that if it is at all possible to speak of Europe today this is exclusively due to the protective power of America, must accept these ideas as a matter of course. It may thus be said that developments have already far outrun the original conception of a European union and that this conception is becoming increasingly supplanted by that of an Atlantic union, which, as the greater of the two, embraces the European union as well.

54

We now come to the *third* consideration. There is some justification for saying that the idea of a European union, including the economic consequences, has to a certain extent grown out of date through the trend of events. In a double sense it comes too late. In the first place it has come too late to prevent the self-laceration of the continent, since this disaster has taken place to such an appalling degree in the second world war that today the European nations have not even the strength any more to attack one another. A new war between them can only be imagined as part of a world dispute which would sweep across Europe. Seen in a clear light, therefore, the sense of a European community can no longer consist in the preserving of peace between the peoples of Europe – this should have been thought of while there was yet time. Its meaning lies rather in organizing the defence of Europe against the danger which threatens from the East, and in preventing individual European nations, even though unwillingly, from finding themselves in the wrong camp. The idea of a European union comes too late on the other hand for the reason already stated that, even under the most favourable conditions, Europe can no longer defend itself alone, but only in association with the organized resistance of the entire West and under its protection. Without the American war and economic potential our continent is hopelessly lost. The forces of Europe must however combine for a twofold reason, firstly to increase this potential to the maximum, and secondly to preserve within this all-over organization of the West the spiritual and political individuality of Europe, which otherwise threaten to become stamped out in the struggle between the Titans.

This special character of Europe – and here we come to our *fourth* consideration – must above all be taken into account in determining the form which the union of the continent is to take if this is to be viable and permanent and able to subsist on its own without the aid of constant propaganda, force or some other artificial means. We would wish for something which is neither a form of imperialistic bloc, an elaborate construction of civil or military bureaucrats, window dressing for ideologies which shun the light, an unending succession of congresses and conferences, nor a new field of experiments in economic planning. The nearest approach to the goal is made by those who point to the example of Switzerland, which in its federal structure demonstrates how unity in variety, and how freedom of the individual members within the order of the whole is possible. But not all those who desire the 'Helvetianising' of Europe have grasped that Switzer-

55

land is the product of slow and organic growth which could only take place in a soil which had been purposefully and patiently enriched by historical traditions and human relations. If we are agreed that Europe can only grow under the aegis of a principle which we call federation, then we must also realize that federalism, if it is to be more than a mere phrase, is not just a matter of administrative technique, but must be rooted in a definite philosophy.

For Europe too, *federalism* means a cohesion of the whole which comes about naturally through the co-operation of the parts, in a spirit of whole hearted union with the small group in which we have grown up and at the same time with respect for the other groups with whom we come together at the higher level to fulfil those tasks which can only be carried out in common; and in the community spirit which develops from this. If we aim at European federation it must be with the recognition that the nation is indeed an indispensable stage of political organization which cannot be dispensed with, but that it can neither do without the sub-national stages if it is not to freeze into a bloc which strangles human beings and their genuine communities, nor can it remain any longer in sovereign isolation and ignore the higher supra-national stage, if the problems of our age, which far surpass the powers of the national unit, are to be solved.

This great work demands a spirit which is directly opposed to that of modern mass civilization and – let it be said – to the spirit of many advocates of the European community, who in their hearts are Jacobin centralists with no idea whatsoever of federalism. Neither on the national nor on the international plane is it possible to be a federalist in the upward direction and a centralist in the downward one. One must make up one's mind. The fact that many disciples of European federation – including economic federation – avoid this decision, or perhaps have never even realized that it must be made, threatens to side-track the whole movement, which then becomes reduced to a dubious paradox, which we shall come across again when we consider the details of the economic side of European federation.

INTERNATIONAL ORDER AS THE SELF-ASSERTION OF THE FREE WORLD AGAINST COMMUNIST IMPERIALISM

Already in the first German edition of this book, which appeared at the end of the war, attention was diverted, with an outspokenness which at that time was understood by only a few, from the recently overthrown totalitarianism of the Axis powers to the new threat to peace and international order presented by the last remaining totalitarianism of Russian Communism [4]. This danger has meanwhile grown so enormous that all questions of international order today must be considered in its perspective. This fact emerged very clearly in the foregoing section. Everything is of a temporary nature, everything is in a state of constant tension, everything is doubtful, as long as the world is overshadowed by this danger. What is the nature of this danger, and how can it be abolished? A book which deals with the fundamental problems of international order must at least give some indication of the lines along which these questions which weigh so heavily upon us are to be answered, if it is not to lack the foundation of hard and fast reality which the middle of this century demands.

It would be acting with complete irresponsibility were we to try to answer questions on the nature of the Russian Communist danger and the possibility of abolishing it in an optimistic or even a semi-optimistic manner. That there is no international organization of states which could unite both the Communist Russian bloc, which in a military and political career of unexampled success has already absorbed the two continents of Asia and Europe with the exception of their southern or western fringes, and that world which is most justly termed free, in any form at all which would finally put an end to the struggles for power between the nations, is a conviction shared today by all reasonable persons capable of learning from the overwhelming experiences of the past. The dream of 'One World' has come to an end, and although we would not wish to say that there is no purpose at all in the organization of the so-called United Nations which was constituted in 1945, this purpose – apart from certain undeniable successes – can only be conceived as at least maintaining contact between the two camps and keeping everything undecided as long as the unforeseen contingencies of historical development remain open, including the possibility that fundamental changes may take place inside the Communist bloc which would abolish the present irreconcilable antagonism of the two worlds. How deep the cleft is today, however, is shown by the fate of that international organization in which formerly the universal humanity of the civilized nations expressed itself most strongly over and above all contests for power, i.e. the Red Cross, with the parallel organization of the

Red Crescent, for which, even under the banner of simple brotherly love, the gap has grown too wide to be bridged.

If therefore the *dualism of world order today* – by which it has become a world disorder – cannot be surmounted, is there at least not the hope of stabilizing this polarity for an indefinite period? Anyone who whishes to build on this hope must begin by admitting that in some parts of the world the course of the dividing line is such that stabilization cannot be seriously considered until a regulation of this line has been effected.

The most neuralgic points are found in those countries which are cut in two by this dividing line i.e. *Germany and Austria*. A stabilization of world polarity which would improve upon the present state of cold war would therefore presuppose that the dismembered unity of these unhappy countries – in particular that of Germany, where the dismemberment is the more ruthless and insupportable – should be restored. As every thinking person must admit, however, with the world in its present state this reunion can only be conceived as taking place through a shift of the West-East frontier either eastwards or westwards. There is no third possibility, which means that the improvements required to stabilize the condition of the world entail in themselves such an alteration in this condition as amounts to a decision in the war of the titans for or against one or the other bloc. The illusion that a third way might be possible is all the more dangerous for the West, which alone succumbs to it, because it affords Moscow the possibility of holding out the enticement of a compromise at a price which seems acceptable to the illusion-seeking West, whereas according to the inherent nature of Russian policy it can be nothing more than a deception which more or less cleverly conceals a victory in Germany, Austria or elsewhere.

The important thing is to recognize this inherent nature of Russian policy. It may be deduced from the character of this totalitarian regime, and all the foregoing experience which the West has undergone with the Soviet Government proves definitely that this is not just theoretical speculation. It is a *policy of expansion, of challenge*, of conquests by every possible means, which excludes the assumption fostered by many people that it is a policy fed by defensive fear, which can be quietened with concessions, with the payment of a 'price', with the satisfaction of 'final territorial demands', in short, with a western policy of appeasement. If fear can be spoken of here, then it is the *offensive fear* of a government which is convinced that no static balance is conceivable between the world of liberty and that of slavery. No less a price than world mastery, however, will suffice to quieten an offensive fear of this kind.

I think I have dealt with the most important aspects of the inherent nature of the Soviet regime and its world policy in a chapter of my book 'Maß und Mitte'. The attempt made there to define the sociology of Communism is the basis of the following remarks:

Not a single discussion should be started on the Russian Communist Empire and the resulting problems for the West, no one who speaks on this subject should even be listened to, no single suggestion which promises to solve these problems should be made or considered, above all things in Central Europe, before two things have been made quite clear. *Firstly*: we are dealing with a real empire, and the aim of its rulers, which has been openly stated, which is the conclusive outcome of its nature, and which has been openly stated, which is the conclusive outcome of its nature, and which has been more than adequately proved by the way they have behaved, is to expand this empire to actual world domination, and that by every means possible. *Secondly*: this empire which unrelentingly strives for world domination is a pseudo-religion within the shell of the Russian State, a sort of secularised Islam, a social creed which is militant to the highest degree and which therefore advances on two fronts at once, the military and the ideological. The unsuspecting guilelessness with which so many people in the non-Bolshevist world allow themselves to be misued as pawns in the Russian game without ever wishing or knowing it, would not be possible to the alarming extent which is the case today were these two facts generally known, above all in leading and educated circles. Their blindness and ignorance are not the most insignificant weapons with which the Russian Communist Empire has up to now achieved its enormous triumphs, and hopes to achieve further ones.

This is the underlying reason why a stabilization of the world dualism of today – which in any case would be contrary to all historical experience – is not a possibility on which any responsible western policy can even reckon. What remains?

To this depressing question two answers have up to now been given, which in a way appear to be at the two opposite ends of the scale. The one is called containment, the stemming of the Russian Communist flood by the dyke of a western world which can finally match up to the East on the political, moral and military levels. The opposite answer is that only a war can put an end to the present tension, a purely military decision, regarded as both a necessary and adequate condition for the final solution of the problem of world peace which Soviet Russia has created, a gigantic struggle along fronts which, according to the traditional rules of warfare, would not only cut of the Russian Government from the West, but with it the people of Russia. Only historical importance can be accorded to *containment* as a remedy today. In the period succeeding the war containment was a necessary phase, firstly to put an end to the disastrous policy of capitulation and secondly to organize a defence against a series of provocations. Nec plus ultra was all very well as a beginning. In the meanwhile every thinking person must have become convinced that it is impossible to stabilize world peace on the basis of a status quo which indubitably gives the Soviet Union, clearly bent on world domination, the possibility of keeping the West in permanent suspense through its vagaries and through utilizing its position on the 'inner line' to bring western economy into constant disorder and thereby finally to exhaust it.

Containment today means that the West is to be satisfied with a vestigial Europe which bears an alarming resemblance to the Byzantine Empire which by the later Middle Ages had been compressed by the Turks into a small territory, a Europe that in its longing for quiet abandons Eastern and Central Europe and China to slavery. This is discrediting its own political and moral principles and dangerously blunting the propaganda weapon of liberty. Anyone who today considers that a policy of containment alone can suffice shows that he has not yet grasped the gigantic *motive power of the Communist Pseudo-Islam*. The worst is, however, that after the United States have incomprehensively allowed the great burst in the dyke to take place in China it has become very questionable whether mere repairs to the dyke, here, there, and everywhere, will avail, and whether, above all in Asia, the flood does not threaten to assume proportions which begin to give a tragic aspect to the idea of stabilizing the status quo. To choose a more homely symbol: if the water pipes in the house are rotten through and through, and the water pressure is increased to the maximum, there is no longer any point in panting up and down stairs from the cellar to the attic trying to keep one's thumb on all the holes. One must make up one's mind to turn off the main. In addition, it is difficult to accept the fact that one whole floor is already under water.

There is, therefore, no escaping the unpleasant conclusion that the West must find some way of shifting the present status quo in its favour, as well as of so altering the nature of the Russian regime that it will cease to flood the world. Does this mean that no other alternative is open to us than the opposite desperate idea of a *purely military decision?* It is of the very greatest importance that the answer to this should definitely be no! A purely military decision is neither *necessary nor adequate*, because the final result depends upon decisions taken inside Russia and the countries under its subjection.

The purely military decision is *not necessary*, as long as there is hope that changes or sweeping landslides may take place inside the Communist sphere of influence which may remove the totalitarian regime in an unforeseen manner, or which may create a state of affairs in which the desire for, or at least the possibility of a continued offensive policy is reduced to a degree which would suffice for stabilization. It would be very short-sighted of the West to repeat in Russia's case the mistakes made with regard to the former German totalitarianism, and to fail to see in the Russian people their most natural ally in the struggle against their own Government, an ally which must be mobilized by means of a constructive programme for the time when their country will be liberated; not to speak of the inhabitants of the subjected countries.

The West would be well advised not to let itself be carried away with hate against the Russian people in its horror of the Communist regime, but rather on their part to do everything possible to encourage internal resistance inside the Russian sphere of influence. It is characteristic of a totalitarian regime that it is able to exploit the obvious contradictions within the free world, while concealing its own far greater ones. To reveal these, to bring out into the light the inner weaknesses of such a rule, and at last to turn the tables in the third world war, which has already broken out in the form of mixed military and psychological strategy chosen by Moscow, that is the task which lies before the West, and which has already been clearly recognized by the more far-seeing of its leaders. The extensive programme of possibilities which this opens up cannot be described here. While the West gazes spell-bound, and with a fear which Moscow makes full use of, at atom-bombs, tanks and jet-fighters, it forgets that the other type of warfare, the psychological-political, which in its one-sidedness is far more dangerous for the West, determines the field in which Moscow seeks the actual decision. Here war has long been declared upon the West, and the purpose of the programme sketched out here is to urge the West to take up this challenge.

If the military decision is not a necessary condition of stabilized world order, this does not of course mean that it can be avoided under all conditions. It remains an eventuality for which it is the primary duty of every responsible government of the West to be prepared today. Should it take place, however, it will become evident that a military decision is not only unnecessary, but also that it is *inadequate* for the stabilization of world order. History will repeat itself here and will show, as has long been clear in the case of German totalitarianism, that everything depends upon what takes place inside the conquered country and what becomes of it. The internal future of Russia and its sphere of influence, therefore, becomes a problem which in the interests of international order cannot be considered too early.

Only a fool will demand that the success of such a policy be guaranteed in advance. But one of its greatest advantages is that it does not interfere with a policy of maximum and energetic military alertness and realistic stubbornness and watchfulness with regard to the tyranny of Moscow, but can ally itself with it, and by showing the way can give actual force and accuracy of aim. At the same time it preserves it from a too brutal and warlike callousness, which otherwise might bring about a world catastrophe and overpower the West also with the poisonous atmosphere of mere military encampment. The most human way is also the wisest way here, and wherever fortune points to an opportunity there should be no hesitation in taking it. It is no easy psychological task, to be sure, to assemble all the forces of the West against the Soviet regime and to demand that the greatest sacrifices be made in the economic and military struggle against a government whose own subjects are made its operating tools, without at the same time making use of the emotion stirring poison of hate propaganda against the other people. In the struggle against the totalitarianism of the Axis powers the West unfortunately did not succeed in this task, with fatal results. In the struggle today against the new totalitarianism its success should be all the greater because the need is recognized more clearly.

The two extremes mentioned – with which the policy recommended here may be favourably contrasted – both containment and the policy of a military decision, falls, each in its own way, into the error of ignoring the peculiar nature of totalitarianism. The 'containers' and 'stabilizers' are blind to the vulcanic nature of such a regime, which is incompatible with the idea of a status quo. The others, who conceive of the dispute as a purely military and national affair, fail, on the other hand, to see that this totalitarian imperialism necessarily rests upon a tremendous tension between the government and the population which it keeps in physical and mental slavery, so that old-fashioned ideas of diplomacy and warfare have become out-of-date and inapplicable. One extreme fails to recognize the external driving power of totalitarianism, the other its internal force. The only right policy is one which takes account of both.

The task with which the West is faced, of gaining an influence on the internal mental and political development of the Soviet sphere of influence, which is sealed hermetically against the outside world, and of speeding up and guiding the internal ferment both in these countries and in their ideologies, presents difficulties to which no special attention needs to be drawn. But it would be asking too much to expect that there should be an easy, certain and safe way out of the extremely difficult position into which the West has been brought, largely through its belief in easy solutions. On the other hand the task has been simplified by an event which from every other point of view constitutes an enormous triumph for Moscow and an equally great danger for the West, namely the penetration of the Soviet regime into the heart of Europe. However much the West regrets the decisive aid it rendered Moscow at the time, it has on the other hand become evident that extraordinary opportunities for a spiritual and moral counter-drive are offered, and nowhere are these opportunities greater than in Germany, where East meets West, as it were 'Unter den Linden'.

In the famous 'Maximes et Pensées' of Chamfort the following very true remark is to be found: 'L'âme, lorsqu'elle est malade, fait précisement comme le corps; elle se tourmente et s'agite en tous sens, mais elle finit par trouver un peu de calme. Elle s'arrête enfin sur le genre de sentiment et d'idées le plus nécessaire a son repos'. This is exactly the way the western world behaves towards the nightmare of Communist imperialism. If it is not to be paralysed by perpetual fear, worry and uncertainty, or not to be plunged through unconsidered hastiness into adventures whose outcome cannot be foreseen, we must wish that it may acquire adaptiveness, that its agitation may be quietened and its equalmindedness preserved. To be able to save and invest, without a look of hunted fear, to be able to sow without thinking that the hailstorm of tomorrow will destroy the crop; to be able to concentrate one's powers in trust that the future contains, not only the worst, but also the best chances, and to live without panic leaving the end in God's hands. A life on friendly terms with the worst danger in our history must, however, find its limit where it results in watchfulness being relaxed, and in a cocoon-like existence of illusions, selfish indifference, blindness and pleasant dreams, from which the awakening will be all the more terrible. Readiness is all.

NOTES

1. (p. 33) Machiavellism:

In spite of all the objections to it, MACAULAY's famous essay 'Machiavelli' (first published 1837, later in his 'Critical and Historical Essays') still stands out among the older literature. The most penetrating contemporary discussion is probably 'La fin du machiavélisme', in 'Sort de l'Homme' by J. MARITAIN, Neuenburg 1943, pp. 97 foll. cf also: KANT, Zum ewigen Frieden, Königsberg 1795, Anhang; HANS BARTH, Fluten und Dämme, Zürich 1943, p. 168 foll.; G. FERRERO, Niccolò e il 'Principe', published by B. RADITZA, Colloqui con Guglielmo Ferrero, Lugano 1939. Note following resumé by Maritain (see above p. 141): '1° Il suffit d'être juste pour gagner la vie éternelle; il ne suffit pas d'être juste pour gagner les batailles ou des succès politiques immédiats. 2° Pour gagner ces batailles ou pour remporter des succès politiques immédiats, il n'est pas nécessaire d'être juste; il peut être, à l'occasion, plus avantageux d'être injuste. 3° Il est nécessaire, quoi-qu'il ne soit pas suffisant, d'être juste pour procurer et promouvoir le bien commun politique et la prospérité durable des communautés terrestres.'

Despite the slanderous legend of the 18th century, TALLEYRAND, referred to in the text, is an excellent teacher of foreign politics, who knew where to draw the line sharply between 'Realism' and Machiavellism. This hard-headed realist hated nothing more than war, and for nothing did he fight more honestly and determindly than the peace of Europe. The way in which he reprimanded the Machiavellist Napoleon for the knavish trick of Bayonne, is as impressive as is the funeral oration for the French diplomat Reinhard, which he held towards the end of his life in 1838, and in which he extols trust and good faith as important conditions of successful diplomacy (quoted by DUFF COOPER in 'Talleyrand').

2. (p. 41) The Great Men of History:

'Die wirkliche Größe ist ein Mysterium', writes Jacob Burckhardt in his essay on 'historische Größe' which still remains the classical discussion on this question which is forever cropping up. Among the latest literature, the study by EDITH EUCKEN-ERDSIEK, 'Größe und Wahn', Tübingen, 1950, deserves close attention.

The questionable nature of acclamation by popular plebiscite becomes very clear in the most recent case of Frederick the Great. If ever there was a cynical machiavellist, then it was the author of 'Antimachiavell', and all the same he earned his surname, with the approval of Europe, strangely enough, not through his considerable peaceful achievements, but through his military successes in the Silesian war, the clearest case of a war of conquest. How this was possible is an interesting question, in the answering of which we should forget neither the gratitude of the English, the admiration of the military specialists, the propaganda of the Paris claque of d'Alembert and Diderot, the enthusiastic impression of youthful impetuosity made on the youth of the time in particular, including no less a person than Goethe, nor the malicious relish of the 'century of enlightenment' over the humiliation of the 'old-fashioned' and 'bigotted' Empress Maria Theresia by the clever and unbelieving rationalists. Despite Frederick's personal charm and his dramatic life, it is important, above all in consideration of his mythical force, to draw due attention to his unsuitability as a pattern of political action. Not all those who attack the neighbours they consider defenceless get away with it so easily, just as, on the other hand, those who have got into trouble through their own fault frequently lack the greatness and philosophical insight which makes Frederick so fascinating even to those who have no wish of succumbing to his personality.

65

3. (p. 43) The Crisis of the Nations:

In subjecting the exaggerated conception of the nation which grew up in the 19th century, to a criticism for which the present time has grown ripe, we are resuming contact with the best tradition of the 18th century (cf my 'Gesellschaftskrisis, Part I, Chapter 1). See on this subject: W. KAEGI, 'Historische Meditationen' Zürich 1942, pp. 249 foll.; J. HUIZINGA, 'Wachstum und Formen des nationalen Bewußtseins in Europa bis zum Ende des 19. Jahrhunderts', in 'Im Banne der Geschichte', Basle, 1943; HANS ZBINDEN, 'Die Moralkrise des Abendlandes', 2nd edition, Bern 1941; L. MISES 'Nation, Staat und Wirtschaft', Vienna, 1919. A complement to this chapter on the nation is to be found in my book 'Maß und Mitte', Erlenbach-Zürich 1950, pp. 241–258.

4. (p. 57) Communist Imperialism:

In addition to the chapter of my book 'Maß und Mitte' referred to in the text, reference should above all be made to: J. MONNEROT 'Die Soziologie des Kommunismus', Cologne 1952; J. MONNEROT 'La Guerre en question', Paris, 1951; G. KENNAN, 'Amerika und Russland's Zukunft' in 'Der Monat', July 1951.

PART TWO

THE ECONOMIC ELEMENTS OF
INTERNATIONAL ORDER

'Telle est la condition humaine que souhaiter la grandeur de son pays, c'est souhaiter mal à ses voisins . . . Il est clair qu'un pays ne peut gagner sans qu'un autre perde.'

Voltaire, Dictionnaire phil., art. Patrie.

'In opposition to this narrow and malignant opinion, I will venture to assert that the increase of riches and commerce in any one nation, instead of hurting, commonly promotes the riches and commerce of all its neighbours; and that a state can scarcely carry its trade and industry very far, where all the surrounding states are buried in ignorance, sloth and barbarism.

Were our narrow and malignant politics to meet with success, we should reduce all our neighbouring nations to the same state of sloth and ignorance that prevails in Morocco and the Coast of Barbary. But what would be the consequence? They could send us no commodities. They could take none from us: Our domestic commerce itself would languish for want of emulation, example, and instruction! And we ourselves should soon fall into the same abject condition to which we had reduced them. I shall therefore venture to acknowledge that, not only as a man, but as a British subject, I pray for the flourishing commerce of Germany, Spain, Italy, and even France itself.'

David Hume, Of the Jealousy of Trade, Essays and Treatises, I.

I

THE ECONOMIC SYSTEM AND
INTERNATIONAL ORDER

After giving a general description of the problems of international order in the introduction, in the course of which actual political questions were discussed as far as seems suitable for the purposes of this book, we shall now pursue those questions which seem to us to be most important. We emphasized that international order should be viewed first and foremost in the light of national order and must be developed out of it; that international peace, if it is not to be uprooted by every tempest, must be deeply and firmly grounded in a society which displays healthy spiritual, moral, economic, and social characteristics i.e. steadfastness, simplicity, justice, and humanity. Since the international crisis is only one part of the general crisis of society today, it is understandable that it can be overcome only by the solution of this general crisis. The programme of social and economic reform, therefore, which was developed in my earlier books 'Die Gesellschaftskrisis der Gegenwart' and 'Civitas humana' is also a programme of a new international order which shall supply the real foundation for a specifically political and legal programme of international political organization.

If the necessity, or at least the advantage, of such a sociological foundation for all questions of international order is acknowledged, it follows that the economic elements of international relations are accorded a special importance. This will therefore be the main subject of the following chapters. In point of fact, of the motives which throughout all times have led to international conflict and finally to war, those which, not always with great precision, are termed economic have always played the most important part. From the battles of primeval times and of the undeveloped races of today for hunting and pasture grounds, for salt deposits and fertile river valleys, the chain stretches by way of the predatory and conquering expeditions of the maritime and merchant states to the struggles today for room for expansion, possession of raw materials, colonies and markets.

A problem immediately presents itself. If a phenomenon exists in which a careful distinction should be made between appearance and reality, between motives which are objectively compelling and those which are merely subjective and pretended, then this phenomenon is war. Since a maximum of passionate devotion on the part of the masses who have to do the fighting is necessary, in order that reason, which otherwise exerts a restraining influence on war, may be put out of action, the first law of warfare, with the exception of a plain and obvious war of defence, has always been that of psychological propaganda. Those responsible for carrying the war must ensure that the masses see the war in the light of those motives which guarantee a maximum of warlike emotion, irrespective of the motives which influence the leaders themselves. Regard must also be given to allies and neutrals. Thus real and apparent motives become interwoven without its being possible to distinguish one from the other and the result is a highly complicated picture which only very few can see in the right light. The fact that it cannot always be assumed that the leaders themselves are clear as to their own motives and interests makes the matter still more involved.

It is therefore not surprizing that it is very difficult to determine what part is played in war by motives of an *economic* nature. All the more so since such clarification presupposes a very comprehensive knowledge of economics, sociology, and history, which not everyone possesses. Certainly the question presents itself in a different form at different epochs of political history because economic conditions have varied very greatly at different times. We may therefore leave out of consideration here the economic motives behind the Fourth Crusade, which led, not to the freeing of Jerusalem, but to the plundering of the Christian city of Constantinople, or those behind the Seven Years' War. We shall limit ourselves rather to the present epoch of history which is characterized in the economic field by the predominance of very definite economic conditions. The uncertainty and multiplicity of opinions to be met with here are common knowledge. Everyone knows how widespread was the opinion during the first world war that the actual cause of the German-British conflict was the trade rivalry between the two countries, or that economic and financial motives largely determined the entry of the United States into the war. Many people still hold this opinion today. Was not the world war altogether the inevitable result of Capitalism, and must therefore true peace for the world not be dependent in the first place on the abolition of Capitalism? Must not the Pacifist therefore necessarily be a Socialist? What part is played by the armaments industry? What importance should be accorded to pressure of population as a war factor?

If we turn to the second world war the confusion and contradictions of opinions become quite unbearable. Are not the main causes again to be sought in economic tensions, in the contrast between 'poor' and 'rich' countries, in the 'unequal division of raw materials', in the unequal division of gold, in the policy of self-sufficiency, or in the tension between overpopulated and underpopulated countries? But why was it that only a few of the countries alleged to be 'victimized' had recourse to war, and why just those which had replaced the principles of free market economy (commonly known as 'Capitalism') by others which can only be termed collectivist or socialist? How is it possible that voices should still be heard which try to put the responsibility for the second world war also upon Capitalism, despite the fact that in Germany, Italy and Japan the most important feature of Capitalism, namely free market economy, was lacking, and had been replaced by a principle of economic organization which essentially characterizes Collectivism, namely, controlled economy. How is the fact to be explained that the other great example of uncompromising Collectivism, namely Russia, went shares with Germany at the beginning of the second world war in dividing up the booty of the East European countries, attacked little Finland and has meanwhile, by methods which are peculiar to Communism, conquered an empire which stretches from Lübeck and Eisenach to Tibet and Indochina? Or is it to be regarded as the fault of Capitalism that the capitalist countries of the West, England, France, and the United States, from fear of war or from military weakness, have displayed an inexcusable forbearance towards the collectivist aggressor states? Is this not making Capitalism responsible for a pacifist attitude, after always having asserted the opposite, and can it be denied that the policy of appeasement has been widely approved of in Socialist circles, and that the military policy of Socialist Governments in England and France are not least of all responsible for the inadequate armament of those countries? At the beginning of the second world war, as Germany and Russia were still united by a pact, did not Communists in all countries decry as 'imperialistic' the solidarity regained at last by the capitalists states against the collectivist aggressor states and try to sabotage it?

It is obvious that we get no further with the mechanical theories of ortho-

71

dox Socialism. A new approach must be made which disengages itself from this stereotyped way of thought, and which takes, not words, but actual facts and conditions, as its starting point. The subject 'Capitalism and Imperialism' as presented to us by Marxist theory needs to be thoroughly overhauled. After a beginning was made in the last chapter of my book 'Civitas humana' we shall continue here by going further over back ground.

THE THEORY OF INTERNATIONAL ORDER AND THE
SOLUTION OF THE PROBLEM IN A LIBERAL AGE

If the relation of the economic system to international order is to be recognized clearly, we must begin by presenting the problem of international order in the form under which it is seen from the economic standpoint. How do matters stand?

We must begin with the observation that an intensive trade, which involves a highly-graded division of labour and therefore an intricate interdependence of one individual upon another, can only develop and be maintained under one important prerequisite. Those who enter into this condition of interdependence must feel confidence in the moral, legal, and institutional framework which protects their system of interchange and their claims that result from it, and that to a degree that makes them willing to accept continually the risks involved in this prosperity-creating relationship. Above all, *two prerequisites* must be fulfilled.

Firstly, there must be an inviolable rule of law and a *code of standards, principles, behaviour, and scale of values,* which although unwritten is still generally recognized, to ensure for all members of the working community that minimum of mutual trust and sense of security and continuity which permits of making reasonable plans and dispositions for the future. *Secondly,* a general means of exchange must exist in the form of a generally acceptable, everywhere freely convertible and stable currency which assures material security for the claims arising from trade.

Only when and as long as these two prerequisites are fulfilled can the risk be sustained which arises from the utmost mutual interdependence of individuals linked by the division of labour and exchange, thus enabling the enormous advantages of such economic integration to be freely enjoyed. Only then and only to this extent is economic integration possible. In other words: economic integration – as far as its geographical extent and

72

its intensity are concerned – always presupposes a corresponding non-economic 'social' integration which provides the setting described. The economic integration cannot in the long run extend further than the social integration, and its intensity is also determined by the degree of the latter. This is the cardinal law which governs rise and fall, expansion and recession of trade in the history of mankind [1]).

Every trained economist of course knows that there is no essential difference between the character of international and domestic trade. But the actual problem of its development becomes obvious if we compare the former with the latter. We recognize that the difficulty consists in finding and guaranteeing a legal, moral and institutional setting for international trade which in some measure approaches that of the *intra*-national. The problem of social integration is always infinitely more difficult to solve in the field of international relations than inside an individual country with its fixed constitutional structure and its political and moral cohesion. In international trade we may seek in vain for an international setting corresponding to that of the national state. A world state does not exist, and world economy therefore lacks a genuine world constitution, which would lay down uniform standards and compel them to be observed by direct and effective sanctions. And because there is no world state, world economy is unable to establish a uniform world monetary system, i.e. an international currency system, such as we are familiar with from our national currency systems, which are under national control and defined and protected by national legal standards, which would guarantee the three essential conditions of a healthy currency system, homogeneity, universally free usability and the stable value of money.

The subtle disputes of the nature of the 'international society' and international law may be left out of account here. The incontrovertible fact suffices for us that international social integration, as the setting for international economic integration, must always, compared with intra-national social integration, be a highly fragile and imperfect structure. How has it despite this been possible that during the past two centuries world economy expanded in an unexampled way and that international economic integration of a nature and intensity developed which differed only in degree, and that not even very much, from the integration existing within each national economy? A world state and a real world currency did not exist at that time any more than they do today. How then was the problem of international order as a prerequisite of international economic integration solved at that time? That is the question, the exact meaning and entire importance of which must be grasped, if we are to understand, not only the past, but also the present.

The problem we are discussing found a solution which may be termed the *'universalist-liberal'* one. What is meant is this:

(1) Instead of the *world state,* which is an indispensable setting for a world economy, but which did not exist, a practicable and robust *substitute* was found, and that in a way with which, on a limited scale, the Res Publica Christiana of the Middle Ages may be compared [2]. This substitute was the international 'open society' (Henri Bergson) [3] of that liberal age, a sort of unwritten *ordre public international,* a secularized Res Publica Christiana, which for that reason spread all over the globe. It is the 'communitas seu res publica hominum sub Deo' of St. Thomas Aquinas, to which natural law gave the double roots of universalism, which postulates the brotherhood of man, and of personalism, which postulates the inviolability of the individual, but replanted out of the spiritual earth of Christian Theism into the loose soil prepared by the Renaissance, by Humanism, Enlightment and Liberalism, while the addition 'sub Deo' was gradually suppressed and finally dropped [4]. No description can be given here either of the complicated structure of this international 'open society' of the 19th century and its manifold workings, nor of the theological, philosophical, moral and sociological forces which underlay this effective substitute for a world state and which penetrated among even the lowest intellectual classes [5]. It must suffice to say that these forces which created the universalist system of the 'open society' of the 19th century are for the greater part rooted – as indeed is only to be expected – in the same soil which produced the predominantly 'liberal' social, political and economic systems of the same age. What first strikes us in considering this order is the respect it enjoyed, which is only accentuated by the bad conscience or apologetics accompanying cases of infringement, which made it possible for international law to be regarded as a genuine law, on a par or even superior to that of the national state; for the world to be united through a network of long-term agreements which therefore made for the stabilization of international relationships; for tensions between large and small states to be continually adjusted – the unjustly suspected 'balance of power' – and for a high degree of agreement to exist regarding legal concep-

tions and national standards of justice. This external order was, however, fostered by the moral and political atmosphere of the 'open society', of the *secularized Res Publica Christiana;* to which a considerable and by no means unwholesome measure of Pax Britannica was added.

(2) If the international 'open society' of the 19th century was the creation of a 'liberal spirit' in the widest sense, which need not be explained in detail here [6]), this origin appears very clearly in another respect, and in the narrower and more usual sense attached to the expression 'liberal', – not as associated with Thomas Aquinas, Suarez, Victoria, Erasmus or Grotius, but with David Hume and Adam Smith. This point is of the greatest importance as explaining the secret of the international order of the recent past. It is the *liberal principle that economic affairs should be free from political direction, the principle of a thorough separation between the spheres of the government and of economy,* between sovereignty and the apparatus which provides material goods, between the Imperium and the Dominium, between the political power and the economic power (MacIver). This reduced the economic importance of the existence of sovereign states, with their different legal provisions, their frontiers, their independent administrative systems and civil rights, to a minimum. The economic process was thereby removed from the sphere of officialdom, of public and penal law, in short from the sphere of the 'state' to that of the 'market', of private law, of property, in short to the sphere of 'society', and this did away with the greater part of the causes of conflict and problems of order of an *economic* nature which arise from the side-by-side existence of sovereign states. This principle also solved an extremely important special problem of international integration, which as we said above was of decisive importance in addition to the problem of international law, i.e. *the problem of an international monetary system.* Just as the universalist liberal 'open society' of the nations was able to create something like a world state, an acting substitute for a non-existent world government, with a common code of law for all nations, so did the application of the *principle of separation* to money give rise to a working substitute for world money and to establish a really international monetary order in the form of *gold standard.* The lack of a uniform world monetary system which would guarantee free exchange of currencies at stable rates was compensated for by the fact that all the leading countries accepted the gold standard and supported it more or less scrupulously in a manner which merged the whole globe into a pay-

ments union and lent the same qualities of homogeneity, stability and convertibility to international payment transactions as characterize national payments. By this means, by the free and universal convertibility of money at fixed rates and the resulting multilateralism of trade – it became possible for the first time to speak of international economic integration in the exact sense in which we speak of economic integration inside a national economy [7]).

Nowhere is the essence of this liberal world order which is characterized by its disassociation from political direction so clearly shown as here. This international monetary system was not dependent upon a world monetary authority nor a world monetary union or any other international pact, which would have tempted the nations to default and made monetary and credit policy controversial questions and the subject of diplomatic contests. It rested, on the contrary, entirely on the law of the individual state, and even the much praised 'co-operation of the Central Banks' proved, as it came to gain in importance, rather to be an anti-doctrinal deterioration and evasion of the gold currency than an encouragement to it, let alone an indispensable support of the international mechanism of gold currency. Since the validity of the individual national currencies depended upon gold, the fact that money = gold not only effected a fixed and free coupling of national currencies, but also compelled national governments by means of their national currency regulations to behave in matters of monetary and credit policy in such a way that this fixed and free coupling remained an undisputed permanent institution, irrespective of all trade fluctuations. As will be shown later, a further advantage was that the evil of an adverse balance of payments, and of international shortage of a currency were completely unknown in international case histories. While the governments clung to their national currency regulations, and in the firm belief, which had become a tradition, nay, even an article of faith, that they were serving, not world trade but their own interests, defended the free convertibility of their currency and their parity with the delicately-formed tools of monetary and credit policy, the result, by no means aimed at in the first place, was a genuine international monetary system – the only one which our age has up to now known. Gold currency thus illustrated the saying of Adam Ferguson [8]) (1723–1816), so essential to liberal convictions, that 'peoples find themselves unexpectedly in possession of institutions which are indeed the outcome of human action, but not the result of human intention', and it is a proof of the further realization that in the wide field of society and economy such spontaneous co-operation is generally superior to conscious planning. It was a monetary system which rested upon 'the structural similarity of the national systems' [9]), and which made currency dependent, not upon political decisions of national governments and their direction, but upon the objective economic laws, which applied once a national currency was linked with gold. It was an 'economic' and not a 'political' currency system. But it was at the same time a phenomenon with a moral foundation. The obligations, namely, which a conscientious conformity with the rules of the gold standard imposed upon all participating countries formed at the same time a part of that system of written and unwritten standards which, as we have seen, comprised the liberal order public international. The gold standard collapsed as one country after another, for one reason or another, began to disregard the rules of the game, which meant that the gold standard was no longer understood, while at the same time the international order crumbled and the final change of the essentially liberal character of the prevailing economic system to one in which interventionism and collectivism played an increasing part deprived the gold standard of its foundation. *The increase of political direction in economic life must necessarily result in the destruction of the monetary order, which rested on the principle of the freedom of economic affairs from political direction.*

If we try to sum up the character of the liberal solution of the problem of international order in a few words, we may put it as follows, which at the same time explains the close connection between the two main elements of this order named above: the liberal idea, by creating an ordre public international which was legally and morally effective and which was kept together by manifold institutional links, achieved the closest possible approach to the (unreachable) goal of setting up an international equivalent of the national state which was indispensable to international relationships. At the same time the separation of the political and economic spheres, by which economic activity became a private affair removed from political direction, was not only a decisive aid in the creation of this quasi world state, but also limited the burden placed upon this framework of the international economy, so that this international substitute set-up sufficed for the actual requirements of an international order. In other words it combined the actual practicable maximum of international order with a minimum of demands upon it. *These historical forces created an international order without dispensing with national sovereignities, and combined this with an economic system, namely the liberal one, which, in contrast to the collectivist system, requires only a minimum of organizational set-up.*

A tremendous achievement which it were opportune at last to understand and duly respect, and whose significance we only fully realize now that this framework no longer exists. On the other hand, now that the liberal idea of order has been supplanted by the collectivist, the meaning of the attempt made above to characterize the liberal international order becomes painfully clear to us. If we examine more clearly the popular idea of today, to erect an international controlled economy on these ruins of an international order, by means of fragmentary Quota, Clearing and barter Agreements and daily varying payments and trade arrangements between the individual states, we cannot help observing its absurdity, and that for a reason which is very instructive in this connection [10]). Two things immediately become clear: (a) that an international planned economy – we must constantly come back to this – representing as it does the domination of politics over economics on an international level, cannot manage with the international quasi-order of the liberal epoch but presupposes a real super state, and (b) that it was exactly a triumph of the collectivist idea over the liberal one which destroyed this loose quasi-order. *International collectivism demands a measure of international statism which would presuppose a very much stronger international frame that that which the liberal age created and which collectivism destroyed.* We shall meet this paradox later in another form.

If this completes the picture as we see it of the nature of the problem of international order and its liberal solution, it only remains to say that we have only tried to give an interpretation of *international law* in the 19th century under the aspect of its economic function. Thus seen the traditional system of international law appears to us as the liberal solution of the problem of international order which has arisen from economic development, this means that this system entered upon a process of disintegration as the liberal idea of order began to decline.[11]) This contention ought to be substantiated in detail by concrete examples. We shall however content ourselves by a single one of predominant importance, the treatment of *private property* in international relations.

It was in accordance with the principle of the separation of Imperium and Dominium, upon which the liberal world order rested, that private property was practically dissociated from the question of the territorial supremacy of the states and nationalities of the owners and the conflicts connected with them. This broke with an age-long aftermath of tradition from Feudal times. While colonial imperialism still clung to the idea that a territorial supremacy of the State over the areas in question was necessary, in order to 'secure' markets, sources of raw material and possibilities of settlement, this was but an anachronistic sophism which thoughtlessly ignored the established principle of liberal world order. 'Political power has determinate frontiers, economic power has freedom of the world' (MacIver) [12]). This principle of the separation of sovereignty and property was of special importance in cases of war, in which respect for the private property of the enemy was an obvious consequence of the liberal universal international order. After disregard of the private property of the enemy had became the rule among the belligerents in the first world war, the extension of this disregard by the victors after the second world war in forcing neutral countries to follow suit constituted a high point of that legal cynicism which has dissolved the old liberal world order. Some years ago I wrote the following, to demonstrate the length to which matters had gone: 'Let us imagine that at the time of the Chinese Boxer Rising (1900) – which bore a distant resemblance to National Socialism – Swiss property had been damaged, and let us further assume that someone conceived the idea of confiscating assets, which had been entrusted by individual Chinese to Swiss banks, to compensate the Swiss who had suffered damage. Can the slightest doubt exist that at that time the very idea would have been swept away by a storm of unanimous public protest? Meanwhile, however, a passport no longer has the qualities of a patent of nobility and an insurance policy, but has also become equivalent to a mandate of expropriation, an order of deportation, a document of moral condemnation, an order for arrest and in the extreme case to a sentence of death [13])'.

IMPERIALISM

The 19th century, then, applied a 'liberal' solution to this problem of international order, which held the separation of Imperium and Dominium to be a factor which furthered international integration, and the renunciation of this solution an unsociable international element. How, though, does this theory match up with the undeniable historical state of affairs known as 'modern imperialism'? Have we not learnt that this is the regrettable attendant circumstance of 'modern capitalism' [14])?

We shall only be convinced of the assertion that imperialism is a necessary concomitant of capitalism if an empirical proof in two directions is provided: (1) that imperialism has never existed without capitalism, and (2) that capitalism has never existed without imperialism. It is only necessary to demand this proof to know in advance that it can never be brought.

The assertion that there has never been imperialism without capitalism is refuted on almost every page of the history of mankind. The proof demanded under (1), therefore, cannot under any circumstances be brought.

Nor is the situation any better as regards the proof demanded under (2), namely that capitalism has never existed without imperialism. The bottom is knocked out of this theory by the fact that there are plenty of states which are entirely capitalistic without being in the least imperialistic. It suffices to name Switzerland, Sweden, Denmark, or Norway as examples. The Netherlands may also actually be counted as belonging to this capitalistic but not imperialistic group. Although up to recently this country owned rich colonial possessions and displayed a considerable power of expansion in acquiring them, it would be ridiculous to count it among the 'imperialistic' powers, since the urge for expansion was entirely absent, which according to the economic theory of imperialism, we must assume to be a prerequisite of it. The fact that there are capitalist countries which are in no wise imperialistic, is all the more unfavourable for the economic theory of imperialism, since this group also includes countries which are among the richest and those playing a leading part economically. They are as strong on the economic side as they are weak on the political side. There is no denying, for example, that Switzerland owes her wealth in no small measure to the fact that for centuries she has not been imperialistic, i.e. that she has never pursued an expensive policy which was destructive to peaceful trade relations, and during a century of undisturbed peace has been able to build up her capital assets by means of unremitting industry and exemplary thrift.

The example of Switzerland might give an obstinate advocate of the economic theory of imperialism occasion to ask whether imperialism must of necessity use *political* means to attain its end, namely the obtaining of a ruling position. Has not 'Switzerland' 'conquered' northern Italy through its banking connections and its electric power companies? No deep consideration is necessary, however, to discover the misconception contained in such an idea. Let us suppose that the possession of banks, electric power, railways or gas companies confers influence and power, and that perhaps upon people who are domiciled abroad. Is there any point at all in calling this 'imperialism'? For this word to have any meaning at all it is essential that the imperialistic policy should be pursued by a political body, i.e. a foreign state. This is just what is lacking in our example. It is not 'Switzerland' which is expanding in Italy, but individual Swiss – through the media of juridical persons – who carry on business there and hope to make a profit. This is an example of the wrong thinking which is remarkably frequent, and highly dangerous, in economic considerations, and which Whitehead terms the fallacy of misplaced concreteness [15]). It consists of turning a conception – in this case 'Switzerland' – into an acting reality which founds electric power companies in Italy. It is the same fallacy which before the first world war led to the fatal and poisonous idea that 'Germany' was a trade rival of 'England', although it was not 'Germany' and 'England' who were rivals of one another, but certain individual Germans and Englishmen, while at the same time there were far more Germans and Englishmen who competed just as bitterly with their fellow-countrymen and who were associated with nationals of the other country by means of friendly relations as suppliers or purchasers.

If we return to the example of Switzerland, for example, we may be permitted to ask what difference there actually is between the foundation of subsidiaries abroad and the expansion of a business enterprise *within* the country itself. Does the establishment in Geneva of a branch of the Schweizerische Bankverein denote imperialism on the part of Zürich? The question requires no answer. Anyone familiar with the theory of foreign trade, will recognize that the fallacy exposed here is only one example of the very widespread idea that a socio-economic process changes its nature as soon as nationals of different countries participate in it.

It is therefore inadmissible to speak of imperialism when a foreign business is established in a country, as long as the government of the foreign country does not back that company by means of power politics, as was for instance the case formerly in Turkey. One should of course avoid falling into the other extreme of denying the non-political foundations of enterprises in a foreign country any importance beyond pure business. A banking house or a power station naturally bestows considerable economic influence, and there are of course sufficiently weighty reasons why a country does not willingly concede this influence to a foreign firm. In most cases, however, the unbridled exploitation of the economic influence which a foreign company enjoys by its private business would appear objectionable only under the same conditions in which a business company of the country itself would be open to the same criticism, i.e. whenever a monopoly is involved.

Our investigation, therefore, has led to the conclusion that imperialism can exist without capitalism, just as capitalism without imperialism. This removes the supports from the economic theory of imperialism, which represents imperialism as an *inevitable* concomitant of capitalism.

That it is possible to grow rich by force at another's expense is no new or startling discovery. This temptation has existed at all times and under all economic systems and has certainly always been one of the major causes of war. It is, however, inherent in the nature of capitalism that the responsibility for adjustment of production to demand lies in the hands of the private entrepreneur and not in that of the State, that sovereignty and the economic sphere are kept distinctly apart and that 'the nations, who would not be preserved from violence and war through the conception of cosmopolitan justice, are united through reciprocal self-interest' (KANT, 'Zum ewigen Frieden', Königsberg, 1795, p. 64). In the same book Kant writes, 'It is the *commercial spirit* which cannot exist together with war, and which sooner or later takes possession of every nation. Since, namely, of all the powers (means) which the ruling power has at its disposal, monetary power is probably the most reliable, governments ... find themselves compelled to further true peace, and wherever war threatens to break out in the world, to stave it off by means of negotiations, just as if they were in a permanent state of alliance'. It is thus not a typical characteristic of capitalism for the State to appear in the rôle of organizer and protector of imperialistic exploitation. Should it do so, then of its own free will, but not as a mystical essential of capitalism.

Modern imperialism, then, is at bottom not an economic, but a political phenomenon. On the other hand must it not be clear to everyone, that an economic system, which in contrast to capitalism, is characterized by the fusing of trade and politics under the command of the State, must by its very nature tend to use state coercive measures for economic ends? This economic system, however, is Socialism, which we are asked to believe will free us from economic imperialism.

That this is the only possible interpretation of the facts, and that the Marxist theory of imperialism – which, like many other Marxist ideas has, consciously or unconsciously, also influenced non-Marxist circles – has distorted reality, is shown by the fact that the various 'capitalistic' States behave in entirely different ways, the one is peaceful, the other aggressive; the same state may even at one time be imperialistic and at other times not. The Boer War, for example, would seem to be a very obvious result of economic imperialism but why then did Holland, which had particular reason to do so, refuse to consider the political annexation of the South African market as a necessity of a capitalistic economy? The example of the United States is also particularly instructive; under the influence of a pacifist public opinion, the USA has distanced itself more and more from the old 'Dollar Diplomacy', without becoming any the less 'capitalistic' thereby. Now that a 'Gun-Boat Policy' has become a thing of the past, any further remarks on this point are totally superfluous.

In the same way, the *relations between debtor states and creditor states* have undergone a basic change in the course of the past few decades. The idea that investments abroad force the debtor country to become a submissive vassal state has lost every vestige of reality. The latest economic crisis in particular has demonstrated the relative impotence of the creditor states with regard to debtor states which have become insolvent, an impotence which is sometimes so exaggerated that it might almost be said that the debtor states have the pull over the creditor states. The United States, for example, have accepted the loss of thousands of millions of dollars, which they had invested in certain states of Latin America, without even attempting to undertake military action of the kind which England and Germany dared take against Venezuela in 1902. Since 1931, Germany has managed to throw off the greater part of its foreign debt without any other consequences than those which accrue to the insolvent debtor in private life, and has indeed been smart enough to take advantage of the repudiation in its trade policy. Nor do the popular notions regarding the chief campaigns undertaken by European imperialism up to 1914 bear any relation to the truth. Although the theory of economic imperialism assumes that capital interests abroad are always the cause of diplomatic conflicts, in actual fact the reverse has been true in many of these famous cases, politics have taken the lead and harnessed capital interests in the service of an expansionist policy [16]).

These conclusions may be summed up in the following sentence: imperialism is not only not an essential component of capitalism, but, quite apart from all the economic links in the chain of cause and effect, is a concomitant which is foreign to, and even opposed to, the capitalistic system. A bellicose policy by no means furthers the interests of capitalism, but is directly opposed to them. An economic system which rests upon division of labour and exchange needs peace if it is to flourish. The objective and reasonable interests of all those participating in buying and selling demand peace. In the age of world trade and a technology of warfare which develops parallel with technology for peace, war has finally lost any economic meaning, if it is to be anything more than brutal plundering, by which the enormous losses caused by the destruction of the international system of trade can be temporarily compensated for. For the majority of people it has ceased to be a profitable business, although, of course, not for certain groups.

There was no need for the participating countries to wait for the outcome of the *first world war* to learn how senseless it was economically, as senseless as was the second world war also. There are no objective reasons for making any conflict of an economic nature responsible for its outbreak. The economist in particular has every reason to contradict the popular exaggeration of the economic causes of both the first and the second world war. This might only be considered to apply seriously in respect of the conflict between Germany and England. But it should be stressed here that the cause of the break between the two countries was not trade rivalry – as is known, each was the best customer of the other – but a political rivalry which arose from the German programme of new naval construction, and the danger that Germany would subject France and Belgium and so be able to threaten England directly from the Channel coast. The so-called trade rivalry between Germany and England was nothing more than an ideological disguise for a real conflict of political interests, the logical fallacy of which we have already met with. On purely economic grounds the conflict must of necessity have been forbidden on both sides. In actual fact, as in many wars, economic logic only played a minor part, in contrast to instincts, feelings and passions. The atmosphere created by free market economy i.e. the principle of economic organization inherent in 'capitalism', serves rather to curb and suppress atavistic bellicose emotions than to stir them up. Those responsible for the war spirit mostly come from those social classes which are furthest removed from capitalism [17]).

In conclusion: not only is capitalism conceivable and viable as 'pure' capitalism without imperialism – just as a 'pure' capitalism can exist inside a country without exploitation; on the contrary, imperialism is the source of the greatest friction and disturbance which up to now have prevented capitalism from demonstrating the power of creating prosperity which it contains. There are three principle reasons which explain why capitalism has not brought the maximum of masswell-being to mankind of which it is capable: the reckless group egoism which with or without certain state interventionism reduces productivity, the gigantic increase in population during the last hundred years, and – imperialism. All three causes are closely related to each other.

Imperialism, as we have said, is basically a *political phenomenon* and as such a creation of *feelings, passions and instincts.* It was believed formerly that an optimistic conclusion might be drawn from this, and that the need for peace as dictated by economic reason would more and more curb irrational bellicose instincts. We are far from thinking so optimistically today. We know that instincts, feelings and passions rule mankind far more strongly than the optimistic rationalism of earlier days was prepared to admit, and that the world is governed far less by facts and calculations than is good for it, especially in an age which is dominated by mass movements and mass instincts.

It remains to us to draw *two conclusions* from our rejection of the theory of economic imperialism. In the first place there are obviously no grounds for assuming that the world-wide slump which developed in 1929 was due to expansion abroad meeting with geographical limits; thus arguing a fatalist prognosis for the future of capitalism. The idea that capitalism is only possible as long as its geographical sphere of influence can be regularly expanded is entirely unfounded. The decisive factor for the success of capitalism is not the number of square kilometres that it covers, but the amount of purchasing power, which again is determined by the amount of production and by a smooth exchange of the goods produced on a basis of division of labour. The second conclusion is that if imperialism is to be

85

attacked, there is no need to turn against capitalism. The opponents of imperialism should not believe that they must become anti-capitalists, as the Marxist theory has tried to drill into them. This applies, not only to highly developed countries, but also to those other countries which up to now were objects of the imperialistic policy of the great powers, and which now wish to liberate themselves from it.

In order to round off our considerations and to cut off the defendants of the theory of economic imperialism from all possibility of a retreat, let us in conclusion present an *ultimate clarification*. However valuable it is to recognize that the aggressive foreign policies of our age are phenomena which are determined by politics and not by economics, we still cannot avoid the question of the extent to which political decisions which dictate an aggressive foreign policy are, influenced by economic factors of a manifold nature. This has no longer to do with the problem dealt with by the theory of economic imperialism, since we are not discussing an inevitable link between capitalism and imperialism. But this new question we put ourselves is all the more complicated and comprehensive, especially if we take into account, not only economic factors which are objectively established, but also (true or false) opinions on such facts, fixed ideas along economic lines, ideologies and the measures relating to economic policy which they ordain, self-deceptions or suggested deceptions regarding the true economic interests of a nation, an assertive attitude on the part of private interests (for example the armament industry or foreign capital interests) and many more. In putting this question we are once more illustrating the oft-proved saying of Epiktet, that it is not so much facts themselves that mislead people, as the opinions on the facts.

Let us take some known examples. We showed that the first world war could by no means be explained as being due to an objectively established conflict of economic interests. Although it was driven into the minds of the masses both in Germany and England that trade rivalry between the two countries was bound to make war inevitable, this trade rivalry was by no means an economic fact, but a purposefully nourished economic deception for popular consumption, for reasons which we have already met. Had both countries acted in their real and plain interests, they would not only have preserved peace, but each would of necessity have wished the other the greatest possible economic success, in the sense of the two hundred year old extract from David Hume quoted at the beginning of this section

86

of the book. The true state of affairs was so twisted on both sides by political ideology, that the masses were made to relish the actual 'political' rivalry, which at bottom was a naval rivalry arising from senseless German ambition. The fact that certain firms on both sides rejoiced at the prospect of being relieved by military force of inconvenient foreign competition only goes to prove that the interests of the individual often lie in a different direction from the interests of the nation as a whole. But it is the task of politics in particular to subdue private interests to the interests of the nation, both then and at all times, and this task is considerably lightened if egoistic private interests are brought to light.

Another example, which is unfortunately of topical interest today, is supplied by foreign trade policy. Although a moderate tariff policy needs by no means be considered an insurmountable barrier to peace, it contains dangers which become obvious today in the tensions caused by a policy of self-sufficiency. It would, however, never occur to anyone to describe this economic policy as unalterable and of compulsory origin. It is rather the outcome of certain political ideologies and certain political conditions. It corresponds further to an internal economic policy which aims at converting our economic system into one of state intervention and collectivism. A real and active peace policy, therefore, must start by attacking these ideologies and conditions.

It is therefore frequently possible to prove that in individual cases 'economic' factors play a part in an aggressive foreign policy, when private pressure groups understand how to make use of their national government for their own purposes, or the true economic interests of the nation as a whole are falsely depicted. It is shown over and over again, however, how little these examples go to prove that the prevailing economic system of necessity and by reason of its intrinsic structure results in an aggressive foreign policy. It is true that in such cases the chain of cause and effect contains economic links, but it ends finally in the field in which, contrary to the materialistic interpretation of history, all decisions take place: the field of politics, power, ideology, psychology, sociology, emotionalism. Everything which at a superficial glance seems to indicate that capitalism is the villain of the piece proves upon more thorough examination to be entirely fallacious. It only proves that, under the present economic system as well as under any other, stupidity, egoism, greed and falsehood can carry on their evil work against peace, as long as reason, public spirit, moderation

87

and truth are not able to keep them under control. Not the imaginary inescapable fatalism of the economic laws of capitalism are to be denounced, but human default. And this default is the direct opponent of the spirit and meaning of this economic system. *The idea that the economic system which rests upon the regulating function of the market and the separation of political sovereignty from economic activity is that which compulsorily drives nations into war, must be completely rejected.*

NOTES

1. (p. 73)

The ideas developed in the text I first submitted partly in more detail in my English book 'International Economic Disintegration' (3rd Edition, London 1950, p. 67 and the following). There some observations on the question of the reaction of economic integration upon social integration can also be found. I have nothing to add to them on this occasion, except perhaps for the remark, that today I should emphasize the mutual effect even more emphatically. The world situation at this very moment gives one reason to point out, that there is a healthy element of compulsion in the choice, either of continually adapting the degree of international economic integration to the catastrophically lessened international social integration or of once more raising international social integration to the level necessary for vital international economic integration.

2. (p. 74) Res Publica Christiana:

Concerning the degree and the nature of the international community of the Middle Ages information may be obtained specially from: R. F. WRIGHT, Medieval Internationalism: the Contribution of the Medieval Church to International Law and Peace, 1930; R. WALLACH, Das abendländische Gemeinschaftsbewußtsein im Mittelalter, 1930; J. HASHAGEN, Internationalismus und Nationalismus im Mittelalter, Friedenswarte, 1938, I; R. O'SULLIVAN, Internationalism, European Civilization, its Origin and Development, Vol. V, New York, 1937, p. 1261 and the following; HENRI PIRENNE, Histoire Economique de l'Occident Medieval, Bruges 1951. How this international social integration in the Middle Ages corresponded to a high degree of international economic integration, was specially shown by: F. RÖRIG, Mittelalterliche Weltwirtschaft, Blüte und Verfall einer Weltwirtschaftsperiode, Jena 1933. A 'communis omnium nationum mercancia' corresponded to the Res Publica Christiana, as stated in the letter (quoted by Rörig) of a Florentine businessman in Bruges to the Hansa of 1457. When in 1531 the inscription 'In usum negotiatorum cujusque nationis ac linguae' was introduced over the Antwerp Stock Exchange this epoch of 'medieval world economy' was already approaching its end.

3. (p. 74) HENRI BERGSON, Les deux sources de la morale et de la religion, Paris 1932, p. 27 and the following.

4. (p. 74)

This is the moment, when one should let the development of the humanitarian international law of the New Era unroll before one's eyes in its various stages, which are specially characterized by the courageous pioneering work of the Spanish Jesuits and the Dominicans of the late scholastic school (Franciscus Suarez, Francisco de Vitoria, Ludovicus Molina a.o.) – aptly so called, as it is linked with the great legacy of Thomas Aquinas – and by Hugo Grotius and Burlamaqui. SUAREZ (Tractatus de Legibus et Legislatore Deo, II, cap. 19, n. 19) explains as basis of the Jus gentium 'quia humanum genus quantumvis in varios populos et regna divisum semper habeat aliquam unitatem... quam indicat naturale praeceptum mutui amoris et misericordiae, quod ad omnes extenditur, etiam extraneos et cuiuscunque nationis'. From this nature of the international 'public society' VITORIA derives on moral and theological ground the commandment of free trade, which compels by the very law of nature ('...quia etiam hoc videtur jus gentium, ut sine detrimento civium peregrini commercia exerceant' quoted from R. O'Sullivan, loc. cit., p. 1275), – a commandment, which then in the paragraph prefaced to my book as motto

89

is translated by David Hume from the language of natural law and moral theology into the secular terms of economic profit calculation. In contrast with these great moments of concept of an international 'public society' in the history of human thought stands the other fateful series, which begins whit Bodin, the actual inventor of the modern conception of sovereignty, and Machiavelli and – armed with the lesson of the depravity of human nature so effectively presented and disseminated by Luther – is continued via Francis Bacon and Hobbes to Hegel and Treitschke and finally supersedes the humanitarian and universal conception of national relations first in the course of the 19th century in theory and then in the 20th century in practice also. In so far as the humanitarian and universal conception of national relations had been superseded in the course of the 19th century, it is only in line with the law of historical interference (which I have explained in my 'Gesellschaftskrisis der Gegenwart', 5th Edition p. 90–103), that it was only after that that the *practice* of international law harvested its full fruits. It is in the light of this that one should consider the following survey, which shows how the number of cases settled by arbitration annually increased in the 19th century (according to R. O. SULLIVAN, loc. cit. p. 1288)

1789–1848 on an average 1 arbitration every 2 years
1848–1860 on an average 1 arbitration per year
1861–1880 on an average 2 arbitrations per year
1881–1900 on an average nearly 5 arbitrations per year.

5. *(p. 74)*

I refer here to my 'Gesellschaftskrisis der Gegenwart', 5th Edition p. 378 et seq. In this overall picture of an international order the dominating role of the leading world political and world economic power or group of powers has been given a very important place. I have expressed my opinion of this several times (International Economic Disintegration p. 16 et passim; Gesellschaftskrisis der Gegenwart, p. 385; Civitas humana, p. 290 et seq.). Along the same lines: F. PERROUX, Entwurf einer Theorie der dominierenden Wirtschaft, Zeitschrift für Nationalökonomie, 1950, No. 1.

6. *(p. 75)*

I refer to my book 'Maß und Mitte', Erlenbach-Zürich, 1950, p. 9 et seq.

7. *(p. 76)*

I have set forth this idea in more detail in my essay: The Economic Integration of Europe, Measure (Chicago), 1950, No. 4.

8. *(p. 76)*

Ferguson is quoted according to F. A. HAYEK, Individualismus und wirtschaftliche Ordnung, Erlenbach-Zürich 1952, p. 16.

9. *(p. 77)*

WERNER STARK, Währungsverträge, a publication in honour of Oscar Engländer, Brünn p. 265. The difficulties of currency pacts therein described, as also those of the Latin coin union illuminate in a very interesting way the basic weakness of the 'political' type of an international monetary order compared with the 'economic', as I have named these 2 types in the text.

10. (p. 78)

I first developed this idea in detail in my English book 'Crises and Cycles' (London, 1936, p. 10 et seq.).

11. (p. 78)

In the past it has always been emphasized, that international law 'in spite of the anarchistic lack of organisation in the community of nations was true law' (G. RADBRUCH, Einführung in die Rechtswissenschaft, 2nd Edition, Leipzig 1913, p. 128) and thanks to the 'pressure of international public opinion' (an impressive point made by R. M. MAC-IVER, in particular, The Modern State, London 1926, p. 284) is even more conscientiously observed than national law (sic. RADBRUCH loc. cit.). But it is clear, that this is not a characteristic of international law as such, but of the *liberal* international order in which disputes are settled as outlined above.

12. (p. 79)

R. M. MACIVER, loc. cit., p. 294. By way of illustration: In the year 1913 the entire British colonies in Africa supplied less than 1% of British export. Their importance was roughly equal to that of Chile. As market for British products the Argentine was about three times and as supplier country about six times as important, without costing the British tax-payer a single penny (according to LEONARD WOOLF, Economic Imperialism, 2nd chapter).

13. (p. 79)

W. RÖPKE, Kollektivschuld und deutscher Widerstand, Neue Schweizer Rundschau, August 1946, p. 203. I have already expressed my opinion of the lack of monetary logic in the idea of 'suitable compensation', over which the execution of the Washington agreement concerning the confiscation of German assets in Switzerland finally failed and which is rooted in the same 'Nationalization of the economy', which is castigated here, in my essays 'Offene und zurückgestaute Inflation' (KYKLOS 1947, p. 70) and 'Repressed Inflation' (KYKLOS 1947, p. 244). The importance of the liberal *principle of separation* for international law as hitherto practiced and the unsolved contradictions arising with its abandonment, are evident in such a singular case as that of *shipping*. Previously it was the rule that foreign government ships enjoyed immunity, because it could be presumed that merchant shipping was of an exclusively private character and that state ships were to serve solely for the exercise of functions of sovereignty, and because merchant shipping was assigned to the sphere of private property, state shipping, however, to the sphere of sovereignty. Now however the removal of this division by the rise of state-owned merchant marines makes the application of this principle more and more impossible (S. MAIWALD, Die Entwicklung zur staatlichen Handelsschiffahrt im Spiegel des internationalen Rechts. Die Staatsfreiheit des Handels als Kardinalprinzip des Seevölkerrechts, Stuttgart, 1946). Of a similar type are the growing difficulties, which are developing in the present efforts to re-liberate international trade ('Liberalization', GATT) by the extended state trading practised by a number of countries.

What importance the principle of separation – especially in the protection of property and international transaction of payments from the arbitrariness of national politics – has for international investment and the development of new countries is obvious. The development of the 'underdeveloped' countries in the 19th century was completed under the working and the protective influence of this principle and therefore soundlessly and

91

without international government programme. That therefore, operating in reverse, the present removal of this principle causes one of the most difficult obstacles, for the development of the 'underdeveloped countries', is a subject we will deal with later.

14. (p. 80) Imperialism:

In the first edition the essentially Marxist theory of 'Imperialism' as a supposedly necessary consequence of 'Capitalism' was given a detailed examination, which patiently showed its theoretical untenability and its incompatibility with the historical facts. The author has refrained from repeating this part here, and contents himself with a few comprehensive sentences, for the entire subject has greatly lost in interest. Today a policy of genuine imperialism is only pursued by that world power, which has made the struggle against capitalism its warcry and one of its intellectual weapons in this campaign of conquest is the attempt, successful only in the case of some backward peoples and individuals, to accuse the remaining 'capitalistic' world of 'imperialism'. The Marxist theory of imperialism is only believed by Communists, that is to say, by those, who support the Communist empire in its imperialistic advance. Anyone, however, who finds fault with the shortness of this paragraph, should consult the 1st German edition. Furthermore the following works may be referred to: L. ROBBINS, The Economic Causes of War, London, 1939; W. SULZBACH, Nationales Gemeinschaftsgefühl und wirtschaftliches Interesse, Leipzig 1929; W. SULZBACH, National Consciousness, Washington D.C., without year; W. SULZBACH, 'Capitalist Warmongers': A Modern Superstition, Chicago 1942; F. A. HAYEK, Der Weg zur Knechtschaft, Erlenbach-Zürich, without year, p. 271 et seq.; J. FREYMOND, Lénine et l'impérialisme, Lausanne 1951; F. DULBERG, Der Imperialismus im Lichte seiner Theorien, Basel 1936.

15. (p. 81) Fallacy of misplaced concreteness:

W. SULZBACH, Nationales Gemeinschaftsgefühl und wirtschaftliches Interesse, Leipzig 1929; L. MISES, Nation, Staat und Wirtschaft, Wien 1919; A. N. WHITEHEAD, Science and the Modern World, New York 1926.

16. (p. 84) Reality of Imperialism:

That actually in many cases it is not the 'Capitalists' who have misused the governments, but the latter who have misused the 'Capitalists' for imperialistic purposes, is shown by: E. STALEY, War and the Private Investor, New York 1935. A really classical example of this was the Mexican adventure of Napoleon III. In order to obtain an economic excuse for his intervention he first had the Swiss banker Jecker, who had given the Mexican President Miramon a loan, made a Frenchman and had his certificates of debt bought up by the French government (LORD ACTON, Historical Essays and Studies, London 1907, p. 150 et seq.).

17. (p. 85) The Contrast between War and Free Market Economy:

The idea that war in an economy of exchange, depending upon division of labour is an economic paradox – a 'false reckoning' – has found its most popular expression in our time in NORMAN ANGELL's wellknown writings (The Great Illusion, Fruits of Victory and others). It would be worth while following it from its first beginnings up to today (see E. SILBERNER, La guerre dans la pensée économique du XVIe au XVIIIe siècle, Paris 1939). In addition to the paragraph from KANT already quoted in the text a worthy place should also be given to BENJAMIN CONSTANT (De l'esprit de conquête et de l'usurpation, 1814, 2nd chapter). Compare moreover the still highly informative work of

P. J. PROUDHON, La guerre et la paix, Paris 1861. Compare furthermore: L. MISES, Nation, Staat und Wirtschaft, Wien 1919; S. RUBINSTEIN, Herrschaft und Wirtschaft, München 1930; R. BEHRENDT, zur Grundproblematik des Kapitalismus, Zeitschrift für schweizerische Statistik und Volkswirtschaft, 1933; M. B. HAMMOND, Economic Conflict in International Affairs, American Economic Review, March 1933. In his famous inaugural lecture ('Du caractère logique des différences d'opinions que séparent les économistes', Genf 1897) M. PANTALEONI said: 'Les rapports entre les hommes sont de trois genres dont deux ne sont pas régis par les lois économiques. Ces genres sont si différents les uns des autres, que je ne saurais bâtir aucun pont qui nous conduise de l'un à l'autre. Il y a, d'abord, des rapports violents, des rapports d'oppression, des rapports qui consistent en ceci que les uns détruisent ou bien qu'ils exploitent les autres... Il y a, en second lieu, des rapports d'altruisme, que l'on peut appeler des rapports de tutelle. Enfin, nous avons un troisième genre de rapports, des rapports constractuels, dans lesquels la violence qui préside au premier genre de rapports est exclue tout autant que l'est l'altruisme des rapports de tutelle.' One must simply understand that imperialism belongs to the first and the free market economy to the latter category, to realize that the heterogeneousness of imperialism as a system of repression and exploitation and of the free market economy as a system of contractual relations cannot be more sharply characterized. The more the free market economy is permeated with elements of exploitation (monopoly), so much the more does it on the other hand approach the first category. When R. G. HAWTREY, Economic Aspects of Sovereignty (2nd Edition, London 1952), thinks he can put forward the objection to Angell's theory that 'the economic ambitions of states are to be expressed in terms of power' (p. 18), and that here national interests clash, this assertion, which is moreover only right up to a point, does not touch the heart of the matter. It is just this theory put forward by Angell, which emphasizes that a national cause of conflicts lies not in the field of economic interests (in so far as the economic system keeps them entirely separate from the political sphere) but in the field of the power interests of the states. This conflict is however not only not essential to the liberal economic system but even in contradiction to it.

93

II

CAESARO-ECONOMY

The mistake of those among the contemporary socialists, who have made Capitalism responsible for war and imperialism, is however much greater and more fateful than we have up to now imagined. Not only is the accused, that is to say capitalism, wrongly blamed for such a serious crime, rather is it the accuser, i.e. socialism, which seems to be more and more heavily indicted in the course of the criminal trial instigated by itself. This conclusion was already glimmering through the statements of the preceding chapter and must now be substantiated in detail.

We have already tried once to clarify the nature of the liberal world order, which is not always easy to understand, by means of the photographic negative of collectivist order, the essence of which is the removal of the separation principle, the giving of a political character to the economic sphere and the fusion of empire and dominion. Now we have the task of exploring the importance of collectivist economic order for the international community precisely and in detail. We shall endeavour to determine the most essential points as follows.

PRE-COLLECTIVISTIC INTERFERENCE WITH INTERNATIONAL INTERRELATIONS

Before examining the effect of collectivism in the strict sense of administrative control (i.e. political direction) of the economic process, we must take into account that the advance of modern intervention and the welfare state tends to produce a step-by-step removal of the liberal principle of separation and to this extent increases national integration at the expense of international. Tending in the same direction is the national isolation policy of the Trade Unions which is thoroughly compatible with a high degree of international solidarity in the case of strikes. Even in this precollectivist stage that process was becoming clear which I have characterized in my book 'Maß und Mitte' as the increasing nationalization of man. It is quite indicative of this process that it is no longer a mistake but a service to the cause of accuracy to substitute the word 'national' in every case where an intervention is described as 'social', and in all word-combinations made up with this adjective. 'Social justice' is a postulate which when considered in a clear light is intended to cover the nation only and not to include Bulgarians, Persians or Indians; 'social insurance' is a 'national insurance' and 'socialization' turns out to be 'nationalization' (as in other languages it is honestly so named). We should also not forget that the enforcement of exchange controls, which hinder the individual debtor in the fulfilment of his payment obligations towards the foreign creditor, amounts to a 'nationalization of insolvency'. In this connection a particularly detailed special chapter would have to be devoted to the extraordinary effect – towards integration on a national, towards disintegration on an international level – of a continued rise in the amount of the national income claimed by the state (fiscal quota), which has long ceased making merely a difference in degree. Public finances, a normal ingredient of a liberal order, which, because of its low fiscal quota, caused no serious infringement of the principle of separation, has developed into an apparatus of an increasingly comprehensive nationalization of the expenditure of income (Fiscal socialism).

The combined effect of all these forces on the decomposition of international interrelations needs not be further examined here. It is sufficient, if we illustrate it by the outstandingly important example of the *Decay of the International Monetary Standard,* which we have described, and which was finally brought about by the pressure of the disintegrating forces generated by the modern interventionist, welfare and fiscal state. This example is of such outstanding importance for 2 reasons: *firstly,* it shows the process of the decomposition of international interrelations at a central point, for with the destruction of the international monetary system, which guaranteed the stability of exchange-rates and free convertibility, world economic integration received a fatal blow. *Secondly,* the failure of all previous attempts to find a substitute for the destroyed international monetary standard, has a deep and depressing meaning, for it illuminates the inherent impossibility of replacing the liberal solution of the problem of international order as a whole by another, and exposes the close correlation between national and international order in a thoroughly concrete and illuminating manner [1]).

Here a last remark must be appended. The process described of the increasing dependence of economic conditions on a state intervention which is no longer guided by any objective logic of economic interdependence, means that state boundaries are becoming more and more lines, to separate from one another the widely differing markets whose conditions of supply and demand are, however, uniform within each nation and collectively determined. What is just as important: these collective conditions, since they are dependent on decisions by the national state which may be reversed at any moment and are fixed for shorter and shorter periods, are neither forseeable within reasonable limits nor subject to the influence of individuals. So a growing *element of political arbitrariness and instability* which is incompatible with international order is introduced into international economic transactions. Whereas it makes the national economies stiffen into rigid bodies, it makes world economy more and more fluid and into an area of the haphazard, approximate, continually fluctuating and arbitrary. That is true especially of international conditions of competition. Whereas for the individual within a national economy they are still mainly determined by individual achievement, the competitive ability of the whole economy in international transactions is more and more determined by the national economic policy or the national monopoly policy. The process which was effective in old style 'dumping' reappears wherever market differentiation of any kind is practised and is rather becoming the rule: *The national boundaries are becoming simultaneously the dividing lines of various theatres of competition which cover a number of enterprises and are collectively determined.* To them apply both the principle of national collectivity and the other of arbitrariness: 'vérité au deça des Pyrénées, erreur au delà' as also 'aus der Wolke ohne Wahl zuckt der Strahl' (lightning may strike indiscriminately from any cloud). By a devaluation or a revaluation of the currency the substance of thousands of contracts is decisively changed over night, and we have reached the point, where countries which are dependent on the import of essential raw materials must often pay almost double the prices valid in the country of production. Export subsidies of all kinds – more or less in the form of repayment of the internal turnover taxes – and the no less manifold import regulations are very usual. The formation of prices in international competition is so arbitrary that, as I expressed it a decade ago, the various national economies are becoming like huge department stores, which distribute the aggregate national costs over the various classes of goods according to what the market will bear[2]). The whole system is finally crowned by exchange control, which makes the act of payment which is so essential for economic transactions dependent on the decision of a civil servant, and, in this way, as we have already seen, 'nationalizes solvency'. The disintegration and arbitrariness linked with all this is the extreme opposite of law, order, community, and economic reason. It is on every geographical scale tantamount to the disintegration of society.

EXPLOSIVE EFFECT OF COLLECTIVISM

This development towards the interventionist, welfare and fiscal state shows already essential features of socialism. It lies exactly on the line which the latter follows to its logical end: *the subjection of the economy to political forces*. What is already true for the *step-by-step* 'political direction' with its increasing accentuation of the economic importance of national boundaries is all the more to be expected from the complete political direction of the economy, to which the superseding of the free market economy by dirigisme actually amounts. In fact it is only now that the process of the 'nationalization of man' is being completed. It is no longer a mere tendency, which within certain limits can be avoided, but a logical necessity.

The deciding point, for the comprehension of which one cannot take too much trouble, is exactly that now the economic process as a whole – not, as in the case of the interventionist, welfare and fiscal state only its conditions, its profits and the distribution thereof – is being turned into a responsibility of the state in the sense that the decision about the use of productive resources is no longer left to the price mechanism ('the current consumer plebiscite') but delivered up to the authorities. The economy is becoming as entirely a responsibility of the government as the army, and in fact the expression 'militarization of economic life' would not ill suit many important sides of the process. The process of transition from a free market economy to dirigisme can also be illustrated here by the example of the relationship between state and church: if the free market economy corresponds to the principle of the separation of state and church, so does dirigisme correspond to the unification of the highest authority in one despotic hand, that fusion which is described as Caesaro-Popery. The collectivist dirigist economy would therefore be nothing but a *Caesaro-*

economy, and if we dare to venture this comparing word-creation, perhaps it is in the hope that the new term has at least the merit of making matters clear.

If however the economic process is dependent on the highest political instance, which 'plans' it and enforces this planning by the powers of the state, it is clear, that the following general law becomes valid: on whatever geographical scale the free market economy is being replaced by the collectivism and dirigisme, the fusion of economic process and government sovereignty will always set a political and economic barrier between these spheres of command and the rest of the world. This maximum degree of concentration towards the interior will always be at the expense of disintegration towards the exterior, in the precise sense that that payments and market community (convertibility and multilateralism) is destroyed, which made the once-existing genuine world economy in spite of everything, appear as a mere geographical extension of the integration which prevailed *within* the national economies. The sphere in which the compulsory control of the economic process takes place must be identical with the sovereign political unity where authority enforces its economic plan. Within this unit an extreme concentration of power in the hand of the government now prevails. So much the deeper yawns the cleft, which separates this order-cell from the other political monads. In short: since within the sovereign sphere of command only a single plan and not the competition of different regional plans can be tolerated, the placing of the economy under official control means, an extreme 'concentration of power' – *accompanied by the break-up of the next highest communities.* Or to express the same idea in another way: if the 'sovereign' of the economy was previously the 'market', under collectivism it is the state, but while the sovereign 'market' as such belongs to the non-political private sphere and therefore as for all natural things 'space is scarcely enough' (Faust II, 2, Laboratorium) for it, the new sovereign is literally the national governing power itself, with everything that this implies.

This law is valid, as we have noted, for political organizations on every geographical scale. Let us consider first the lowest scale; in this way interesting results are reached, the very ones which are confirmed by the experiences of our generation.

On the one hand: if within a nation a collectivist body is organized on a regional level, it must disrupt the national body. An excellent example of

98

this is supplied by Germany after 1945, when the Reich collapsed into a number of independent spheres of command, all of them given to independent planning and practically amounting to as many 'national economies' which concluded regular 'trade agreements' with one another, whereas previously under the rule of a free market economy not even the separation by state-boundaries, languages, customs or currencies had prevented the entire globe from being a single coherent economic system. If today West and East Germany could at least have such dealings with one another as Sweden and the Argentine previously enjoyed, then the highest degree of economic unity between Dresden and Stuttgart that one could hope for, would be reached. Today, however, thanks to the explosive effect of collectivism, they are farther from one another in their economic relations than Lapland and Patagonia were previously under the system of a free market economy.

On the other hand: a collectivist and dirigist economy, which is anchored in national centralization, must show itself to be incompatible with *federalism* and *regional-communal* self-administration, for its compulsory co-ordination of the economy according to a central plan leaves little room for a genuine decentralization of the administration. The result is therefore, that collectivism and federalism are in any case incompatible with one another, since in the case of collectivism from below the lower political bodies (cantons, provinces, states) destroy the central authority and in the case of collectivism form above the central authority stifles the members. In any case collectivism means that the state-structure degenerates towards one of the two extremes: to centralism or particularism. In this connection too German development after the second World War offers instructive examples. It especially showed very impressively that, if one wished Western Germany to be a federated state and saw a worthy political goal in genuine self-administration, the choice of a free market economy as economic principle of order was the indispensible preliminary condition.

These considerations are now valid for international relations also. In fact we need only apply our findings concerning the relationship between the regional political bodies and the nation on to the next highest geographical level, to realize that here too domestic concentration can only be achieved at the price of isolation from abroad and an excessive integration on the lower levels at the expense of a corresponding disintegration on the higher. National collectivism – the more radical it is, the more complete –

must lead to the disruption of the international community. Now collect-ivism on a national level is the rule, whereas regional collectivism is merely a curiosity, and the supra-national type, for reasons still to be discussed, a Utopia. As a result the phrase may be permitted, that economic collect-ivism must disrupt international integration and harmony. This can also be expressed as follows: collectivism means total control by the state and, as the national government is the normal political commanding instance, to which it is correlated, complete control by the national state. As in this way the responsibilities of the state become unlimited, it means: increase of national sovereignty to the nth power.

To this corresponds – with grim irony for the internationalistic ideology, from which socialism has taken its beginning – the practice of collectivist foreign economic policy, which with compelling rigour must try to keep away from the national planned economy all disturbing effects from out-side, which escape its grasp, and to preserve it in its centrally determined compactness. To this corresponds especially *exchange-control,* about which Marx and Engels had said not one word, but which now turns out to be the indispensible keystone of the entire system of collectivist commanding force, so very much so that foreign exchange control has become an indispensable – although, by itself, insufficient – feature by which collec-tivism, is identified. On the other hand an exchange control, for whatever reasons it may be introduced, has a tendency to impart the collectivism of foreign trade and of the exchange market to the entire national economy.

The explosive effect on international relations, which collectivism provokes especially by exchange control, becomes clear only when we realize, that it is usually combined with a *constant inflationary pressure.* The connection between collectivism and inflation, upon which we stumble here and which justifies us in speaking of a *collectivistic-inflationary* style of economic policy after the second world war, is twofold [3]).

In the first place national collectivism leads to inflation for reasons, which merit an exact and sober analysis and among which the following must be emphasized: (1) 'Collectivism of every kind and every degree includes the control of the flow of money and credit by the planning government, but at the same time disconnects the automatic steering signals, which the gold standard had at its disposal. How will the planners make use of the leeway, which they can now use at their own discretion? In all probability they will follow an inflationary course, because it is the line of least resistance, and because it corresponds to the ideologies of 'full-employment', of the 'welfare-state' and of 'cheap money'. If, deprived of the navigation-instruments of the gold-standard, on can moreover no longer steer the course of financial policy by fixed landmarks and must reckon with a broad margin of error, one will in a collectivist state develop a tendency to steer rather to the left towards inflation than to the right towards deflation, and at best wrench round the steering-wheel only when inflation remains no longer in doubt even to the most obdurate and has caused serious devastation. The ship of collectivism will therefore show a strong and scarcely resistible drift to inflation, especially as the wind of Keynesianism blows powerfully in the same direction. Experiences since 1945 give ample proof of this. (2) Planners are people, who are optimists for compelling reasons and therefore always subject to a tendency, to issue more drafts on the national economy than it can honour. Impatient and ambitious, they have a tendency to want to achieve too much at once, to spend money with generous hands (which achieves under all conditions the effect of 'full employment'), letting loose on the national economy by an excess of investments and mass-consumption more demands than can be satisfied at current prices from production and paid imports, and in this way so overtaxing the national economy, that it gives way at its softest and most sensitive point, namely, in the purchasing power of money. The monetary system becomes in this way the account, on which all lapses against proved principles of economic policy are booked up to the point of insolvency. This permanent overtaxing of the national economy is in addition no longer adequately compensated by saving, for an inflationary policy of economic planning, combined with an overpressure of taxation, by which it is usually accompanied, and the psychological effects of a welfare state create an extremely unfavourable climate for saving. (3) While savings are inadequate, a collectivist economy has, on the other hand, invariably an almost irresistible tendency, to drive investments to a maximum volume. From this follows the temptation to resort to forced saving by a credit expansion which diminishes the value of money, to illustrate which we can take the famous Monnet-Plan in France, which was to a large extent financed by the watering-down of the French franc. (4) The collectivistic economy needs constant inflationary pressure, i.e. excessive pressure of demand and overliquidity (W. Eucken), in order to offset the paralysing effect of economic controls; otherwise it would be suffocated by its own apparatus of dirigisme. (5) The demands which are made in a collectivistic state on the public budget, are so high, that the budget deficit becomes a chronic source of inflation (France) or, when a balanced budget is achieved, the revenue is derived from inflated incomes, which in the long run alone will render bearable a fiscalquota of 40% or more (Great Britain)[4]).

There is however also an inverse relation between collectivism and inflation. If nowadays collectivism leads as a rule to inflation, inflation leads also to collectivism, because few governments can withstand the temptation to restrain inflation whatever its origin by economic controls. This same apparatus of collectivist compulsion, which is one of the causes of inflation, is used to convert 'open' inflation into *'repressed'* inflation. The indispensible means for this repression is exchange control. If there can be no doubt, that an 'open' inflation, such as was the rule after the first World War, is a most disturbing element in international relations, scarcely a word needs be thrown away on the disintegrating effect of the 'repressed' inflation, for the very reason that it leads to a complete falsification of international value relations and is indissolubly linked with exchange control.

These connections between collectivism and inflation must be carefully taken into account, if we wish to completely understand the statement that collectivism is an explosive force in international economic relations. We cannot however leave this point, without adding two remarks.

The one refers to the law of geographical scales, according to which collectivism exercises an effect of maximum concentration in the descending direction, and one of maximum disintegration in the ascending direction. We have already verified the validity of this law up to the national level, and there is no reason not to apply it to a case which is as yet merely hypothetical: let us suppose that, in spite of the difficulties still to be discussed, a successful attempt is made to realize *collectivism* on *a supranational level,* say in Western Europe. If collectivism on the national level cannot achieve superconcentration in the interior except at the price of a rigid isolation from the exterior this logic would repeat itself in the case of European collectivism, i.e. a collectivism on the level of an entire continent. The national autarky of national collectivism would then be replaced by the continental autarky of European collectivism. If Europe became, let us say, a huge Norway (today the most extreme case of a socialistic country this side of the iron curtain), the isolationist form, in which such a country today regulates its economic relations with foreign countries, would be transferred onto the European level. Every considerable extension of collectivism therefore pushes the problem of international interrelations only on to the next highest geographical level – up to the complete Utopia of world-collectivism.

The other remark applies to the *character of the nationalism* which inevitably accompanies national collectivism. Is it an aggressive or rather a restrictive nationalism? The economic logic previously developed by us obviously makes it in no way compellingly necessary for a government, which adopts dirigisme rather than a free market economy as its dominating principle, to be forced into the path of an *aggressive* nationalism. In no case can such a tendency be discerned in any of the countries, which have followed socialistic ideals since the second World War, although slight traces of it could be found in the ruthlessness with which the British Labour-government was wont to use the 'bargaining power' of the State monopoly for a large part of the foreign trade with small states like Denmark or the Netherlands. On the whole the nationalism of socialistic countries has remained a restrictive and isolationist one. To render it aggressive obviously requires additional and special elements. Above all collectivism as a 'social technique' must be combined with an expansionist and missionary ideology as it was in the case of extreme Marxism and National Socialism. Nevertheless, in the long run there remains the problem whether the fusion of Imperium and Dominium, which is the characteristic of a collectivist system, will not make the ultimately scarcely repressible interest of the state in the progressive extension of the spheres under political domination appears to be a vital interest for the nation and in this way creates the stuff for an international conflict, which even a peaceful and self-isolating socialistic country cannot ignore.

INTERNATIONAL PLANNED ECONOMY

Let us sum up: collectivistic 'dirigisme' with planned economy, 'full employment' and 'repressed inflation' at home and exchange control towards the outside world has – as it can no longer be doubted, and is recognized by more and more socialists, – necessarily the effect of making world economy in the sense of free co-ordination and genuine integration of international economic relations impossible. It must destroy the very basis on which in the liberal era the problem of international interrelations could be solved. It is just as clear that here we find the ultimate cause for the disintegration of world-economy and for the obstinacy with which the international economic confusion has resisted all attempts to overcome it since the second World War. The collectivist and inflationary course of the national governments has led not only at home, but also in international dealings to a state of affairs, the untenability of which cannot much longer be denied, even by convinced socialists. The call for international 'integration' is the general answer to it.

The need for removing national 'dirigisme' cannot therefore be doubted even by a genuine socialist, if he thinks things out to the end, and fortunately there is no lack of such socialists. Before, however, a socialist draws the only logical conclusion, albeit one which is tantamount to a capitulation, that the restoration of international economic integration can only be achieved in a free market economy, there is for him a last line of retreat. The obvious idea would be to overcome the national disintegration which national collectivism has caused not by the restoration of a free market economy, but by transferring the principle of a planned economy which has been compromised on the national level on to the international level. He would then seek the way out of the impasse of national collectivism in an international collectivism. Will he find it? The right answer to this question is of exceptional importance for the decisions, which our time has to take in the sphere of international interrelations. We shall at a given moment in a later chapter of this book have the opportunity to return to this point again, when we discuss the question of the economic integration of Europe. Only the most important basic considerations are here anticipated.

The question, I repeat, runs, whether in order to overcome international disintegration, it would be sufficient to convert national collectivism into international collectivism and to transfer the style of national economic planning, which is responsible for disintegration, from the national level onto the higher international level. The answer results from the character of the collectivist economic order, i.e. the economic order which replaces the market by plan and compulsion as a political direction of the economic process, i.e. as a controlling dirigisme.

The first result of this is, that the attempt to solve the problem of international order in this manner would be bound up with a serious disadvantage

104

under all circumstances. As in point of fact economic planning which by its very nature implies a radical political direction of the economy always presupposes a state, in which the threads of the planning and directive force meet, it can only extend as far as the sovereign political power extends. International economic planning must therefore remain limited to that sphere, for which the creation of a genuine international state is not completely Utopian. A world state is out of the question, likewise a planned economy of world dimensions. It may also be doubted whether even a comprehensive European state must not still for some time to come remain a mere dream, but it is all the more certain, that this is the utmost we can expect in our European position. Then however the conclusion is unavoidable that by means of economic planning we can hope at the most for a European, but no universal integration like the earlier one of the world economy, that is to say a continental 'closed' instead of the 'open' economy of the pre-collectivist period, an economic block of the European countries, a 'vast unit', whose plus in integration would have be acquired at the expense of less close relations with the rest of the world.

A way out, which would admittedly weld together the nations of single continents, but would drive the continents themselves all the farther apart, would therefore be no commendable one. Furthermore: it is not a possible way out. In order to realise that, we must again remember, that a collectivist order which brings the economy entirely under political control presupposes a state corresponding to the sphere of planning. A European planned economy would therefore, as we have seen, demand a European superstate, which must possess over all the individuals of the continent the same rights of command as national collectivism possesses over the individuals within the national boundaries. Not only however does this European state not exist and is also by no means near to realization, but the very circumstance that it would have to be equipped with the concentrated power of a collectivist state, makes it, in as much as it is to come about by a voluntary decision of the nations and is to be able to count permanently on their voluntary agreement, into something that common sense must call a Utopia. The salient point is that it would have to be not just any kind of state, but a special type, namely a collectivist one, which like a collectivist national state, could only be one centralized to the utmost. It is scarcely imaginable, that the European nations could be ready to transfer to such a superstate powers of authority, which not a few of them are wise enough to withhold even from their own national government in jealous defence of the rights of freedom and in mistrustful repulsion of bureaucratic dictatorship. Will they let themselves be treated as minors by a distant European government, which is rooted in no tradition, like the Norwegians and formerly the English by their own socialist governments, and become reconciled to a Europe resembling a huge Norway or a Labour-Great Britain?

Not even convinced socialists will dare to answer these questions in the affirmative. They show this in that they consider the consolidation of Europe into a superstate possible only in the loose form of a federation which preserves the individual national life. They know as we all do, that Switzerland gives us the lesson, that only the federative type of state is suited to embrace in freedom different nationalities with their own traditions, languages and cultures into one state, and that that, which is true for Switzerland, firmly rooted in the soil of centuries-old historical experience, is naturally valid for Europe to a far greater extent. Switzerland however gives us a second lesson, which after previous explanations we no longer need to substantiate: not only can it only exist as a federated state, but even as a federated state only when the predominating economic order is the free market economy and not some degree of collectivism; with, of course, the exception of wartime. And this is also doubly and trebly true for Europe. From these considerations it is clear, that the functioning of a European planned economy, if it is to take place in freedom, presupposes a European state of a type which would be incompatible with that form in which alone a political union of Europe which preserves right and freedom is possible, that is to say the federative.

Having established that the paradox of a national socialism consists in the fact that it must in practice deny the internationalism, in which it has its historical roots, we now stumble on the *paradox of international socialism.* It consists in the fact that international socialism on the one hand makes a corresponding international state absolutely indispensable, but on the other hand – always supposing that such a state is to be based on the free co-operation of the peoples and not to be welded together by some despot or other into a 'block' – makes it impossible, because as a collectivist state it would have to be centralized to the utmost. Therefore just at the moment when we would need the Eueopean state most urgently, it would most surely slip away from us.

All experiences we have been able to acquire up to now confirm this statement. Both the long drawn out difficulties of the economic union between Belgium-Luxembourg and the Netherlands (Benelux) and also the uselessness of the efforts of the Marshall Plan-Administration to carry out an all-European investmentplan not as a mere addition and a diplomatic adjustment of the national investmentplans, but as a European central plan following the pattern of national economic planning, must be understood in the light of these considerations [5]). Here, in this inexorable economic logic of international planning, lies also one of the main problems, provided by the European Community for Coal and Steel (Montan Union according to the so-called Schuman plan).

This logic is often confused in discussion by frequent reference to the *rights of sovereignty,* which the nations would have to sacrifice in the common European interest, and from time to time it seems even to be supposed that exercises of the kind of the Schuman plan are excellent on the sole grounds that they demand such a sacrifice from the national governments. And what could lie more clearly on the way to peace and progress? In this way the impression is created, that the refusal to submit the native industry to the controlling and commanding power of a supra-national planning authority lies in the same direction as the obstinacy of hardened governments, who reject a limitation of their freedom in foreign affairs, i.e. ultimately of the sovereign right to war, which it would be so necessary to agree upon in the interest of peace and international co-operation.

This is an astonishing confusion. Subjection to the order of the supranational planning authority, would mean to give up a right which belongs so little to the attributes of a government, that most of them, namely the non-socialist, have in the previous course of modern government history never had recourse to it, for the reason that they consider it an inadmissible extension of national 'sovereignty'. In the case of these governments therefore the 'sacrifice' of sovereignty would mean that they would grant the supra-national planning authority the right to give orders to their own citizens in a sphere, which they themselves have up to now wisely left to the 'sovereignty' of the market. They are thus asked to sacrifice a 'sovereignty', which they themselves in no way possess, because according to their 'ordre public' they leave it to the market – the sphere of Dominium and not of Imperium. If it is, on the contrary, a socialist government like the previous labour-government, it does actually possess the sovereignty in

107

question, but it cannot sacrifice it, if it does not want in this way to deliver up an appreciable piece of its national socialist system to an international superstate.

It is not the sovereignty of the European states which is, when carefully considered, the evil, but the excessive use which so many have made of it in the period of national collectivism. Certainly here an energetic retrenchment is called for. But little would be gained, if the sovereign right, which today the governments invoke to intervene in economic life, were taken away from them solely for the purpose of transferring it to an international authority. A Europe, which exercises the sovereign right of pursuing a planned economy, of submitting the exchange market to controls, of socializing industry and of shutting off the continent by customs barriers and other obstacles to trade, would not be much better, in many respects even worse, than a single national government, which does the same. Certainly the lessening of national sovereignty is one of the most compelling commands of our time, but the excess of sovereignty should be *abolished* and not *transferred* to a higher geographical unit. Not to understand this is a failure in comprehension which afflicts most of what is today being said and written about the economic integration of Europe. Sovereignty does not only mean the unquestionable right of the state towards other states, but also that towards its own individuals. In the first case it is a question of the seat, in the second of extent, but it only becomes a real problem, when it becomes a question of extent. A mere transfer of the seat of sovereignty leaves the problem of the extent untouched, even aggravates it.

We shall conclude with three remarks. The *first* is intended to draw attention to the difference existing between the single measures of international economic planning, as the Schuman plan according to the wishes of the originators was obviously intended to be, and an overall system of international economic planning, which is so comprehensive, that by it the national system of collectivism is really removed and welded into a higher international unit. It would be dogmatic, to exclude the possibility, that in an exceptional case the governments and nations in spite of everything might unite for higher political reasons in a pact providing for a planned economy. But such cases cannot be multiplied at will, without finally difficulty becoming impossible. There is reason to suppose that the Coal and Steel Community represents the utmost in international economic planning that the European nations could be prepared to accept for higher European reasons.

Secondly it is necessary to stand up from the beginning against the attempt to evade the problem of international economic planning by a fictitious solution. It consists in understanding by international economic planning something quite different from that which is named 'economic planning' on the national level and alone earns this name, that is to say, not an international central planning, which directs the international economic process according to a uniform plan and enforces the execution of this plan as national authorities would, but that kind of international trade, which results from dealings between national planned economies[6]). That this does not result in international order requires no further argument. It will no more lead to international order than the dealings between the regional planned economies in Germany, 1945, which were barely maintained by barter agreements and black marketing, were able to produce a property-functioning national economy. It is this very co-existence of national planned economies which has led through bilateralism, restriction of monetary transactions, autarky and extreme instability of economic relations to the present anarchistic condition of the international economy, which more and more socialists are at last ready to term untenable.

And now a *third* and last remark. We have revealed that it is an illusion to try to escape international economic disintegration, for which national planned economy is responsible, by international economic planning. So we may state: *the Nation is the highest geographical political level, on which a collectivist economic order is possible.* From this follows, that collectivism just as it is, is at home a 'road to serfdom', to an inescapable 'super-monopoly' and to smaller economic yield, it becomes in external affairs 'a way to international disorder'.

THE PARADOX OF SOCIALISM

We have already twice had the opportunity, to speak of the paradox of socialism, that of national and international socialism, and only now is it fully clear to us, how socialism reveals itself to be a typically paradoxical idea, probably the most paradoxical known to the history of human thought. You demand – so would one like to address the socialists – a socialist order in the name of the freedom and dignity of man? But how in

109

practice can it have any result other than the 'prison state'! You praise the socialist order in the name of maximum productive efficiency, which overcomes the contradiction between 'progress and poverty' and puts an end to the 'capitalist anarchy' with its waste, its crises, absurdities and miscalculations? But, while you shatter the market with its competition and its pricesystem, you put in place of this regulating drive a central planning authority, which floats without steering, compass, stars and sextant on the vast ocean of the economy! You crave for the socialist order in the name of the struggle against excessive power, privilege, arbitrariness and monopoly? Since however such an order includes the highest possible degree of concentration of economic decisions and this maximum of concentration is at the same time a concentration of political power, that is to say a maximum monopoly of naked force, the socialist crusade against excessive power and arbitrariness must end in an insurpassable and incurable worsening of the existing condition! And finally: In the socialist order, you want to march under the banner of internationalism and the brotherliness of all mankind? As however such an order can mean nothing else, but the imposition of a maximum of controls and welfare functions in the hands of the concrete national state, national integration must likewise increase to a maximum and pay the inevitable price for this in corresponding international disintegration.

It is the lastnamed paradox, with which we have here been occupied, and it is all the more provocative as the socialists have taken the international unifying effect of their programme to be a foregone conclusion just as they took it for granted that 'capitalism' is hostile to the international community. It is this paradox, which among all the paradoxes of socialism was the last to be unmasked, only in our own day, under the pressure of experiences, which no one can now escape.

This last paradox is probably the crassest of all. For when we compare the part, which internationalism has played in the socialist ideology, with the reality which has resulted with such compelling logic, one must acknowledge the justice with which a particularly well-informed ex-socialist, Franz Borkenau, states in his work 'Socialism – National or International' (London, 1942), that there is scarcely a point in the socialistic creed, in which the gulf between ideal and reality yawns so deeply and hopelessly as here [7]). With a blindness and an obstinacy, for which it is difficult to find a reasonable basis, the problem existing here, has remained as good as unacknowledged, although every attempt from Fichte onwards to imagine a concrete picture of a socialistic order, ended with a regularity, in which an inner necessity should have been recognized, in the construction of a programme of action, the political centre of which is the national state, the geographical framework of which is the nation. Even Marx, when at the end of his 'Communist Manifesto' he developed his socialist programme, had to make suggestions, which of necessity amounted to a 'national socialism' and a 'nationalization of man', which did not prevent him from concluding his pamphlet a few lines later with the fortissimo-chord of the summons to the unification of the proletarians of all countries.

A true monument to inconsistency, moreover, has been provided by those socialists, who have not been content with international lip-service, but who with inner conviction have interceded for the concrete aims of a liberal trade-policy. We remember that English labour-leader Philip Snowden, in whom a quarter of a century ago a modern Cobden could have been acclaimed, until the hard reality of the labour-state with the new figures of a Sir Stafford Cripps or a Hugh Dalton plunged the memory of a figure like Philip Snowden into the twilight of legend [8]).

It remains noteworthy, that even the opponents of socialism recognized only very late and then only with slowly developing clarity the nature of the problem of the international consequences of socialism and here discovered one of the most serious paradoxes of socialism and one which is most difficult to refute. Yes, we scarcely say too much, when we maintain, that the discussion on this point is even today in its infancy. If it were otherwise, the discussions how to shape the new international order and about the individual projects arising in this connection, (Benelux, European Federation, Schuman plan, International Control of Investment etc.) would not still be conducted in a fashion, which must be considered inadmissible by the few, who know what is actually at stake. In the light of this, how incomprehensible and naive appears the role of judge, which socialism has for so long delighted to adopt towards the 'imperialism' of 'capitalism'! In fact an economic system, which nullifies the division of Imperium and Dominium, of nation and economy, of politics and economies effected by a free market economy, and leads to a thorough impregnation of all economic conditions with a political colour, must have as its object the employment of governmental powers for the purposes of the economy. Only now, after in contrast to a free market economy, nation and national economy are fused into one,

111

does the economic welfare of the people become a function depending on the size of the area and on the natural wealth within the politically governed territory. Only now does 'room to live' (the concept of a nation) develop from a political propagandaphrase or the slogan of the greedily ambitious vested interests of the monopolies into a real problem which affects the nation's existence. Only now is the struggle for square miles, men, mineral wealth and transportroutes becoming really serious, because these have all become real and indisputable reasons of state. Only now is imperialism as a struggle for the maximum size of the autarkic and collectivist economic area becoming the most essential and inescapable vital law of nations. And now it is becoming evident, that the international economic relations which socialism brings with it are of the type most unforgettably made known to the world as the formation of economic blocks. The iron curtain of rigorous exchange-control, strict bilateralism, nationalization of foreign trade, inexorable supervision of immigration and emigration, destruction of the international monetary mechanism – those are all inevitable consequences, and we know now sufficiently what they mean: not only the shrinking of world-trade, impoverisation, bureaucracy and inflexibility, but also domination, power, hegemony, repression of small countries and unbearable increase of the points of international friction. All that will become even clearer in the next chapter.

NOTES

1. (p. 95)

It might be objected, that the cleverest of the substitute-plans, that is to say, the Keynes-Plan of the World Clearings Union, has received no opportunity to prove itself. Even if we do not want to attach a deep sociological significance to the mere fact, that no one has been able to resolve to try it out even once, yet it must be said in addition to all the individual technical criticisms which may be levelled at this plan, that even the Keynes-Plan could in the long run only have worked under general conditions of international order and international balance, which are also the conditions for the working of the gold-standard. The same elementary philosophy might be valid for the so-called Graham-plan (cf. WALTER EUCKEN, Die Wettbewerbsordnung und ihre Verwirklichung, Ordo, II, p. 76 et seq.) and for the European Payments Union.

2. (p. 97) International arbitrariness as a consequence of collectivism:

Cf. W. RÖPKE, International Economic Disintegration, London 1942, p. 47 et seq. There I developed the idea described in the text in more detail. In this connection must be mentioned also the collectivist falsification of international conditions of competition through the policy of the cheapening of groceries by the state and the state control of housing. It is now one of the main obstacles, between the Netherlands and Belgium in the further operation of the Benelux-Union.

3. (p. 100) Collectivism and inflation:

Cf. W. RÖPKE, Das Zeitalter der Inflation, Schriften der Volks- und Betriebswirtschaftlichen Vereinigung im rheinisch-westfälischen Industriegebiet, Duisburg, 1951; F. A. HAYEK, Vollbeschäftigung, Planwirtschaft und Inflation, in his complete work 'Vollbeschäftigung, Inflation und Planwirtschaft', published by A. Hunold, Erlenbach-Zürich 1951. For the understanding of repressed inflation: W. RÖPKE, Offene und zurückgestaute Inflation, Kyklos, 1947; W. RÖPKE, Repressed Inflation, Kyklos, 1947.

4. (p. 102) Fiscal pressure and inflation:

In this connection the following should especially be consulted: COLIN CLARK, Public Finance and Changes in the Value of Money, Economic Journal, December 1945. In criticism: JOSEPH A. PECHMANN–THOMAS MAYER, Mr. Colin Clark on the Limits of Taxation, Review of Economics and Statistics, August 1952.

5. (p. 107) International investment-planning:

Here the very appropriate remarks are to be quoted, which WALTER EUCKEN made in the supposedly last of his essays (Investitionssteuerung durch echte Wechselkurse, Zeitschrift für das gesamte Kreditwesen, of February 15th 1950).

6. (p. 109) So-called 'international economic planning':

The following examples are given from literature: G. D. H. COLE, The Planning of International Trade, in 'Studies in World economics', London 1934; CLARK FOREMAN, The New Internationalism, New York 1934. Such organizations for so-called planning organizations as the International Cotton Advisory Committee, (ICAC), which actually only obligates the member-states to supply statistics and to pay membership contributions, are here naturally completely disregarded. But not a small part of what is today called 'International Planning', is nothing but such drapery.

7. (p. 110) The paradox of international socialism:

The above named publication by Borkenau is very praiseworthy, but does not penetrate to the decisive points. It is worthy of note that the standard work, which Marxist Socialism had produced on the question of international complication (OTTO BAUER, Die Nationalitätenfrage und die Sozialdemokratie, Wien 1907), scarcely touches the essential economic issues. It is characteristic that even SCHUMPETER'S well-known work (Kapitalismus, Sozialismus und Demokratie, Bern 1946) completely evades the delicate subject. Informative supplements to this may be found in: L. MISES, Die Gemeinwirtschaft, 2nd. edition, Jena 1932, p. 197 et seq.; F. A. HAYEK, Der Weg zur Knechtschaft, Erlenbach-Zürich, p. 271 et seq.; L. ROBBINS, Economic Planning and International Order, London 1937; B. BRUTZKUS, Die Lehren des Marxismus im Lichte der russischen Revolution, Berlin 1928 (also in English in the collection published by F. A. Hayek 'Collectivist Economic Planning', London 1935).

About the connection with the history of the ideas of socialism: F. BORKENAU, loc. cit., especially p. 36; W. RÖPKE, Wirtschaftssystem und internationale Ordnung-Prolegomena, Ordo, IV, 1951, p. 261 et seq.

8. (p. 111) Socialist Inconsistency:

About the moving figure of Philip Snowden: F. W. HIRST, From Adam Smith to Philip Snowden, a History of Free Trade in Great Britain, London 1925. A last echo of Snowdenese inconsistency was the well-known ejaculation of the late foreign Minister, Ernest Bevin, who stated in the House of Commons, that he longed for the time, when it would be enough for a round-the-world-trip, as previously, to go to Victoria St. Station, buy a ticket, and to get into the train with sufficient pounds. A particularly depressing example of the horrifying lack of coherence in the political and economic thinking of our time, since a socialist minister of all people should know what the realization of his ideal means for the 'nationalization of Man'.

III

THE INTERNATIONAL PROBLEM OF
RAW MATERIALS AND COLONIES

INTERNATIONAL 'SOCIAL JUSTICE'

It was once said, somewhat unpleasantly, of the English imperialism of the 19th century that it said 'Christ' and meant 'cotton'. That is one of those unjust generalizations, which have so much contributed to the poisoning of the relationships between peoples and is especially ill-suited, when it is expressed with pharisaical self-righteousness. It refers to a period in which the great powers were scarcely in a position to reproach each other, and to a country, which unlike others can at least say for itself that it had shown itself to a high and exemplary degree, capable of self-criticism and reversal of policy.

The remark nevertheless contains some truth, in as much as political expansion has always worked with certain 'covering lies', in order to provide the real aims with a façade most suited to the changing spirit of the time, and to justify them on those grounds considered at the time as the most legitimate. There was for example undoubtedly a time in the 19th century when the argument of the dissemination of religion afforded great service, also in lulling the conquering power's own conscience. It is only a later secularization of this argument, when expansion is justified by the idea that backward – the word today is 'underdeveloped' – peoples must be raised to the level of European civilization.

It would need a thorough investigation, one scarcely undertaken up to now, to determine the real character of such 'covering lies' and to avoid too crude a conception of them. At this point we must content ourselves with a hint that it would be wrong to talk here of mere 'swindle' and naked 'hypocrisy'. Even though the façade does not correspond to reality, the deception caused by it is at least to a great extent also a self-deception. It is an interim world between appearance and reality, complicated and very interesting from the sociological and psychological point of view, and is best described by expressions like 'cant' and 'ideology'.

Now it is certain, that the period in which the European colonist and conqueror found it expedient to justify his policy of expansion to himself and to others as a religious or civilizing missionary work, must today be considered at an end. The propagandist camouflaging of the conquest of Abysinnia as a campaign against cruel barbarians, to whom Roman civilization must be presented, seems today to be almost a piece from a romantic opera. In general the West has become since the First World War too unsure of itself and its civilization, to remain any longer insensitive to the ironical undertone, with which reference is made to 'the burden of the white man', on whom Providence has conferred the arduous duty of the 'culture-bringer'. Instead a new cant has appeared; the economic one. 'Christ' is no longer spoken of in connection with naval gunners, but instead all the more is said about raw materials, markets, exchange-difficulties and room for surplus-population. If previously one virtuously sought to embellish a policy of expansion mainly with cultural aims, it seems today to be an economic disguise which can best give such a policy an appearance of justification. Today one says 'cotton' and means, if not 'Christ', then the political reality which hides behind the economic façade. Hunger for power, lust for prestige, increase of 'national honour', political or cultural missionary spirit, the urge to get things done and the hunt for a job and many other things, which are in no way of an economic nature, but which have in great measure determined European expansion. Were one to examine what great economic benefit the European colonies brought the Mother-Land, one would reach a sobering conclusion and in the case of Germany and Italy discover an almost absurd disparity between expenditure and profit.

Before we take a closer look at the situation today, it would be very useful to take a glance at the *last 100 years of European colonial policy*. We shall then be able to distinguish *roughly five main phases* [1]).

In the *first* phase dominated by early liberalism the predominating feeling about a colonial policy was scepticism, which found its best-known expression in the famous words of the subsequent leader of English imperialism, Disraeli, who declared the English colonies were 'mill-stones round the neck of the mother-country'. Most of the arguments used today against the claims of the 'Have-nots' – that it is not necessary to possess colonies in order to be supplied with raw materials, that colonies are only an expensive hobby, that the important thing is an international exchange of goods which is to be as far as possible undisturbed, and not an equal

116

distribution of territories – were at that time familiar to every educated person. A great part of the colonial expansion of England in the 19th century was achieved in continual conflict with this liberal colonial theory, and it is well-known, that Bismarck himself at first rejected the acquisition of colonies.

This scepticism about a colonial policy gives place towards the end of the 19th century to the *second* phase: the epoch of 'imperialism' and 'world policy'. Carried by the public opinion of their countries, the great powers enter upon a vigorous race for the last colonial territories, protectorates and 'spheres of influence', – which poisoned international relations. That this new eagerness in the struggle for colonies rose out of no economic necessity and cannot be laid to the charge of 'capitalism', we have already made sufficiently clear. Particularly the German colonies – that is to say the colonies of that country, whose economic prosperity was specially striking at that time – were of no economic importance, whatever either as suppliers of raw materials or as markets or as areas for settlement; in view of the irrefutable statistics there can be no dispute about that.

After the First World War, we enter into the *third* phase of colonial ideas. A new scepticism gained ground, this time strongly supported by the feeling that the time of real colonial policy was past and that Europe's old trustee-relationship towards overseas possessions could no longer be maintained. Everywhere national and racial consciousness was beginning to stir; European privileges, such as had existed in Turkey, in Egypt, in China and related countries, were crumbling; the measure of self-determination, which had to be granted to countries of more or less typical colonial character, grew perceptibly.

It was only in the thirties that the world suddenly entered into a *fourth* phase. It is characterized by the fact that the countries which have 'come off badly' (the 'Have-nots') discard all touches of colonial fatigue and persistently demand an even distribution of the colonial booty, and this in the name of international 'social justice'. What does this imply?

These 'hungry' states were in the main Germany, Japan und Italy, i.e. those countries, whose 'dynamic force' finally led to the Second World War. Now from the very beginning one of the most effective methods of propaganda has been to transfer the idea of the class-struggle–which was specially familiar to an old socialist like Mussolini – together with its phraseology, to the relationship between nations, and in the name of

117

'proletarian peoples' or, according to the German variation, with the claim to 'Lebensraum' (room to live), to demand a fresh distribution of political domination in the world in favour of the have-nots. So the call for 'social justice', which was to eliminate the difference between rich and poor from individual to individual within a country, was partly complemented, even partly replaced by the shout for 'international social justice', between those nations which are 'rich' in square miles of political domination and their economic resources, and the others, which are 'poor' in them. This propaganda-campaign was carried on with great skill, with unusual intensity and with a success, which one must term gigantic, and we may say, that in this unparalleled success one of the main causes of the Second World War must be sought.

In fact: here was a slogan, which allowed the dynamite of internal social contrasts to be thrown outward among the nations, to convert the dissatisfaction of the lower and middle class into nationalism and an impulse to conquer, the attention of the people to be diverted from the internal causes of economic decay and from the responsibility of its own government and to be directed against foreign governments and peoples. That was all based on a few indisputable, although easily distorted facts and demanded in the name of a 'justice', which could here as well as in many other fields be successfully misused as a covering for other aims, because it contained a germ of truth. It was indisputable, that the distribution of the politically dominated square-miles among the nations was extraordinarily unequal and the sovereignty over the economic resources of these square miles even more unequal, and it was and remains an undisputed fact that, if one takes as a standard the number of the politically administered square-miles together with their resources, the nations of the world are graduated into millionaires, middle-classes and proletarians. This was common knowledge, and so those 'dynamic' governments could appeal with an equally decisive a success to the greed of their own nation as to the bad conscience of the others, drowning the few voices, which exposed all that as complete mental confusion, went to the bottom of the facts of the case and asked, by what rights and in what circumstances the terms 'poor' and 'rich' could be transferred to entire nations and with the number of politically dominated square miles as a standard.

How colossal the success of this intellectual campaign was can be judged by the influence it had on that world political and world economic post-war

118

programme, which Great Britain and the United States announced in 1941 under the name 'Atlantic Charta'. Along with 'social justice' in internal affairs there was at that time scarcely another programme point so undisputed and so accepted by all sides for the new order of the world as the demand, that a balance between the 'owning' and 'non-owning' peoples should be aimed at and that for all the same 'access to the raw materials' or their 'just distribution' should be ensured.

In this a very remarkable change took place shortly after the Second World War. In seeking to characterize it, we describe at the same time the *fifth* phase in the development of the ideas, which determine the attitude of the West towards the 'colonial' world. This will be discussed later, when in a further chapter we deal with the modern programme of the 'development of the underdeveloped countries'. The idea of a 'class-distinction' between the peoples continues to be effective, but has now taken on a new form. Nowadays little is said about the 'privileges', which single countries of the West hold over others, through the easier access to raw materials which they possess thanks to their colonies. The colonial period is in any case irrevocably approaching its end. What has taken the place of its characteristic tensions and endeavours is on the one hand the claim to an equalization of wealth, which the former 'colonial' world itself – the whole group of countries now described as 'underdeveloped' – makes on the whole group of the western countries. On the other hand, however, it is the desire of the latter, to meet this claim in a manner compatible with their interest in the expansion of world economy, in the satisfaction of their ever-increasing demand for raw materials, and in political and economic influence. It is the former colonial world itself, which now as a new group of 'Have-nots' emerges from its passiveness with stormy claims, but at the same time there can be no doubt that much of the expansionary, missionary and protective endeavours from the earlier colonial periods revives unquestionably in the role, which the western countries here take over, although in such a way, that it is not easy to recognize the old content in the new form. The only country, which openly continues a policy of imperialistic colonization is, as previously noted, Communist Russia, but the remarkable thing is, that it does it in the name of a struggle against a non-existent imperialistic colonialism – or one existent only in pitiable remains – on the part of the West and with this downright cynical mockery of the truth can still achieve success.

119

THE REAL PROBLEM

This latest phase of development in colonial ideas makes admittedly little difference to the fact that the question of international 'social justice', as it has occupied minds in the fourth phase, remains one of the most important and the most interesting.

What is the point at issue? We start from those two facts, which we have already acknowledged as indisputable. The *one* that the size of states which share the political domination of the globe, differ widely in size, with the giant empires of Russia and the United States at one end of the scale and small states like Switzerland at the other. To this must be added the *second* fact, that the natural riches of the world are not evenly distributed over the earth's surface, but irregularly, so that the great and greatest empires often have an even greater share in the political dominium over natural resources, than would correspond to their size. In this way the inequality which already results from the unequal size of states is further accentuated by the relative size of the raw material areas under political domination.

Now the real importance of both these facts would not be understood, if we did not add a *third*. Such a striking inequality in political domination over raw material areas will certainly always have serious consequences, yet will not become a burning and vital national problem, as long as the level of economic development and transport technique sets narrow geographical limits to international economic relations. Up to the beginning of the last century the demand for a just international distribution of the world's raw materials would have had no sense, since the share of foreign raw materials in the international trade was slight, and most of the nations had in any case to be content with the natural resources of their own territories. It is this very radical change, which has taken place since then which must be added as a third to the two facts already named, in order that we may fully understand the problem. More and more raw materials have entered world-trade and have gained a vital importance for all more or less developed nations, the world has gradually become an economic unit, in which the inequality in political domination over raw materials has become a highly acute problem. It is for all countries a problem of existence, that they should obtain regularly and on the same conditions as everyone else, rubber, petroleum, tin and the other organic or inorganic raw materials, but here they are faced with the fact, that a

120

great part of these raw materials is found on the territory of a few large states.

These three facts, however – the inequality (both political and economic) and the dependence of all developed countries on the overall availability of the world's raw materials, are still not sufficient to give rise to a problem of the 'just distribution of raw materials' or the equal access of all countries to the world's raw materials. A *fourth* must be added, and just because so many ignore this, they become a prey to mistaken ideas and ambiguous slogans.

In all questions of international economic relations, the analysis of which we find at first difficult, we do well to proceed from the relationships between the various districts of a single country, and this clarifying method proves its value here too. It is indisputable, that even the individual cantons in Switzerland are not only very unequal in size and natural resources, but must ensure that these natural resources, which are so unevenly distributed over the political and economic subdivisions, are treated as a whole and are equally accessible to all. Here too all three facts previously mentioned are found together. But why does no one talk of 'poor' and 'rich' cantons in the sense that the first are small like the canton Zug and the second large like Graubünden or rich in coal like the Valais? Why is there here no problem of 'just distribution of raw materials' and no popular movement in Switzerland, for this canton to get its shares in the coal-deposits of the Valais? The answer is obvious: in this case no one falls into the ever-recurring fallacy of misplaced concreteness, which would in our example cause us to put the number of square-miles dominated by a nation, on a par with individual wealth, i.e. to confuse sovereignty with property, public with private right, empire with dominium. In this example of Switzerland all are guarded against this error, because the canton governments themselves separate these very different matters and do not misuse political domination over raw materials areas to make of them a privilege for the citizens of the canton and to establish conditions for the acquisition of raw materials by a cantonal economic policy, which are more unfavourable for strangers to the canton than they are for the natives.

THE LIBERAL SOLUTION

It is to be recommended that this unreal example should be thought out from all sides and possibilities in order to return then with greater clarity to the international raw materials problem. We repeat: that triple fact confronts mankind with a great difficulty. All countries need the raw materials of all areas, but the political map of the earth shows the greatest inequality in the size of states. Did not the only solution consist in transferring conditions within a country to the entire world and in building a world-state? And does not the impossibility of this way-out mean that one must allow international 'injustice' to poison the relations of peoples?

By no means. It was just the much abused liberal epoch of the 19th century which found a solution to the problem, that was so natural, that one was first aware of it when it had been given up and sacrificed to the new spirit of collectivism. We know the solution already [2]). If no world-state could be created, the next-best thing was to lessen the economic importance of unequal domination of the world's resources to the greatest possible extent, by separating where possible the spheres of politics and economics and creating what we call world-economy.

By this *free-market solution* it was made possible for international economic transactions to be so carried out, as if there were a world-state, and the individual countries stood in the same relationship to one another as the Swiss cantons or the provinces of some other country. No one spoke of a 'raw materials problem' of the 'have-not peoples', no one of the necessity of 'the equal access of all peoples to the world's raw materials', and if anyone would have done so, he would not have been at all understood. The struggle for colonies stood, as we saw, in absurd contrast to their economic necessity; a country like Germany experienced at that time an unheard-of economic prosperity, although the share of the colonies in German foreign trade was ridiculously slight, and little countries like Switzerland were leading in their prosperity and economic progress without having even in their own country appreciable raw materials at their disposal, to say nothing of possessing colonies. Raw materials were bought on the world-market, like stamps at the post-office counter, so to speak, without any difficulty about the necessary legal tender, for the multilateral character of the world-economy – which amounts finally to the much-reviled basic law of buying in the cheapest market in the world and selling in the dearest – made all countries into one big market. Neither were they bought on conditions graduated according to state-boundaries, apart from the monopolies already existing at that time, many of which sold more cheaply to foreign countries than at home (dumping), whilst the German Potassium Syndicate offered the example, rare at that time, of inverse price-differentiation (in favour of the home-market).

There was even a joke at that time, that it was almost a misfortune for a country to possess raw materials, since, thanks to the price-policy of the monopolies, it would then have to pay only more dearly for them. For a few important goods like iron and steel, coal and sugar, that was literally true. The largest state, the British Empire, followed, both in the Mother-country and in the crown-colonies, the principle of practically complete free-trade, whereas the Dominions maintained a system of protective tariffs, but were bound neither to each other nor to the Mother-country by a comprehensive preference-system.

THE RAW MATERIALS PROBLEM AS A RESULT OF THE DECAY OF THE LIBERAL WORLD-ECONOMY

In this way it was proved, that no so-called raw materials problem need arise out of our three-fold set of facts in the world any more than it would in the relationship of the Swiss cantons to one another. In this liberal world-economy national boundaries were without any appreciable economic importance, and the world-market was practically a unit with basically equal economic conditions for everyone, without consideration for citizenship or for the size of the state. The secret of the solution was the separation of the political and economic spheres, and in this liberal world the demand for political domination over raw material resources, to secure the supply of raw materials must have appeared as a parodox or as an attempt to obscure purely political or strategic aims. Nowhere could hate for the British Empire be successfully raked up, because it 'monopolizes' so great a part of the riches of the world.

To that extent, however, to which the governments of the world permitted the decay of this liberal world-economy, all this was bound to undergo a profound change and the problems of 'a just distribution of raw materials' was bound to develop out of a figment of the imagination or an empty propaganda-phrase into a real and more and more serious question. The raw materials problem and the problem of the economic 'living space' of the peoples simply appear now as part of a greater problem; growing out of an economic policy which is turning more and more towards collectivism and does exactly what a liberal economic policy had carefully avoided doing, namely, subjecting the economy at home and abroad to political direction, with the result that the economic importance of national boundaries and the size of the politically dominated area tend to increase more and more.

If it is a fact, that the parts of the earth's surface under the political domination of various nations differ widely in size, and if on top of it they are fenced in by economic boundaries, then this must in face of the highly differentiated character of our modern economy and in face of the uneven pressure of population in the individual countries lead to an untenable situation which imperatively demands a solution. There is no longer any point in answering the handicapped countries with arguments only suited to a liberal world-economy: that the acquisition of raw materials is, just as in a home market, merely a question of money, that political sovereignty has nothing to do with private possession, and so on and so on. Dominium and imperium are in fact two basically different things, – but only in a liberal world. In millennia of absolution and feudalism they were coupled together, and if modern collectivism should triumph, we shall return to this archaic state. Then however it will no longer be possible to divert the world's attention from the fact, that the colossal structures of the great empires mean at the same time economic privilege, in contrast with the past liberal world-economy. Then it will be difficult for example to invaliditate the assertion that, since the British Empire was fenced in against the outside world by the Ottawa Treaties (1932) and the other giants, such as Russia, the French Colonial Empire and the United States have also shut themselves off more and more, the exchange of raw materials for manufactured goods within these empires is easier than between them and the rest of the world. Then the small countries, poor in raw materials, have most to fear for their economic future.

The unrest of countries standing outside these empires can only be stilled, if the great empires give palpable proof that they have understood the responsibility towards all mankind (the earth today having become an economic whole) which their colossal scope places upon them. Men are detecting that just as the conception of property according to civil law includes more and more a social responsibility, so political 'property' must today also acquire a trustee-character, if it wants to appear justified, and only when the agglomeration of politically-dominated square

124

miles is given this character, will human beings in the long-run put up with it.

To anyone who has read these remarks attentively and with understanding, it need not be said that the trustee-character is to be sought not in any division of sovereignty, but in the liberal division of sovereignty and economy, the exact opposite of what the propaganda of national-socialism and fascism had demanded. That is true however not only for the relationship between the 'Haves' and 'Have-nots', but also for that between the Haves themselves, since the raw material resources of the world are so distributed geographically, that even the empires are not in a position to obtain all the raw materials on their own territories and are for some of the most important – e.g. rubber or tin – dependent upon a reciprocal exchange. If we are not successful in creating a world-order, which makes the national resources of the earth accessible to every country on the same conditions, a dangerous seed will be sown among all peoples – between the great and the small just as among the great ones themselves. We have seen how much of it has already borne fruit, and we are very likely to see more of it.

A special problem, which should not be confused with this general problem of division or combination of imperium and dominium, is presented by the great *international raw-material monopolies,* especially when they are dominated by a few countries as in the case of potassium, rubber, copper or tin. Even when they pursue no dumping-policy similar to the former iron and steel monopolies they often represent an element of arbitrariness, differentiation, exploitation and uncertainty. As it is largely a question of raw materials of great strategic importance, they can easily let loose a diplomatic struggle among the great powers for a secure supply of raw materials, for which petroleum offers a particularly well-known example. The propagation of 'equal access to raw materials' actually simplifies the specific demand, that the privileged position of the international raw material monopolies should be broken. Now this highly-justified demand is already to a large extent being taken into account by the fact that in many cases sooner or later a competitive production arises, if stimulated by the price policy of the monopolies. The breaking of the Chilean monopoly in saltpetre by synthetic nitrogen-production, the opening-up of potassium-deposits throughout the world and the development of rubber production in new areas of the earth are well-known examples. We are dealing here with a serious problem in the international combating of monopoly, which would best be solved if governments were to review their pro-monopolist policies and to restore to the best of their ability the free play of competition.

AN IMPOSSIBLE SOLUTION

Let us return once more to the general problem; it is clear that something effective must be done. We are however once more faced with the great danger that under the influence of a collectivist ideology, which interprets the experience of the liberal past in a manner which is fundamentally wrong impossible solutions are attempted and the obvious is overlooked. The formulae of 'just distribution of raw material resources' or 'equal access' to them are highly ambiguous. Is it intended to take such a 'distribution' literally and to give each state a just share in the political rule over the area with the valuable resources. What is the idea, i.e. how should the division be carried out? According to what standard should the claims be determined and according to what formula satisfied? According to the size of the population? That would be a very approximate and unsatisfactory procedure. How are the different raw materials to be reduced to a common-denominator? How is the fact to be taken into account that the bases of distribution are continually changed by the discovery of new sources of raw materials, new kinds of raw materials and new methods of use and by the economic development of all countries? Is the world to be politically 're-shuffled' again and again, and whose fantasy is sufficient to imagine however vaguely this procedure with its worldcongresses and quarrels? Or should all raw materials of the world be harded over to a world planning-committee and in this way make a suggestion which is always made when no practical proposal can be found, but which, even if it were practicable, would only eternally prolong the evil of the political direction of international economy?

It is clear that all such suggestions turn out to be impossible fake solutions, even more than that: as an extremely dangerous acknowledgement of a principle, which needs to be sanctioned only once in order to throw open the doors to eternal conflicts and agitations of all kinds. So the world can do nothing but return to the only solution which exists, as long as we possess no worldstate and the individual national economies are not fused into a single world-embracing one: the liberal solution of a genuine world economy with its multilateral character and all its further essential features.

THE RETURN TO THE LIBERAL SOLUTION AND ITS CONSEQUENCES

We have in fact reached a point in history, where the earth (at any rate economically) has become a unit. As, however, the world, as before, is divided into a series of states of the most varying sizes, there arises an extremely serious contradiction between the political and the economic and physical world-map, a situation of political and economic overlapping similar to the distribution of the denominations all over Switzerland. Just as the solution of this denominational mixture cannot be found in the principle of the Diet of Augsburg 'cuius regio, eius religio', but only in the removing of the political character from religion and in mutual tolerance, so also does the problem of world-economic – and world-political over-lapping admit only of one solution: the removal of any political character from the economy, i.e. the liberal solution in contrast to the collectivistic system.

Only in this way is a 'just' distribution of raw materials and an 'equal access for all nations' to them possible. No turning and twisting and no suggestions of whatever nature will alter the fact that we are faced with an immensely serious choice: either we must be prepared for a never-ending struggle for political domination over the earth's surface fought out among the nations with the downright prehistoric embitterment of the ancient struggle for pasturage and sources of salt – or the barriers erected out of short-sighted group-egoism must be torn down again. The one or the other: a never-ending scuffle for the greatest possible extension of com-mercial enclosures or a return to the scorned principles of a liberal world-economy with tolerable tariffs, most-favoured-nation treatment, the policy of the open door, an international monetary-system and no 'economic blocks'. Anyone who thinks this return Utopian, will have to explain to us clearly how he intends to evade the uncomfortable alternative.

The problem of a just distribution of raw materials is therefore no political problem of a new territorial order or an international organization, but an economic problem of the new world-economic order, and in fact a problem of one such as is alone worthy of this name, i.e. the liberal one. The demand

127

for a re-establishment of the world-economy is accordingly, and necessarily one of the most forceful, as it becomes a demand in the name of international justice and peace. It should be put with special urgency to the great empires, for they carry a double responsibility; as political dominators of a large part of the world's resources of raw materials and as dominating economic powers, on whose policy it depends in the first instance whether a return to a world-economy is Utopian or not. A change of mind is also requested in circles fully appreciate which the alternative here developed and realize the inescapable necessity of returning to a liberal solution of the international economic problem, while persisting in their failure to recognize the fundamental contradiction between such a return to reason and a collectivist and monopolistic course of the internal economic and social policy.

Once again however and in the most terrifying fashion does the 'Great Error' of our confused era disclose itself at the close of these considerations: the claim of collectivism of all types and grades, to deliver us from evil in the name of freedom, justice and peace and to promise us a new and better world-wide-order. In fact the surest and most direct way, to take us still further away from these ideals is collectivism, which itself belongs to that world, from which it wants to liberate us. It will not be necessary to explain again all about the compatibility or otherwise of collectivism and freedom. All the more urgent seemed to us the need, to make it clear once more, that collectivism is not only the fatal enemy of freedom, but also that of international justice and peace. That many collectivists are far from intending this, makes the case only more tragic and confirms the words of Thomas à Kempis, that all men indeed desire peace, but only very few the things which lead to it.

NOTES

1. (p. 116) Phases of colonial policy and colonial ideology:

Cf.: R. MICHELS, Die Theorien des Kolonialismus, Archiv für Sozialwissenschaft, Bd. 67, 1932; RENÉ MAUNIER, Sociologie coloniale, 2 Vol., Paris 1932–36; W. K. HANCOCK, The Wealth of Colonies, Cambridge 1950.

2. (p. 122) The liberal solution:

Further reading: L. ROBBINS, The Economic Basis of Class Conflict and other Essays in Political Economy, London 1939, S. 81 ff.; NORMAN ANGELL, Raw Materials, Population Pressure, and War, Boston 1936; GROVER CLARK, The Balance Sheets of Imperialism, New York 1936; Raw Materials and Colonies, Royal Institute of International Affairs, London 1936 (valuable statistical compilations); H. D. HENDERSON, Colonies and Raw Materials, Oxford 1939.

IV

THE INTERNATIONAL POPULATION PROBLEM

THE DEVELOPMENT

The entire problem of raw materials and colonies cannot be fully understood, if it is not set in relation to the population problem. In this way however there arises for us in a quite general sense the question of the relationships between the population problem and the peace problem.

That under primitive social and economic conditions the *overpopulation* of an area can turn into a real cause of warlike expansion, is really not seriously doubted either by historians or by ethnologists. It is however true for this stage that one should not conceive the relationship between cause and effect as a particularly simple one. The over-population of a tribal area is indeed no coincidence, but the result of a conscious renunciation of all those manifold means of population-control, which exist at all times and among all peoples. Behind such a renunciation stand possibly the same motives for developing a domineering force which then lead to warlike expansion. In contrast, we come across examples indicating that a strict policy of population-control constitutes the essence of a policy directed towards the seclusion of the country and the warding-off of all external enlargements. (Japan up to the end of the Tokugawa-Period in the year 1868.)

It is necessary, to point out these connections, in order to refute from the very beginning the *naturalistic conception of history,* according to which there are natural forces such as increase of the population, which force the peoples with the inevitability of fate on to the path of warlike expansion. The increase in the population is, as we saw, as a rule the result of a certain spiritual dynamism, the causes of which must first be examined, if one really wants to get to the bottom of things. It is to be expected, that the Cimbri and Teutons – the model examples of our school text-books – were from their early days a restless and pugnacious people, the growth of whose lust for conquest are only two forms of expression of the same spiritual tendency. Our own time too gives us an opportunity of making these observations, for we also know 'Peoples without living-space', who have justified their desire for expansion by over-population, but who simultaneously strive by all possible means for a further increase in the population. The best example of this was offered by Fascist Italy, which by restriction of emigration and the encouragement of large families itself helped to make the Italian population problem more acute, at the same time however continued to use over-population as a justification for its conquest claims. Among the steadily changing excuses of the national-socialistic policy of conquest the supposed claim to living-space by the German population, who were simultaneously driven to multiply by all possible means, likewise played an unforgotten part. In both countries a grievance, in which there was actually a germ of truth, – as in the raw materials problem – was cynically misused as a screen for naked imperialistic aims, so that it could no longer be taken seriously.

The international population problem of the present-time can only be understood, if one bears in mind the *development of the economy and population in the last hundred years*[1]). In this period there has taken place in the entire civilized world an increase in population, which in its extent and tempo has no parallel in the entire history of mankind. Its cause is to be sought less in an increase in the birth-rate than in a fall in the death-rate – especially in the case of infant mortality – alongside a steadily high birth-rate. Whereas in previous centuries out of ten children perhaps two survived, by the 19th century thanks to the progress of medicine and hygiene and thanks to increasing prosperity it became possible to keep them all alive. As, however, the birth-rate was not immediately adapted to the fallen death-rate, it was inevitable, that the population-figure shot up sharply. That is the procedure carried out in the 19th century in the countries of western civilization and which is repeated before our eyes again and again, as soon as a country has adopted this civilization. Here there is a 'historical interference', by which the rationalist spirit of modern civilization lessens mortality in a first phase and within short time, whereas the birth-rate, persistent as it is, continues for a long time to move on along the old way. By chlorination of drinking water, by protective injections and measures against malaria one can immediately and by direct means force down the mortality rate, but not the birth-rate. Sooner or later the moment used to come in every land, in which the birth-rate is 'rationalized' and adapted to the death-rate, so that the stormy increase in population

131

slows down and finally reaches stagnation. Most countries of the west, who are indeed the pace-makers in the entire development, were at this stage a short while ago. But how little in spite of everything the development allows itself to be moulded into a rigid form, is indicated by the fact that recently many of these countries have entered into a new phase of population increase.

The enormous increase in population of the last 100 years is therefore to be considered as a historically unique process, which contains in itself the possibility of coming sooner or later to a standstill or even of turning into the reverse process. The same intellectual forces, which inspired it, can end it, as soon as they have broken down the persistence of the birth-rate, and even before the First World War not a few serious observers were seized by anxiety that the modern rationalistic spirit, which we have to thank for the decline in the death-rate, finally, as soon as it begins to have the full effect on the birth-rate, may overshoot its goal, undermine the moral health of a people, devalue the family and force down the birth-rate far below a bearable level.

How incautious it would be to depend upon the 'development-laws' of the population and to dare prognoses in this field with too much assurance, has just been demonstrated by the period, which has elapsed between the first German edition of this book (1945) and this one. The anxiety, which had just been under discussion and which had given rise to manifold theories, had proved in the meantime to be unfounded. The western world itself has, as already mentioned, experienced an almost general boom in population during the last decade, which has drawn with it even a land like France and has reached an all but sensational level in the United States. In the last-named country the average annual increase in the population has nearly doubled in comparison with the preceding decade (1.4 % in comparison with 0.71 %), and in the last five years from 1945 to 1950 the average annual increase has even amounted to 1.73 %. In this case the U.S. are as already stated, only a specially striking and important section in the development of the entire western world, although one should not overlook the special position of a few countries (especially England, Sweden and Denmark), which persist in the two-children system.

We realize today, that nowhere has a self-assured prophecy suffered such a wretched shipwreck as in this sphere of the development of the population, and it is high time that we became aware of this fiasco with all its conse-

132

quences and accommodated ourselves to the radical volte-face in our thinking, which is in this way forced upon us. Whereas an increase in the population of the 'underdeveloped' countries – which is due not to an increase in the birth-rate, but to a reduction in the mortality-rate –, is progressing, there is added to it a great new flare-up in the population increase of the western countries, attributable both to a further fall in the mortality-rate and more especially to an unexpected and hitherto rather unexplained fresh rise in the birth-rate. The total result is a swelling in the world-population, which exceeds not only all prophecies, but also all historical examples. While it increased from 1850 to 1913 more or less regularly by about 0.95 % a year, on the basis of today's figures an average rate of $1\frac{1}{4}$ % (Colin Clark) must be reckoned with for the next 20 years which applies to an entire world-population, amounting already to $2\frac{1}{2}$ billions [2]).

The portent of these facts is enormous. They mean, that the never too well-founded anxiety about the economic stagnation and other possible consequences of a *decrease* in the birth-rate must now give way to the contrary and highly-justified anxiety about the economic, cultural and political consequences of an *excessive* increase in the birth-rate [3]). We have every reason to be concerned about the bare basis of existence of mankind, and even more reason, to fear the extra-economic consequences of such a human high-tide. If even today two thirds of the population of the world are insufficiently nourished, what is to happen, if, with mankind's present rate of development, an additional population of the size of that of all North America, has to be fed within the next 10 years out of the available resources of the world, whereas at the same time the destruction of the soil in wide-spread areas of the globe is increasing to a horrifying extent? What will become of the world-supply of raw materials of all kinds, of wood, ores and everything else, to think only of water for the population of the highly industrialized countries which is concentrated more and more in the great towns and industrial centres? What has become of the theories, which only 10 years ago seriously put the question how, without a massive expansionary policy on the part of governments savings could be converted into investments, thus avoiding continued depressions? Does not the increase in the population which has meanwhile become recognizable force us to a radical 'readjustment' of our thinking in the direction of the opposite problem, how the increase in investments which has in this way become necessary, accompanied as it is by a world-wide political necessity for gigantic permanent armaments, can be so far financed from genuine savings, that the danger of continued inflation can be avoided? Does it not make it further necessary for us, to give the production of food and raw materials an entirely different and more favourable prognosis than was given only two decades ago?

These and other questions are to be taken up by us in a later part of this book, when we speak of the problems of a new world-economy, especially of the problem of the development of the 'underdeveloped countries'. At this point we want to limit ourselves, to dealing with questions, which the gigantic growth of the world-population raises for international relations of an economic and political kind. For this we must go back a little further.

It is known, that the 19th century whose population-development we portrayed in its broad features, was introduced with a precept, which expected from population-increase only need, hunger and poverty (*Robert Malthus*). As one of the means which correct an incident over-population with gruesome relentlessness war was named in the pessimistic doctrine of Malthus. Has this pessimistic doctrine been fulfilled? The answer to this is given by the fact, that the population of the industrial countries has since then multiplied, but that the average prosperity has greatly risen. The catastrophe prophesied by Malthus did not occur, because the productivity of the world – in agriculture as in industry – has risen much more markedly than the population. These very historical forces, which on the detour via a forcing-down of the death-rate have led to a sharp rise in the growth curve, – the spirit of science, of progress, of the liberation from tradition – led to industrialization, to a world-economy and to the settling of vast, rich new countries.

England, Germany and all other countries, for which Malthus had prophesied over-population, have solved the problem of population-increase in two ways. First they have sent millions of people to the new countries overseas, which lay open in the 19th century to mass-settlement. Secondly they have superimposed on the agrarian foundation of their national economy an industrial storey, whereas at the same time in the new countries overseas huge surpluses of food were produced, largely by the very people, who had emigrated in masses from the old countries. Only in this way could the gigantic population of the 19th century emerge. Had it not been for the *industrialization and the internationalization of the economy*

134

– two sides of one and the same process – it is not to be doubted that an increase in the population of this tempo and extent would have led to those melancholy consequences, which Malthus had prophesied, and it is more than probable, that the over-pressure of the population would have exploded in a war. But the very unfolding of industry and a world-economy – in a word what is generally meant by the expression 'international capitalism' – relieved the pressure of the population and stopped up this source of warlike developments. In fact none of the wars of the 19th Century has its direct or indirect cause in pressure of population.

It is true that since the turn of the century *indications of tension* were beginning to be perceived. While this very period up to the outbreak of the 1st World War is characterized by a further powerful development of industry and the world-economy, yet the possibilities of peaceful expansion towards the overseas territories (by mass-emigration to foreign states or by conflictless occupation of colonial-territories) approached the point of exhaustion and within the industrial countries the problem of the concentration of the proletarian-masses began to weigh more and more heavily on politics, in no country more than in Germany.

This was the first time broader strata of the society were beginning to feel a very real uneasiness concerning the world economic and industrial development. Not a few began to realize that the unparalleled increase in the population had brought the world into a situation full of dangers and problems, which would one day show themselves in all their enormity, as soon as the conditions, under which the additional millions had come to life, started to waver. Even then the realization was ripening, that *modern mass-civilization, which has bestowed upon us the growth of the population, leads to serious manifestations of social instability* and burdens it with moral and political tensions of all kinds, which also have a dangerous reaction on foreign policy. In this way however, it was possible to argue even at that time, arises a really tragic confusion: the earth has only been able to bear and nourish an increased population, because its entire productive power could be adapted to the purpose of supplying the masses by a complicated scheme of international division of labour, but the conditions necessary for the enormous mass-supplying apparatus are peace, order, freedom and security, in short a series of laboriously acquired principles of human communal life, which must be guarded as laboriously as they have been acquired. Mass-civilization however, implies powerful

135

tendencies, which loosen rather than strengthen those principles, for which concentrated masses tend in general to have very slight respect.

An amorphous mass is the best soil for all well-known political movements, which carry into internal and external politics that unrest and decomposition which seem to be our fate. It is just this mass which is extremely sensitive to those words, so appealing to the lower instincts, of aggressive nationalism, of arrogant boasting, of inconsiderate disregard for the interests of others and of national autarky, and it is by their sheer number that the mass becomes in the end an unfluential factor in politics. Only by its preponderance can the worst form of nationalism, that of the *totalitarian mass-state,* be explained. In this way however the gigantic population increase of our time is on the point of destroying by its political and sociological reactions the foundations on which the entire system of modern mass-production rests. Malthus took revenge on his optimistic critics a century later, but in a way, which was in no way clear to him and to his time. That is the situation in which we find ourselves to-day.

THE PRESENT SITUATION

We are once more throwing a glance back on this peculiar century, in which the multiplication of the population has gone hand in hand with the unfolding of the modern industrial production relying as it does on a world-wide division of labour. This combination has had two effects: it has converted the increase in the population from a factor for misery into a factor for prosperity and in this way from a factor of political tension into a factor for peace: it has at the same time united all nations by the solidarity of economic interests. The free circulation of goods and people, which a characteristic principle of the liberal world-economy, has opened the entire globe to the economic activity of every individual, without requiring a shift of the political frontiers: he could either emigrate to a foreign country or send his products there, in order to exchange them for others. On the other hand every country had the economic power of the entire globe at its disposal, without the necessity for political submission: it could get men and capital from everywhere and make sure of getting the products of every other country by international exchange, the higher profitability of which needs no more proof. Thanks to this economic system an extension of the political frontiers for the alleviation of the population-pressure had not only become unnecessary, but at the same time nonsensical, since the entire system was based on peace and reciprocity. Among civilized nations war had become an unprofitable business and in this way a completely valueless means of alleviating population-pressure.

If all nations and their leaders had solely and with total clarity borne their economic interests in mind, the *First World War* – of which the Second is only a worse continuation – need never have broken out. The fact that it did nevertheless break out, proves however that the spiritual and sociological foundations of the system had fallen into disorder, and thus very thoroughly and disastrously. Never before had an objective and nationally developed interest in peace been greater among all peoples than at that time, never before had the bare existence of such a number of human beings been directly dependent on the preservation of peace, and yet this terrible war, from which everything else started, broke out, the first great war, which was borne, fought out and suffered by the same masses, the same masses to whom, as a whole the war was suicide. Every explanation of this horrible paradox, will remain a superficial one, if it does not take into account the fact that the invasion of the masses, who easily become a tool of those who know how to arouse, to direct and to use their anarchistic instincts, endangers the principles which assure the security of civilization.

To express this previously-stated idea in another way: *modern mass-civilization has become economically possible thanks to principles which do not really fit in with the sphere of human thought.* Modern mass-civilization lives on a spiritual and moral capital, which has been collected in more aristocratic, more individualist days, with Christianity and a humanity rooted in the tradition of classical antiquity as a foundation. Whatever may be said western liberalism was its last form and nothing proves our thesis more clearly, than the very fact that the masses can do so little with it. 'Live and let live' is indeed a maxim, for which one can not expect the man of the masses to understand 'Die and let die' is better suited to him. Hitler, Mussolini and Stalin, these figures which are so representative of mass-civilization, have astounded the world by the flexibility with which they clothed themselves now in this, now in that ideological toga. (Almost every contemporary current – Socialism, Marxism, the middle-class movement, and any others.) They have cynically tried in the course of their pragmatic politics to direct into their mills. Never however have

137

they asserted they were representatives of liberalism. They knew why; they perceived that an unbridgeable gulf separated them and their masses from this strange world of liberalism.

The First World War – which appears to us to-day as the first phase in a new 90 years war – means in nearly every respect the beginning of a *new epoch* and puts the population problem on a new basis. Tendencies which up till then were still latent or subdued, now advance free and change the face of the world. The rule of the masses makes gigantic strides and with it the shaping of the world, which corresponds to it: nationalism, economic seclusion, collectivism, the softening of fixed standards. We are still in the middle of this process of dissolution and can now ascertain with the deepest concern, that the population problem, which until then was only a cultural and intellectual problem, is, through the resulting reactions becoming a threatening economic problem. The liberal world-economy of former days has given place to a multiplicity of international economic ties, un-related to each other and subject to the pressure of thousands of crippling controls; this has ended an era in which an increasing population was diverted over the entire globe by free movement of people and by free exchange of goods. *If in the liberal world-economy the population problem found its continued solution in the individual sphere regulated by civil-law, of non-political movement of people and goods, so how does the nationalization and political direction of the economy mean that the solution is being sought in the political and collectivist sphere.*

In this way the size of the politically dominated space is becoming of more and more importance for the existence of the present and further popula-tion of every nation. The multiplication of the population is becoming in this way, as it was in prehistoric times, a factor of unrest. If the channels of world transactions are more and more blocked, if the daily changing friendships and enmities are opening and closing markets, if the entire intricate mechanism of the liberal world-economy is rusting, if a leading country like England, which has first shown the peoples the way to a world-economy and with exemplary fidelity to principle, first ensured its smooth running, could after 1931 short-sightedly deny this glorious past and shake off its responsibility for the world-economy, if international movements of capital become solemn exceptions, if everywhere the doors of immigration are closing and there are fewer and fewer countries in which one could become even a dustman without possessing the appropriate

138

passport – then the political frontiers do indeed become a really serious economic problem, then the question of raw materials and colonies is no longer a mere phantom, then there are satiated and proletarian peoples, and then there is for many countries a population problem in the sense that the relationship between the size of the population and the politically dominated area is more unfavourable than elsewhere. But then the favoured peoples – the great empires – who neglect their trustee duties towards the geographically-restricted nations, have every reason to be displeased with themselves and to fear an 'international class-struggle'. We are not exaggerating: it is dynamite which is being piled up here. In order to be completely clear about the matter, one must visualize the connection once more in a somewhat different way.

The development of industry and a world economy with a division of labour extending over the entire globe has brought about an extraordinary increase of productivity of labour, which has in great part been absorbed by an equally extraordinary multiplication of the population and has created the necessary conditions of existence for countless additional millions. The level in the division of labour which was thus reached cannot suddenly be lowered, without endangering the existence of millions and millions and in this way our social order in general – just as one cannot lower the temperature of a saturated solution without getting an undissolved deposit. Once the multiplication of population of the 19th and 20th centuries had taken place, one cannot pull from under the feet of the additional millions the conditions, under which they were born, without producing a catastrophe. We cannot simply turn back economic history, without at the same time screwing back the population-capacity of the world to the low level of the past. That is all the more dangerous for international peace, as the individual nations are very unevenly affected by this reversing process, which is at the same time the process of subjecting the economy to political direction according to the status of their population, i.e. according to the relationship between their population and the quantity and quality of the politically dominated area. No economic theory or political philosophy of any kind can change these hard facts in any way.

All this would be true, even if the increase in the population had to-day reached a standstill in all important countries. It is however particularly true for the present situation and more especially for those countries, the growth of whose population will continue over a considerable period and at an appreciable rate. If these countries have not, like Russia, the good fortune to possess room for further expansion at hand, they must realize that for them, the problem of population increase becomes more and more difficult to solve, in contrast to the time when the old industrial countries like England and Germany had to deal with the same problem. Japan is doubtless the best example of such need. Italy too belongs to this category although in a less striking manner. These countries might well be given a timely admonition to apply the brakes to their population development. But that in no way alters the fact that in the meantime the population of these countries is growing further while the old safety-valves for pressure of the population have been more and more blocked up. The political reactions of the resulting over-pressure, contribute appreciably and in a disastrous manner to the destruction of the world-economy, and the extremely nationalistic policy, in which those countries, certainly not solely on account of pressure of population, had indulged, leaves behind an economic burden, which only further intensifies the population problem.

THE PROBLEM OF INTERNATIONAL MIGRATION

The most effective means of levelling up international differences in the status of the population and in this way solving the international problem, doubtless consists in removing all barriers to emigration and immigration, and so to create complete freedom of movement for men over the whole globe. In this way we should return to the conditions which on the whole existed during the 19th century and at the beginning of the 20th century, before the strict barriers to movement of to-day were erected. If men would only act upon rational considerations, they would distribute themselves over the globe in such a way that there would no longer be either over- or underpopulated countries. If there were added to this complete freedom in the movement of capital, the marginal productivity of the factors of production, soil, capital, and labour would tend to even out as between countries; hence, the level of incomes from soil, capital and labour would be the same everywhere within each category and that finally these would no longer be 'poorer and richer peoples, but only more densely and less densely populated and more or less intensively cultivated managed

140

countries' (L. MISES, Nation, Staat und Wirtschaft, Wien 1919, p. 52) [4]). Reality will never completely correspond to this theoretical scheme, since it would be an unreal assumption to think that – in their choice of a place of residence – men would only be influenced by economic calculations. But these and many other complications in no way alter the fact that unlimited freedom of movement for men and capital would make of the relative poverty of a country a self-chosen fate, against which men would probably have neither the right nor the inclination to react with dissatisfaction and political restlessness. The international population problem would lose its economic and social meaning and could never serve as an excuse for an aggressive foreign policy.

Now our task would be easy, if we could assert with a clear conscience, that *all* barriers to international movement could only be created out of unreasonableness and narrow-mindedness. This is not however the case. There is certainly enough unreasonableness and narrow-mindedness in these spheres: the limits of reason are certainly over-stepped almost everywhere. Likewise many of the alleged *motives* are incapable of standing up to serious criticism. Nobody who is a friend to peace and humanity and an opponent of national egoism will even at best get rid of a permanent feeling of uneasiness, and only with the most extreme reluctance will be admit to himself, that here may exist a real and genuine case of disharmony between the interests of the individual nations and the overall interest of humanity. To this we have obviously to resign ourselves in so far as we are dealing with principles.

First intellectual honesty demands of us that, in spite of the unbounded misuse, which has been applied to the idea of rational eugenics, we should acknowledge a germ of truth in the fear of a country like the United States, Australia or New Zealand of being inundated by an unrestricted immigration from the over-populated countries of the Mongolian peoples, and that we should understand the efforts of such a country to erect effective dams against this tide. Furthermore: every land must have the right to protect its intellectual and political tradition from an influx of immigrants, who might endanger it by their incapacity to be assimilated or even by their sheer numbers.

Immigration restrictions can be justified, however, on purely economical grounds, as a measure which protects a land from an increase of population, which would exceed the optimum ratio of people and resources and would lead to a worsening of an already existing over-population. It seems at first sight that such a policy is only the logical application of the idea of tariff protection to the human labour force, as it is mainly highly-protected countries which have introduced a specially strict immigration legislation (U.S. and Australia). This analogy is however only a superficial one, as the influx of human beings cannot be compared with the import of goods. Immigration means an increase in population, which cannot really be judged differently from a natural increase in population due to the surplus of births. Its restriction can therefore be considered as one of the means of curbing the increase in population. Viewed from this angle restriction of immigration appears as a *quantitative* measure in pursuit of a given population policy, just as, in the argument above it appeared as a *qualitative* act. Has not a country the right, in the same way as it seeks to protect its biological and intellectual inheritance, to strive to achieve the most favourable relationship possible between the number of human beings and its resources, that is, to strive for the optimum ratio of the population? No one will wish to dispute this. And yet the most notable and highly disturbing feature in restriction of the population is that it is an act of national population-policy, which affects not the unborn, but the people of other countries, who are now compelled to remain in a relatively over-populated country. Here there exists a genuine collision of interests, which will only lose in acuteness when the increase in population of the relatively over-populated countries will have come to a stop.

If we therefore with a heavy heart see ourselves compelled for the sake of intellectual sincerity, to make some basic concessions which result from the ratio of a qualitative and quantitative population-policy, this in no way implies a defence of the present-day practice, which has become more and more narrow-minded. This narrow-mindedness proves, that it is no longer a question of a well-considered population-policy, but an indefensible expression of economic nationalism. The theoretical possibility that the economist may under certain circumstances have to acknowledge a limitation of immigration as being in the general national interest, is conditional on such intricate combinations of circumstances that the present-day practice of international limitation of immigration can scarcely be justified by it.

This practice appears in a still more unfavourable light, if we put its *popular motives* under the magnifying-glass. That is specially true of the opinion that immigration increases the danger of *unemployment,* an opinion which is very often to be found in the crude form of the belief that an immigrant can only find employment at the expense of a native. This idea, unhappily so wide-spread, is based on the error, inbearable for anyone trained in economics, that the total sum of productive work to be mastered is of a fixed pre-established size, a cake so to speak, from which no one can cut a bigger piece, without another's faring badly. After all, we do not work, in order to occupy ourselves, to satisfy but our needs, as well as one can outside the fools' paradise and we urgently need every unit of man-power for this. The absolute limit of the total volume of work to be done is determined by the sum of our wants: in practice therefore it lies in the infinite. It is true that the number of opportunities for employment is actually dependent on the market, i.e. on the effective purchasing-power. Purchasing-power however emanates from work with the proper aim; all produce for all, and it only depends on whether they produce correctly, that it to say for each other's needs. The problem of unemployment relates consequently not to the entire volume, but to the correct composition of production; the problem is one of *equilibrium, not of absolute total volume,* it is of a functional and qualitative, not of a global and quantitative nature. The volume of production to be performed is not determined, by the extent of the consumption but on the contrary the extent of the consumption is determined by the volume of production. The measure of unemployment is a question of the better or worse functioning of an economy governed by division of labour, not of a lack or a surplus of human beings. A drastic lessening of the population in a country suffering from unemployment by mass-deportations which left the pattern of occupations entirely unchanged would not lead one step nearer the conquering of unemployment, but rather once again confirm the truth, that what matters is the quality, the functioning of the apparatus and not the quantity, its mere size.

Here we have to do with a thoroughly tough piece of popular economics, with one of the most common, but also the most obstinate and most dangerous weeds in the garden of our already pretty much overgrown economic science. It has even its botanical name: 'lump-labour fallacy', the English call it, which we can perhaps reproduce with 'Trugschluß vom festen Arbeitsquantum'. We shall meet it in a later chapter (3rd Part, Ch. 2) [5]).

143

Now we can see clearly, wherein lies the crude fault in the argument, that immigration means a danger for the home labour-market. It is to be sought in the idea, that immigration by its mere quantitative effect is bound to create unemployment. That is decidedly not the problem. The true problem, as we saw, is to be sought elsewhere. It is the question whether immigration has a favourable or unfavourable effect on the economic equilibrium.

It is obviously impossible to give an unambigious reply to this. All we can say, is this: since we are dealing with a problem of balance and not with one of a quantitative general level, a lot will depend not only on the economic situation at the given moment but also on the *type* of the immigration and its relationship to the economic structure of the immigration-country. If it is of the 'right type', that is to say, if it fits in with the economic structure of the country of immigration, it can even in a depression very well revive economic activity and so create as many jobs as it needs, if not even more. It can give to the economic life an impulse which is quite incalculable. That is all the more probable, as immigrants belong as a rule to the most enterprising and adaptable type, are in short men, who, because they are moreover already in movement and are used to accepting discomforts, possess exactly that characteristic, which is deserting the resident type of worker to the detriment of the elasticity of our economic system, namely the readiness and the ability to change places of work or residence or both according to the needs of production. It is, to take an example, naturally imaginable, for dockers to immigrate into a country, in which the docks are suffering from unemployment. But in the first place it is not very probable that they would turn to just this industry, and secondly such immigrants would be the first to look around for a new job, even if for this purpose they had to switch over to another occupation. In addition must be considered the fact that the immigration arising from economic motives – naturally not the political – is usually itself subject to fluctuations of the market, of such a kind, that it decreases when the immigration-country is in a state of depression and increases, when it is in a state of prosperity. It therefore increases when it is most needed, and decreases when it could really become a burden; it might even give way to a reflux of emigrants, which relieves the labour-market of the depression – ridden immigration-country – obviously the most useful arrangement from the point of view of the immigration-country, although certainly not always from the point of view of the emigration-country. Immigration doubtless increases the overall flexibility of the economy of the immigration-country, for which Switzerland could be named as an example.

If neither the narrow-mindedness, which dominates the immigration-policy of so many states, nor their more or less untenable motivation gives us the right to demand complete international freedom of movement, yet we have all the more right to stigmatize the narrow-mindedness of national commercial policies, especially when countries combine a strict restriction of immigration with an extremely protective tariff policy. While the restriction of immigration can still be defended by invoking a clear national interest, the policy of exclusion, pursued everywhere with regard to goods, money and capital, cannot possibly be explained, with the best will in the world, by anything but vested interests, which are entirely opposed to the general national interest they are using to promote their own ends. While the policy of immigration may be faced with a genuine conflict between the interests of an individual country and those of an emigration-country, in the field of commercial-policy proper, this conflict is as a rule, only a seeming one and it only serves to hide the real conflict which exists between the vested interests, and the general interest of the country thus shutting itself off. To this survey must be added a further important circumstance. If in the present situation of the world, limitations on international freedom of movement are unavoidable, their effect on relatively over-populated countries can only be kept within more or less bearable limits, if the international movement of goods, money and capital enjoys all the greater freedom and can therefore, work as a substitute for the hampered movement of human beings. If men are compelled to hold out under relatively unfavourable conditions of production, they must at last, by means of a proportionately freer international trade be granted the opportunity of making the best out of their situation and specializing in those types of production in which they are least handicapped (Law of comparative costs). If they are no longer permitted to export themselves, they must be all the more freely permitted to export the products of their work on the most favourable conditions. It is bad enough, that the one permission must be withdrawn from them under exceptional circumstances. If however the one is taken from them together with the other, then all safety-valves are closed.

We can express this idea in another way: the situation of poor countries in comparison with rich countries can be relieved either by the free international movement of goods and services or by that of capital and labour. The last is obviously the most perfect method, but in so far as the international movement of capital and people is restricted, the first will serve as an indispensible substitute. Both lead to the achievement of the maximum possible balancing-out of the level of income and the standard of living of the nations. But this levelling-up serves not only the interest of the poor, but also that of the rich countries, because it is not carried out not so much by taking from the rich and giving to the poor, as by making the production on the entire globe as rational as possible and by exploiting to the maximum the total economic potential of the world.

If we have combined the movement of capital and the movement of human beings into a group, and set it in contrast to the movements of goods, we must now add that the substitution-relationship existing between both groups, is now also valid within the group of capital and human movement. That means therefore, that not only the movement of goods must be all the freer, the more the movement of men and capital is hindered, but also the international movement of capital must be all the freer, the more the movement of humans is hampered.

We cannot conclude these remarks on the modern problems of international movement without making two observations:

The *first* refers to the bearing, which the international restrictions of movement have on the total economic and social order of our time. They must not be judged according to the special arguments discussed here, but also as an expression of the increasing collectivization and nationalization of economic life, which, as we know, are inseparable twin-sisters. It is clear that a government, which under the banner of collectivism and economic planning takes over more and more the responsibility for the functioning of the economic process, cannot leave the comings and goings of men to their own inclination, or it would let slip one of the most important elements of planning. If such a government eventually develops into a totalitarian regime – which is after all a scarcely avoidable consequence of a consistent pursuance of this policy – it will consider with doubled mistrust everyone who comes from outside and might be a dangerous germ-carrier of freedom. For the same reason, it will resist the idea that anyone, who is weary of totalitarian collectivism, might leave the national prison at his own discretion.

146

So in this way we arrive from limitation of immigration to *limitation of emigration*. Whereas, as we saw, we must admit the validity of certain reasons for the former, there is no reasonable argument that could justify limitation of emigration in the eyes of anyone who has retained an elementary respect for the freedom and dignity of mankind. That, even on this side of the iron-curtain we have progressed alarmingly far on the way to the 'nationalization of man', is best proven by the degree, to which even the restriction of emigration, albeit in subtle and indirect form, has become the rule. He who speaks of 'the flight of capital' as a crime requiring forcible prevention by the police, should be clear how near he comes to the spirit of totalitarianism, for which the prevention of the 'flight of labour' is only the logical next step on this path of the 'nationalization of man'!

It is no less obvious that we cannot continually increase the importance of the national government for the well-being of the individual by a broader and broader extension of the welfare-state without subjecting the influx of new receivers of government-manna to a stricter and stricter control. The more we leave the responsibility for our welfare to the national government – in reality of course the collective total of the tax-payers – the more jealously we shall watch over the numbers of those who must share in the booty. The more the passport becomes by means of the extensions of the social services a gratuitous insurance-policy, all the less tolerant shall we be in the issuing of such a document, and in the end anyone who is not firmly attached to a national community is lost. He sinks to the level of a vagabond in a world which has gone back to the feudal principle: nulle terre sans seigneur.

Here, as in other fields – and in this way we advance further to the *second* remark – the problem of an international liberation must be seen in its entirety, i.e. in its inner connection with the problem of the entire economic order. Let us moreover sum up the recommendations for a timely *international migration policy* under the following points:

1. There is no excuse and justification for limitations on emigration.

2. The present restrictions on immigration are especially unbearable where they affect members of the group of the intellectual and economic leaders and entrepreneurs.

3. As far as mass-immigration is concerned, there exists not only the right, but moreover the duty of every nation, to subject it to a *qualitative* control, which protects the spiritual patrimony, the political tradition, the ethical,

147

linguistic character and the social structure of the country from an immigration undesirable from these points of view. Apart from the fact, however, that a warning must be given against a misuse of this argument, it must be emphasized that the process of assimilation is all the easier, if the immigrants do not cling like a rootless proletariat to the big towns and industrial centres, but scatter over the plain land and get an opportunity to take root in a world which is more natural and which simplifies the creation of a community. A proof of this is the experience, that in the case of Italian immigration to France peasants are far more easily assimilated than proletarians.

4. Corresponding to this, there should be in the emigration countries an economic and social policy, which lessens the impetus to emigrate. The last thing we should wish for is a world of wandering nomads, and when we place such emphasis on greater international freedom of movement, it is not because we wish that as many as possible should make use of it. What we have in mind is rather the idea that the greatest possible number of humans should have freedom of migration but that only the least possible number should have the wish to actually make use of it because they enjoy living and working conditions, which make them happiest in the place where they are born, even at the price of a low material income. On the other hand, the more the freedom conceded is one of potential and not actual immigration, the more will the immigration countries be inclined to a liberal policy, and it is this *potential* freedom, not the actual one with which we are mainly pre-occupied. We must consider that for the normal man it is in no way natural, to leave home and country and to seek his happiness abroad, in a strange climate, among people of another language and other customs, and to seek it in a completely uncertain future. On the average it needs a powerful economic, social or political pressure, to drive men to the desperate measure of self-uprooting. If we do everything to lessen this pressure in the emigration-countries, by agragrian reform, by de-proletarisation and evoking a sense of belonging and by combating persecution for political, religion and racial reasons, we shall have made a not insignificant, although indirect contribution to the reduction of the international barriers to migration.

5. Since, as we saw, a lot depends on the right type of immigration and its adaption to the economic needs of the immigration country, it follows that the barriers to migration can be made all the more surmountable,

the more is done to effect this choice and this adaptation. There is a broad and fruitful field for an international migration-policy in the true sense of a co-operation of governments in the international organs, which have been successfully created since the war (IRO, Intergovernmental Committee for European Migration).

6. While all these measures should make it easier for the immigration-countries to adopt a more liberal policy, yet it would be naive to expect the restoration of the earlier freedom of immigration and indeed this could not be unreservedly recommended. Then however countries should realize, that they must guarantee international freedom of movement for goods and capital with all the more zest.

CONCLUSIONS

After this excursion into the territory of international movement we now return to our main question.

We sum up our rather involved trains of thought in a few words and establish that the historically abnormal population increase of the 19th and 20th century has placed a great strain on peace in two ways. In the first place the concentration of masses and the emergence of the type thereby created of the *homo insipiens gregarius,* leads to dangerous manifestations of social fermentation which at least strengthen international tension, if they do not on occasion even produce it. Secondly, however, the process of the dissolution of the world-economy and the nationalization of the economy puts the problem of the population on quite a new basis, for it renders the population problem of the world more acute and the international balancing-out of a population-pressure of varying intensities more difficult. From this result certain conclusions, which can be reduced to three mainpoints.

Firstly in the interests of peace one has every reason to consider a sudden increase of the population with downright uneasiness, to wish the restraining forces complete success and to encourage them as much as possible. That is true in the first instance for Asia and Africa, but the newest development makes it necessary to extent the monition with emphasis to the western world. Henri Bergson is right, when in his book 'Les deux sources de la morale et de la religion', he says: 'Si l'on ne 'rationalise' pas la production de l'homme lui-même comme on commence à le faire pour son

149

travail, on aura la guerre. Nulle part il n'est plus dangereux de s'en remettre à l'instinct. La mythologie antique l'avait bien compris quand elle associait la déesse de l'amour au dieu des combats. Laissez faire Vénus, elle vous amènera Mars'.

Secondly it is in the greatest interests of peace to promote with energy the process of transforming the masses into a community, a process which a slowing up of the growth of the population could under certain circumstances relieve. A social and economic policy, which 'reduces' the masses, appears to be at the same time a peace-policy of the best kind. Structureless masses have always been a better tool of aggressive foreign policy than country-folk and towns-folk. For this reason, the idolization by Marxism of the proletariat as an avant-garde of peace needs correction. On the contrary, it is certain that uprooted masses conceal an emotional explosive of the highest force; in which direction and for what cause it explodes, whether in the vertical class struggle or in the horizontal international struggle, depends in the main on what ideology and leadership devolve upon the masses.

Thirdly the international population problem is once again specially brought home to us by the fact that the disastrous dissolution of the liberal world-economy, the nationalization and the giving of a political direction to the economy and the economic over-emphasis of the national boundaries must in the interest of peace, at last be halted and the work of reconstruction undertaken. If we cannot help conceding certain special rights to the limitation of the international movement of human beings, we emphasize on the other hand that the freeing of the international movement of goods and capital is an all the more urgent commandment.

NOTES

1. (p. 131) Bases of the population problem:

Cf. W. Röpke, Die Lehre von der Wirtschaft, 7th. Edition, Erlenbach-Zürich 1954, p. 80 et seq. and the further reading mentioned there. In addition: R. v. Ungern-Sternberg, Grundriß der Bevölkerungswissenschaft, Stuttgart 1950; R. Mukerjee, The Political Economy of Population, London 1943; G. Myrdal, Population, a Problem for Democracy, Cambridge Mass., 1940; A. M. de Jong, Inleiding tot het Bevolkings-vraagstuk, Den Haag 1946; G. Th. J. Delfgaauw, De economische theorie en enkele economische bevolkingsproblemen, Amsterdam 1947; Alfred Sauvy, Théorie générale de la population, Vol. I, Paris 1952; Landry, La Révolution démographique, Paris 1934.

A survey of past development is provided by the essay 'Un demi-siècle d'évolution démographique', Bulletin Mensuel de Statistique (League of Nations), November 1944.

About the change-over during the last decade: Joseph S. Davis, Our Changed Population Outlook and its Significance, American Economic Review, June 1952; G. Frumkin, Populations Changes in Europe since 1939, New York 1951.

Robert C. Cook, Human Fertility, London 1951, moreover draws one's attention to the important fact that today the reduction of mortality in the underdeveloped countries is proceeding very much more quickly than in the western countries. The curves of mortality and nativity therefore diverge more quickly today than previously. As far however as the *birth-rate boom in the western countries* is concerned, it is a phenomenon of very complex origin. Meanwhile one must however ask very seriously how much responsibility must be laid at the door of the *modern welfare-state*, which does away with the psychological mechanism based on a sense of responsibility, a mechanism which the entire previous population-theory has always pre-supposed; the welfare state may in fact even twist this sense into its contrary, in as much as it makes the production of children into a profitable business. Even that belongs to the fateful vicious circle, into which the welfare-state is bound to slide.

2. (p. 133) Growth of the world-population:

Annual rate of growth of the world-population

1650–1750	0.29%
1750–1800	0.44%
1800–1850	0.51%
1850–1900	0.63%
1900–1940	0.75%

(according to Kingsley Davis, Annals of the American Academy of Political and Social Science, January 1945, p. 3).

Consider also the single fact, that in 1927 the population of Japan amounted to 56 millions, in 1955 however will have increased to 90 millions. The population of Egypt has increased sevenfold in the course of 100 years.

3. (p. 133) Consequences of the hectic growth of the population:

On this point there exists a vast and highly informative literature, which, partly due to a tendency towards exaggeration, is to be used with caution. The following should be especially noted: Colin Clark, Halfway to 1960, Lloyds Bank Review, April 1952; M. Roberts, The Estate of Man, London 1951; G. O'Brien, The Phantom of Plenty,

Dublin 1948; M. D. Dijt, De economische toekomst van het Westen, Haarlem 1950; K. SAX, Bevölkerungszuwachs und Welternährungslage, Universitas, August 1952.

4. (p. 141) The international migration-problem:

Cf.: W. RÖPKE, Barriers to Immigration, in: 20th Century Economic Thought, published by Glenn E. Hoover, New York 1950, p. 605-645. Out of the huge volume of further reading are specially to be recommended: L. MISES, Nation, Staat und Wirtschaft, Wien 1919; L. MISES, Die Gemeinwirtschaft, 2nd. Edition, Jena 1932, p. 201 et seq.; E. A. ROSS, Standing Room Only?, New York 1927; L. ROBBINS, Economic Planning and International Order, London 1937, p. 316 et seq.; JULIUS ISAACS, Economics of Migration, Toronto 1947; H. A. CITROEN, Les migrations internationales, Paris 1948.

5. (p. 143) Lump-labour fallacy:

The locus classicus for this is: J. E. CAIRNES, Some Leading Principles of Political Economy, London 1874, p. 304 et seq. Cf. also: W. RÖPKE, Crises and Cycles, London 1936, p. 77 et seq. In this connection L. HERSCH (Unemployment and Migration, International Labour Office, Genf, 1931, p. 216) comes to the pithy conclusion: 'If it is desired to reduce and prevent unemployment to any appreciable extent, we must try in the demographic field to promote freedom of migration just as in the more strictly economic field we must try to promote international freedom of trade'.

152

PART THREE

THE FEAR OF WORLD ECONOMY

I

THE DECAY OF THE WORLD-ECONOMY

The remarks of the preceding chapter have proved how much the peace, order, security, justice and welfare of all countries depend on the creation of a common will of the nations to overcome the present decay of the world-economy and to find new bases for free and universal international economic transactions. The sources of resistance, which operate against the formation of such a will, are so numerous and so powerful, that one might be tempted to give up hope, to let things take their course, and thus to acquire temporarily the reputation of being a realistic thinker. No one, however, who knows what is at stake can allow himself such resignation. It is quite unjustified as long as no irrevocable decisions have been taken and the hope exists of dealing with the resistance by getting at its psychological roots. The deepest of these roots however, next to collectivistic ideology, is perhaps *fear*.

Fear, defined as an unreasonable and immeasurable exaggeration of possible dangers is indeed a basic trait of the present-day resistance to a world-wide economy. What, then, are the individual sources of this fear of the world-economy?

We are certainly not mistaken, if we seek the psychological basis of this anxiety in the fact that the memory of the once well-functioning world economy has become paler and paler, whereas the decay has persisted for so long, that many can scarcely imagine how international economic relations are to be regulated other than by offices, forms, prohibitions and authorizations, quotas, controls, exchange-control and clearing-contracts. The fear of the world-economy is therefore in a quite general sense a tendency to *shy back from the unknown* and the *familiarity with existing conditions*. So our first task must be to refresh the memory of the world-economy, as it existed heretofore and therefore to depict its decay, in order to make clear to what unbearable conditions people believe we must get used.

THE OLD WORLD-ECONOMY

Just as a healthy human-being worries little about the enormously complicated combination of his organs, which gives him health, and only discovers in illness on how many preliminary conditions it depends, so did the civilized world also accept the functioning of international economic transactions as quite natural and recognized only when it was shattered, its complicated structure and the number of the conditions, on which its functioning had to rely. Actually it is only today, when the world-economy no longer exists, that we are beginning to unveil the mystery of its effectiveness and to realize how involved in fact something was which once seemed so simple and natural. For our purposes we are limiting ourselves to the following main-points:

1. *The world-economy was basically a system of interdependence and intercommunication.*
That is to say: there was a connection between all national markets, which made the world-market practically a uniform whole. What comprehends all economic relationships into a national economy in a manner which seems to us quite natural and brings about what we call economic integration was present to a great extent also within the world-economy: one could buy more or less unhindered in the cheapest market and sell on the dearest and in this way bring about a balance of price and markets by what is called in the language of the stock-exchange 'Arbitrage'. This condition of genuine economic integration within the world-economy was in practice so far fulfilled, that the difference between national and international economic integration was only one of degree and expressed the natural obstacles rather than the enforced and therefore more burdensome ones. Certainly there were tariffs but their importance was on an average not appreciably greater than those of the transport-costs. Both were obstacles, which had to be overcome in international transactions, without their being able to eliminate the freedom of the transactions which linked the individual national markets into a world-market and limited international price-differentials for goods on the world-markets to a minimum.

2. *Representing, as if did such a system of intra-communication the world-economy was also a multilateral system,* actually in a double, not always clearly distinguished sense: (a) in as much as an important part of world-trade *actually* developed multilaterally (*actual multilateralism*) and (b) in so far as that in practice the entire world-trade *could* have developed multilaterally (*potential multilateralism*) [1]). The potential multilateralism was at least as important as the actual, for only the ever-present possibility of

changing over from bilateral to multilateral transactions made of the world-economy a completely interdependent and interconnected system, which, in simple words, amounted to a situation in which one could at any time buy in the cheapest market and sell in the dearest. But whereas the actual multilateralism can be measured statistically, the potential one evades by its very nature every attempt at measurement. All we can say about it, is this: the potential multilateralism stands or falls by certain preliminary conditions of international economic transactions, among which the freedom of international payments and the absence of a 'planned' regulation of foreign trade stand at the head.

3. *The world-economy was, thanks to a really international monetary-system (Gold standard) practically a global payments community.* That is to say: thanks to the stable parities in the very small margin between the gold export and gold import points, thanks to the gold standard's own mechanism for the preservation of these parities and above all to the unlimited freedom in the exchange of the currencies themselves (convertibility), the juxtaposition of national currencies was no factor which exercized an active influence on the flow of goods. As the rate of exchange was subject to no changes, at least not between those countries whose trade made up the bulk of international economic transactions, as such changes were not for a moment considered possible and exchange itself was completely free, the world-economy was a payments community like every individual national economy and the gold standard practically a world-wide payments system. However clear this effect was, yet it is only today, when the world-wide payments system has been wrecked, that we realize that it was dependent on more numerous basic conditions, than at that time seemed to be the case. The effectiveness of the gold standard was in fact simultaneously condition and effect of the entire economic system of that time and along with the latter, subject to the same political, legal and moral hypotheses. We know today that the so-called 'automatic' character of the gold standard was dependent on the constant will of all governments and all Central Banks, to maintain this character and moreover, on a certain measure of conscious control. It was a mechanism, which could dispense neither with constant lubrication by short-term international capital-transactions nor with the guiding hand of London as leading financial-centre of the world [2]).

4. *The world-economy, with the free-trade area of Great Britain as its*

157

nucleus, was paralysed by no kind of prohibitive import duties on the part of the other main countries. Certainly protectionism had constantly advanced since the seventies of the last century and had become a more and more serious problem; admittedly here lay the seed of impending disintegration. It is nevertheless beyond doubt, that government interference with international trade were up to 1914 held within limits which allowed the world-economy to function. Bearable tariffs, the general application of most-favoured nation treatment and the stabilization of customs duties by long term commercial contracts together ensured this result. The animosity with which the issue was fought out at that time between Free-Traders and Protectionists, was certainly not unjustified, but present day experiences however teach us how much it meant, that the protectionism of that period managed to limit itself to 'orthodox' measures. Thus we get the impression today that both schools of commercial thought – the Free-Traders and the Protectionists – had overestimated the importance of their dispute. It should not be forgotten that up to 1914, in spite of all protectionist obstructions, the world-economy had constantly developed. We must further not forget to place the level of customs duties in relation to the reduction of transport and production-costs which took place during the same period, and it must be considered that, if Protectionism was intent upon the aim of holding-up world economic integration, that it achieved this aim far less than commercial liberalism the opposite one.

5. *The world-economy was a system of basic freedom not only in the international movement of goods, but also in the international movement of capital and human beings.*

The fact that the gold standard excluded any monetary risk involved in long term capital investments abroad, the insignificance of governmental interference with the international movement of capital and not least the political and moral integration of the world, which permitted men to trust in peace, fidelity to contractual obligations and legal security, – all this led to gigantic international movements of capital becoming an important symbol of a world wide economy. Added to the international mobility of capital was that of human beings and their working-power. Immigration-restrictions were almost totally absent, and men made use of the opportunity thus offered to them to reach countries of high wages and lies social pressure, to an extent which is unique in history. This intensive movement of capital and men made an appreciable contribution towards

158

the economic integration of the world and helped to even on the conditions of production and levels of income, a process which appears to us quite natural if it is going on inside a national economy. Thanks to the harmonious combination of the flow of goods and capital, thanks to the effectiveness of the gold standard and the smooth functioning of the international credit mechanism the 'transfer' or large amounts of capital caused no difficulties. Moreover nervous movements of capital of a short-term kind ('hot money') were as good as unknown and in this way disturbances were avoided, which were to become so fateful after the first World War.

THE WORK OF DESTRUCTION

Even these few hints make it clear that we must understand by world-economy not a mere statistic total of imports and exports of all countries, but the definite form of an international economic order, which approximates international economic transactions to national in degree, if not in kind. From this it follows that there must be really international markets, a really international formation of prices and that freedom in the choice of buyer and seller which is an indispensible part of any such international economic integration. World-economy, as we saw, can only exist in the form of a really international market, price and payment community, which presupposes an interdependent, intercommunicating and multilateral economic system with an international monetary system, a minimum of import and export restrictions and with basically free international movement of the mobile production factors (labour and capital). Anyone who finds it difficult to comprehend the sense and implication of these conditions, should bear in mind, that such an international economic system must provide for mobility in the flow of money and goods and opportunity to exploit regional price-differentials ('Arbitrage') which we take for granted in a national economy. As soon as this possibility is no longer present within a national economy – let us say between Geneva and Zurich, a real economic disintegration will occur with the result that we can now no longer speak of a uniform national economy, but only of a juxtaposition of more or less incoherent economic relations. If one counted together the turnovers still taking place within the national economy, the resulting figure would perhaps be as impressive as ever but it is obvious that this mere quantum would correspond to a completely changed 'quale'

159

a mere addition of isolated economic acts, which lack all unity and inner relationship. The name 'national economy' would have lost its sense.

> The parts are lying in his hand
> But lacking is the mental bond.

Exactly what would occur within a national economy if it were no longer a market, price and payment community, has happened in the world-economy, since it has stopped to an increasing extent during the last twenty years being a multilateral interdependent and intercommunicating system. Since we have had to deal with a real and vast disintegration of the world-economy, which has been produced by the disintegration of the multilateral network, the international monetary-system, the most favoured nation principle and that minimum of commercial freedom, which in spite of a policy of national protective tariffs has been guaranteed. By the transition from the orthodox interventionism of the traditional protective tariffs policy to the unorthodox (planning, collectivist) methods of the commercial policy (quotas, prohibitions, foreign-trade monopolies, exchange-control and clearing-contracts), from multilateralism to bi-lateralism, from the international gold standard to monetary nationalism, from freedom of payment to exchange-control and from the policy of the most favoured nation principle to that of discrimination and preferences, the world-economy has been made into what a national economy would be, if the market, price and payments community were interrupted from town to town and from canton to canton. Just as such a national economy would be little worthy of its name, so is there little sense in continuing to refer to such a disintegrated world-economy in this way.

This destruction is the work of the governments, who have adopted the above-named measures of economic policy, the ones from evil intention, others from negligence, weakness or lack of insight and still others from self-defence or after extreme resistance and in pessimistic resignation. If we are to lay the chief guilt at the door of Germany with its policy of autarky directed by the vested interests of the vast grain-growing estates and of heavy industry, or the United States, which the more it had, as chief creditor of the world, to open its doors to the goods of its debtors, the higher it raised its tariffs, or Great Britain, which torpedoed a tariff-reduction agreement between Holland und Belgium (Ouchy-Conference of 1932) by an appeal to the most-favoured nation clause, whereas it

160

tied its own commercial bonds with the Dominions even tighter, or small and medium-sized states which competed with each other in narrow-minded economic nationalism? It is in truth extremely difficult to decide the question of guilt, and more useful than all mutual accusations is the common admission: nostra culpa, nostra maxima culpa.

This destructive character of commercial policy results in a small degree from the limitless sharpening of the traditional protective tariff policy, in a large degree however from the advancement of new measures of commercial policy. Their common characteristic is the aim of submitting international economic acts to *a conscious quantitative regulation*. Here we are dealing, in other words, with unorthodox measures, which result together in the new system of a 'planned' commercial policy in contrast to the earlier free economic system, and correspond to a domestic economy, which we term collectivist (arbitrary economy). If it was previously left to the otherwise free foreign-trade, to react to protective tariffs in the desired manner, these reactions should now be replaced by official orders. It is the command of the state, which puts itself in the place of the market and with brutal directness and by conscious planning gives foreign trade the desired form and the desired scope [3]).

And what since then is desired is a foreign trade, which is left as little as possible to the regulating forces of competition and corresponds to an increasing economic nationalism, to which German economic writers at that time gave the name 'autarky'. It is further a foreign-trade which at every moment strictly obeys the wishes of the government and promptly adapts itself to every sudden change in these wishes. Finally it is a foreign trade, which is so steered that it becomes an important part of an over-all collectivist system, its possible disturbing influences are cushioned before they impart themselves to the domestic markets which are subject to planning and control. If protective tariffs fixed by long term commercial agreements were the heart of the earlier trade policy and served the relatively modest goal of protection and the promotion of individual economic branches, the new commercial policy is becoming more and more an instrument of a complete screeming of the whole national economy which is rigid with and dominated by monopoly and interventionism.

Since about 1931 a revolution has taken place in international commercial policy, which has disintegrated the world-economy. It was a revolution of aims and a corresponding one of means. Until this point economic

161

nationalism had almost everywhere a definite and limited aim: to guarantee producers protection from foreign competition according to the conditions of their branch of production. The traditional method of commercial policy was in line with this aim of protecting production from case to case: it was the policy of import duties, which otherwise left the way free for international trade and hindered it neither by exchange-control nor by state trading monopolies. Governments limited their interventions to a merely qualitative (liberal) control of foreign-trade, and the quantitative control, 'unorthodox', collectivist control and 'planning', was only of secondary importance after the removal of the traces left over from the first world war except in Soviet Russia, which in this way showed itself to be a highly-disturbing foreign body in the world-economy.

Then after the collapse of the international credit and payment system in the year 1931 and with the shattering of the national monetary systems, the disturbing change which is well-known to us set in. Instead of the individual protection of the producer another and more comprehensive goal begins to dominate the foreign trade policy of the nations. More important than the protection of the individual producer is from now onwards the screening of the national economy as a whole, the currency and the more or less controlled and planned national economic system from influences and disturbances coming from outside. It is no longer the competitive ability of individuals which stands in the foreground, but the equilibrium of the balance of payments, which before 1914 was never mentioned in the highly developed countries and only temporarily or on the fringe of discussion from 1920 to 1931.

To this radical change of aim corresponded the no less radical change of methods in foreign economic policy. In the service of the new and com-pretensive task there now developed suddenly that system of collectivist isolation, which is crowned by monetary control, and this system has remained till today predominant in Europe as well as in the greater part of the world. The result is the disintegration of international economy, in Europe and throughout the world. That is the point, which for all further considerations in this book we must constantly bear in mind.

THE CONSEQUENCES

What this distinction of the world-economy, which is essentially the work of the new control-by-planning methods of commercial policy, means for the prosperity and peace of the peoples, need not be further explained at this point. We prefer to complement the general ideas, which the reader may be presumed to possess on this subject, by emphasizing the following points:

1. *The dissolution of the world-economy means the tendency to displace multilateral by bilateral commercial relations and in this way the destruction of the international market, price and payments community.* In this way the deep and real sense of the word 'disintegration' is fulfilled.

2. *The dissolution of the world-economy causes an unsteadiness in international trade hitherto unknown*[4]). To the geographical disintegration of the world-economy by bilateralism, corresponds the lack of continuity in time; collectivist foreign trade is, quite characteristically, given to abrupt changes in extent, composition and geographical direction, according to the instructions from the central authorities by which it is adjusted to the continual changes in trade agreements, whose term of validity becomes shorter and shorter and to the ever-changing economic conditions which, under bilateralism, are no longer kept in balance by the steadying influence of the world-economy. Corresponding to the general character of collectivism, the government is now living from hand to mouth in foreign trade, by detecting now here, now there opportunities for buying or selling, by now throttling imports and increasing exports, because the domestic production of a commodity tends to surpluses, now increasing imports and throttling exports, because an item is in short supply. A globe-encompassing world-economy, which represents a coherent whole and is solely subject to the conditions of production-technique, transport-routes, private business-relations and the consumer-habits of the free market economy, conditions which do not as a rule change abruptly, such a world-economy, which furthermore enjoys the stabilizing influence of the largest imaginable area and a long-term settlement of commercial policies and monetary conditions is the very image of steadiness, continuity and reliability. Collectivist foreign trade, however, becomes more erratic, temperamental and unreliable in proportion as it is removed from the stabilizing forces of the world and subjected to the control of the central authority.

Two remarks are necessary to complement these general statements: To actually understand the unsteady, frankly anarchistic character of

163

collectivist foreign trade, one should bear in mind that it is the *essence of collectivism* to change the entire national economy into a kind of *giant firm,* which stands under centralized direction and therefore has the possibility of buying and selling, without having to adjust its prices to the costs incurred in the production of every single article. It becomes a gigantic department store, which can vary prices within the overall costs according to circumstances, whereas the consumer or tax-payer pays the difference. That, however means that such a collectivist state can at any time by powerful and sudden dumping-operations or by the buying-up of goods throw the world-markets into the greatest confusion and in this way become a peace-disturber of the first order, from whom one can expect surprises at any moment.

As long as Russia with its insignificant foreign trade was the sole case of this kind, the rest of the world could to a certain extent put up with such a seat of disturbance. After, however, National Socialist Germany had trod the same path, the disastrous influence of the collectivist principle on the world-economy became evident, and the world has since learned more from the Third Reich than it realizes. In this way we come to our second remark. The national socialist example shows that one country after another came to believe it necessary to meet the collectivist disturber of the peace with the same weapons. In this way, however, not only did the disaster spread, but the collectivist countries were also taught that, the more imitators their example found, the more difficult did their situation become. In this way it was proved that the collectivist principle in foreign-trade, in contrast to that of the freemarket economy is essentially a principle of disharmony and parasitism.

FORCES OF AGGRAVATION AND SELF-HEALING

The remarks just made already indicate that the dissolution of the world-economy by collectivism has a fatal tendency to unleash forces, which drive it further and render a reversal of the process more difficult.

Collectivist propaganda has an infectious effect, in particular as a more or less pronounced inclination towards collectivism is to be found almost everywhere. This infectious effect is strengthened by the fact, that the example of the collectivist countries faces one country after another with the question as to why it should be the dupe. Even if it prefers to defend

164

itself by boycotting and a commercial isolation of the collectivist country, instead of applying collectivist methods itself: (example: the United States towards National Socialist Germany) some compulsory foreign trade is inevitable. Countries remaining faithful to the world-economy as a rule themselves, like Switzerland, forced to apply the control-by-planning methods of bilateralism and of clearing-agreements, when dealing with collectivist countries, and it is not always easy to avoid reactions on the domestic economy or on the remaining free commercial relations. In short, every country is sooner or later faced with the serious question whether, in face of the growing uncertainty and unsteadiness of international transactions it must not thoroughly review its relationship to the world-economy.

The further this development advances and tears down one country after the other into the whirlpool and the more the mere passing of time accustoms all to such a caricature of the world-economy, so much the more does the memory of its origins and the responsibilities fade. People tend to, that just as they have slipped into this whirlpool, there must also be a way for them to get out of it, and every government adopts the habit of pleading its powerlessness and the necessity for 'howling with the wolves'. With a kind of *exceptio plurium* – we are experiencing that once more in the case of the abolition of monetary control in Europe which is recognized as urgently necessary – the responsibility of the individual countries for this unsatisfactory state of affairs is blurred because instead of boldly deciding to reverse the process, every country lays the blame at the door of other countries, the spirit of the time and inevitable circumstances. Every country waits for the good example of another, with the result that all wait in vain. People argue as if the dissolution of the world-economy were not the work of men, but a dark fate to be ascribed to higher powers, whereas in truth individual countries have taken over the leadership in descent and now individual countries too must take over the leadership in the about-turn. *If the plea is made that nothing can be changed in conditions which have once been established, it should also be admitted, that there is no degree of dissolution, which could not be defended with such a comfortable argument.* Unfortunately one must admit that the return is in fact more difficult than the descent. As in nature, where perhaps the deforestation of a country shows sometimes the impossibility of repairing the damage, there are in social life, too, irreversible processes or processes to be reversed only with

165

difficulty. While today's dissolution of the world-economy is not an irreversible process like an advanced inflation, yet one cannot fail to see that it is one not easy to reverse. What weighs most heavily here is perhaps the fact that economic nationalism creates 'vested interests', which defend the status quo with extreme obstinacy and which, in this connection, despise no means. In addition we must consider the fact that this nationalism is closely interwoven with a more or less collectivist pattern of the domestic economy and can only be removed along with it. The further this fusion has progressed and the deeper the interference with the economic process has become, which is the inevitable corollary of a collectivist commercial policy, as, indeed of, every unorthodox interventionism, so much the greater is the resistance which every attempt at a thorough revision has to meet.

These forces of aggravation are, however, opposed by forces of *self-healing,* and it is undeniable that the latter have been effective since 1945. At last there are factors, which put certain limits to the dissolution of the world-economy. It is for once the well-known fact, that even a collectivist trade policy does not succeed in suppressing all the forces of the market, which *intra, praeter et contra legem* urge a liberation and restoration of the laws of supply and demand. Even the most severe punishments and the sharpest controls cannot make the brutal interference with the market 100% effective or eliminate the natural gravitation towards competition. The more state intervention is directed against this gravitation, the more violent is the pressure to be applied, the stronger in turn, is the counter-pressure, and which of them will turn out to be stronger in the end, cannot be prophesied with certainty.

Now there is another special reason why the isolationist and oppressive apparatus of a collectivist commercial policy has something so violent and unnatural about it and why the strongest pressure must be exercised, in order to reach the goal at least in some measure and for some time. The world economic disintegration means a retrogression in the development towards ever more intensive economic relations, and this, moreover, at a single point determined by political circumstances, namely on the state-frontiers. Autarky does not, indeed, signify a romantic reversal of the *entire* economic development to the idyllic level of past centuries, but only of developments extending the frontiers. But what can national boundaries mean in the long run, of which Seneca even in his day said: O quam ridiculi sunt fines hominum? Let us state immediately at this point, that there is no area of the earth where the absurdity of this situation strikes one more and is at the same time more unbearable than in Europe! Nowhere is the contrast between the possibilities of economic development and its actual restraint by the narrowness of a national policy of isolation more challenging than here, where the greatest masses of human and material economic forces crowd together in the smallest space, but bump everywhere into the hedges of a jealous neighbour.

That primitive economic intercourse, to which collectivism is turning back the world economy, may have been thoroughly normal in previous centuries, but it stands in a contradiction which is in the long run insupportable, to an economic system, which is so integrated and rationalized and based on such a highly developed technique of production and transport as we have today. For this reason it is so unconvincing, if one represents the world economy of the most recent past as something abnormal and artificial, which after a brief flowering has been condemned to decline. What is really abnormal and artificial is rather the attempt to bring about this decline by all possible means.

This explains why economically leading countries such as National Socialist Germany had to move heaven and earth to reach only a relative degree of autarky, and why a country is by such convulsive efforts involved in the most severe economic, social and finally even political crises and sinks deeper and deeper into the morass of collectivism. This is further the reason why the romantic economic policy of autarky has in truth the paradoxical consequence of ending in a highly unromantic over-organization, over-bureaucratization and over-rationalization within its boundaries, and why such a policy can never find rest, but be subject to its own dynamic force, which continually set it new and unforeseen problems and tomorrow throws overboard the equilibrium so laboriously established today. And so we may then finally expect with good cause, that the forces of world-economic integration, which are today being suppressed with all violence, will sooner or later once again make themselves felt. Naturam expellas furca tamen usque recurret. It is in fact difficult to block the current of world transactions: somehow it will carve out a new bed for itself, after all the vast disturbances which such a process brings with it, but which could have been avoided, if one had not attempted to fight against the natural course of things.

All these sentences were written more than fifteen years ago amid the outbreak of war. If I examine them today and compare them with the present state of the world, the truth seems to have been well confirmed, that the antinomy between the disintegration of the world-economy and the dynamic overall development tends towards finding a balance. In the re-integration of world economy appreciable progress has been made, which will yet be discussed in more detail and the urge to further loosen up the still existing fetters is unmistakeable. It is, however, just as indisputable, that it is precisely this disintegration of the world-economy, which is still advancing, although admittedly at a lessened pace, which provides as always the drag-chain of the overall economic development of the west. The balance of payments disturbances, the lack of equilibrium in foreign trade, the lack of an international monetary system, exchange-control, bilateralism, trade restrictions of all kinds and not least the continual stoppages in the movement of international capital – everything together produces confusion, misdirection of the factors of production, lack of equilibrium, restriction of development and a paralysis of the productive potential of the entire western world, whose growth can be read from the figures of a production which has meanwhile so astonishingly increased. These figures can and should not however hide from us the fact that there is still something fundamentally wrong with the economic system of the west, and the origin of this confusion is to be sought in the continuing disintegration of international transactions, which deprives the increase in overall productivity of a great part of its fruits and rather increases the tension between the various economic areas of the world. The situation is in truth more paradoxical than ever before.

All that will perhaps be more readily understood in the *small countries* than in the large, and in this way we come to a point, at which a few common misapprehensions must be corrected [5]). We have in recent decades got used to seeing in the great number of *small* sovereign states, a number increased by the last peace treaties, one of the most important causes of the decay of world government and therefore to expect a recovery by the creation of greater economic units. Again and again we hear in this connection of the multiplication of customs frontiers since the first World War, of the 'Balkanization' of Europe and similar things, until we are almost convinced that the freedom of international trade would unques-tionably be tremendously furthered, if the colourful political map were simplified and reduces to a few great economic powers.

In fact we are here dealing with half and quarter truths, which are almost worse than complete errors. Certainly small countries have in recent decades paid homage to economic nationalism in a very stupid and narrow-minded way, but the striking thing in this case was less the damage they inflicted on the world economy than that which in ignorance of their industrial possibilities they inflicted on themselves. The ambition of many of these countries to be at all costs self-sufficient in pencils or motor-cars, was certainly ridiculous and highly expensive. But one would certainly lose all sense of proportion, if one did not admit that it was a policy which was in the first instance very costly for the country itself, and that the protective tariff policy of some large states has inflicted far greater damage to the world-economy than all the autarkic extravagances of the Balkan countries taken together. That this is so often overlooked, is once again a result of the habit of thinking in square kilometers and not in economic power.

To separate truth and error, we must distinguish between *two types of small states,* namely, those which like Switzerland, Holland, Sweden or Belgium have reached a very high economic level and have become exporting industrial countries standing on the fringe of over-population, and the others, which like Rumania or Bulgaria are still in the phase of development from an agrarian into an industrial country. The small countries of the *first* type will on account of their economic structure and on account of their smallness be forced, to a far greater extent than the large states, to acknowledge the advantages of the world-economy and to pursue a moderate trade policy. They are so to speak great free port areas, for which a lively and as far as possible undisturbed exchange of goods is a really vital question, of direct topicality for every moderately perceptive inhabitant. They must, in order to be able to give nourishment and employment to their numerous population, bow to the necessity for exploiting the advantages of the international division of labour. Every attempt at autarky would be suicide for them and they know it.

Naturally even here there will appear tendencies to convert the economic advantages of the small state into disadvantages and instead of, like a free port area, obtaining the goods cheaply from all parts of the world and paying with a few highly-specialized products, to try to produce goods inside the country, for which the cost of production must be high as a result of the very smallness of the country. However the consequences of such a misdirected policy make themselves evident so quickly, painfully and directly, that the authorities must soon call a halt and turn round, if they do not wish to gravely wrong the vital interests of their own country and conjure up unforeseeable economic, social and political consequences. The smaller a country is, the less it is in a position to restore the disturbed equilibrium in foreign trade by a devaluation rather than a continued and flexible adaptation of costs and prices. Once again, it is the smallness of such a country and its great dependence on foreign trade which see to it that the damage of such a policy of national recklessness is usually greater than its usefulness.

As all these inferences are familiar to the inhabitants, they follow far less than the inhabitants of large states the temptations of economic irrationality, propaganda for autarky, exchange-control or devaluation falls here on stoney ground, whereas it is easier than in the great countries to convince men of the necessity for a flexible price and wage system, without which free international economic intercourse cannot exist. An appeal to the necessary consideration for export – and in this way indirectly for import – may, if the domestic flexibility of prices and costs is endangered by interventionism or monopolism (including that of the Trades-Unions), count on meeting with understanding from an unusually large part of the population. For the same reason, cartels (which may be very numerous, as they are in Switzerland) can here pursue their harmful practices only within certain limits, which are not to be overlooked.

So at the present time these small states can become real islands of economic reason. They are not only no decrepit monuments to uneconomic organization and backwardness, not only no disturbers of the peace of the world-economy and obstacles to its development, but apparently especially created so there should still be on the earth nations who are at least compelled by circumstances to show a minimum of economic reason. In fact, if these small states did not exist, they would have to be invented today. Considered like this, they have not only a raison d'être – which is quite obvious –, but are actually an urgent necessity. To give irrefutable proof of this, lies in their own hands.

It is quite different with the *second* group of small states, which have, it is true, a political and military weakness and a smallness of extent or population in common with the first named, but are yet completely different from them regarding their economic importance and structure, in that

170

they are poor and are still more or less on the level of agricultural states. As they have little to fear for the nourishment and occupation of their humble population and foreign trade is for them no issue of absolutely vital importance, economic nationalism finds here a relatively wide scope. Multiplying the number of such small states, such as happened through the splitting up of the old Austro-Hungarian monarchy, means in fact a retrogression in the rationality of the world-economy. As it is however in this case a question of poor countries, the damage for the world- economy is on the whole far less great than one would suppose, if one considered the map instead of world trade statistics. This is the only case which corresponds to the great states' popular idea of the disadvantages of the small countries for the world economy, but this just for a reason which very much lessens their importance for the world as a whole.

So we come to the conclusion that the widespread ideas of the economic rôle of the small states are indistinct and superficial, so much so that they practically reverse the true facts. We are either dealing with an economically highly developed small state, whose commercial policy is of importance for the world-economy: then it is just this economic structure that obliges such a state to show more self-restraint in commercial policy than the great states observe, – naturally presupposing a minimum of intelligence. Or, however, we are dealing with a small state, which, thanks to its slighter economic development can indulge in very daring experiments in autarky; then it is just this different economic structure, which keeps the damage to the world economy within narrow limits. Put in another way: *Small states, which are really of importance to the world-economy, are, because of their smallness, estimable – and today particularly indispensible – supports of the world economy.* The latter can only gain, if such small states are preserved or even increase in number, *at least so long as little prospect exists of the entire world embracing free trade.* It can likewise only gain, if the *small states of the other type unite into larger economic units.* The implications resulting for Europe's new political order, are obvious. They can be summed up in the phrase, that the absorption of the economically highly developed small states by an European Customs Union under present-day conditions would probably only remove an indispensible brake on economic unreasonableness, whereas for the small states of the south-east European type the opposite is true. This is at the same time an earnest exhortation to the economically highly developed small states, to live up to their world economic rôle without side-stepping, we need scarcely add.

It can therefore hardly be maintained, that economically highly developed small states such as Switzerland are a burden on the world-economy in fact, it is just the great states who can make life difficult for such countries. It is not the great countries, who can complain that the commercial policy of such small states disturbs the world economy, but on the contrary those small states, who can complain about the great states, when they put greater and greater difficulties in the way of the foreign trade so vital for the small states. If the large countries continue along this fateful path in the future, they can bring it to the point where our small states, surrounded by trade barriers, are suffocated, but it would be to add irony to injury, if one spoke condescendingly of the economic straits of the small states. It is the commercial narrow-mindedness and pettiness of the great states, not that of the small states, which is at issue.

In this way all that is necessary has been said about the question of a country's *economic viability*, a question habitually put for nations of small extent and with scanty raw material resources. It is now clear, that we are dealing with a very questionable and misleading conception which, as the examples of recent history prove, can have a bad influence on politics too.

The most recent of these examples is still fresh in the memory: *Western Germany* after the last World War. The idea, that this rump, which had resulted from the unfortunate decisions of the victors, was, on account of its separation from the agrarian hinterland of Eastern Germany not economically 'viable', was to a great extent responsible for the fact that the decision to deliver Western Germany from the devastating effects of inflationary economic planning and to set it on its feet by the restoration of a free market economy, with a sound monetary system, was protracted through years of misery and only executed by the reform of the 20th of June 1948. In actual fact there was no sensible reason why, in spite of all the devastation, mutilation and impositions, if only the right course of economic policy was adopted, this country should not develop 'viability' as some kind of 'greater Belgium', i.e. as a predominatingly industrial country which defrays the costs of its existence by paying for the net import of food-stuffs and raw materials with the export of industrial goods and services. What mattered only was that after the evil nightmare of

172

collectivism and 'repressed inflation', an economic order should be made effective, which released the productive forces of the country, after they had been paralysed and squandered by the worst economic confusion which ever a socialist planned economy had brought upon an unhappy land of the industrial west.

The idea of a Western Germany, which was not 'viable', because it is cut off from its agrarian hinterland, is based on a very elementary fallacy in economic reasoning. The agrarian surpluses of Eastern Germany had always had to be paid for with the industrial surpluses of Western Germany, and so the only difficulty existed in replacing, until the hoped-for early moment of reunification, this previous exchange by one between Western Germany and the rest of the world with its surpluses of agrarian products and raw materials and its desire to sell them in exchange for German industrial products. But given these surpluses and this wish and given further the diminished productive energy of Western Germany, why should those difficulties be insuperable, if one only brought the productive forces of Western Germany to life again through a return to economic reason. Everyone knows, that Western Germany's born since 1948 has answered this question in the most convincing manner.

The idea of economic 'viability' suffers, as this example shows, from an unduly organic conception of the 'national economy', i.e. from a mistake in reasoning, which is known to us as 'Begriffsrealismus' or 'fallacy of misplaced concreteness' (Whitehead) with all its totally disastrous effects. It by-passes the truth, that the drawing of a political frontier changes nothing in the substance of the economic process as a constant exchange of goods produced by division of labour, unless such a political frontier is used to hinder this exchange by political means. In this however the 'incomplete state', whose 'viability' is being doubted, has the least interest of all, so that it is as a rule the other 'viable' states, which limit its possibilities of existence by their commercial policy.

Obviously therefore the economic 'viability' of a state is not a function of its size and its equipment with natural riches, as Switzerland proves to our satisfaction. And who doubts that even a mere city-state like Tangier is anything but 'unviable'? Size, density of population and the raw material resources of a country determine solely the degree of its dependence on foreign trade and in this way both its own interest in a free world economy and its vulnerability through the enchaining of free trade.

It is understandable, that the conception of the economic 'viability' of a state always crops up in the discussion, when it is a question of the new creation of an 'incomplete' state by the division of a larger one, not however in the case of a small state already long in existence. In 1919 the 'vital capacity' of Austria was discussed, and after the last World War that of Western Germany or Pakistan, not that of Switzerland or Norway. Just this should be sufficient proof of the true nature of the problem. It lies in the difficulties of a change and adaptation, which we have studied in the example of Western Germany, not, however in a lasting 'unviability' of the new state. It goes without saying that the more economic nationalism and collectivism hamper international exchange, not only the greater are those difficulties of adaptation, but also the less favourable are the permanent conditions of a small and 'non-complete' national economy. But that is only a new aspect of a truth which is already sufficiently known to us, that the modern nationalist and collectivist economic policy, in other words the increasing fusion of imperium and dominium, gives to the size and the natural riches of a state an economic importance, which they do not possess in a free world economy and in a liberal economic order. Whether and in how far a political act, such as the drawing of a frontier, has economic importance, depends on whether and to what extent the predominating economic order of the countries gives economic importance to the state-frontiers. That socialism increases this importance to a maximum, is the catastrophe of our time.

NOTES

1. (p. 156) Multilateralism:

For details see: W. Röpke, Die Gesellschaftskrisis der Gegenwart, 5th edition, Erlenbach-Zürich, 1948, p. 399 et seq.; W. Röpke, International Economic Disintegration, London, 1942, p. 30 et seq.; The Network of World Trade, League of Nations Publication, Geneva 1942; Albert Hirschmann, Etude statistique sur la tendance du commerce extérieur vers l'équilibre et le bilatéralisme, Conférence Permanente des Hautes Etudes Internationales, Bergen, 1939, Institut International de Coopération Intellectuelle, Paris.

2. (p. 157) The Financial Structure of the World Economic System:

The best presentation known to me: Roger Nathan, Le rôle international des grands marchés financiers, Paris, 1938. The transfer mechanism of that time up to 1914 is described and analysed in an exemplary manner by J. Viner, Canada's Balance of International Indebtedness 1900–1913, Cambridge (Massachusetts), 1924.

3. (p. 161) The Destruction of the World Economic System by Collectivism:

Compare M. S. Gordon, Barriers to World Trade, New York 1941; J. B. Condliffe, The Reconstruction of World Trade, New York 1940; W. Röpke, International Economic Disintegration, London, 1942, Description of important stages in the futile defensive battle: E. W. Rappard, Le nationalisme économique et la Société des Nations, Cours de l'Académie de Droit International, Paris 1938; W. E. Rappard, Post-War Efforts for Freer Trade, Geneva Research Centre, Geneva 1938; Commercial Policy in the Interwar Period: International Proposals and National Policies, League of Nations Publication, Geneva 1942.

The distinction between free market (conforming) and collective (non-conforming) trade policy was presented clearly for the first time by: G. Haberler, Liberale und planwirtschaftliche Handelspolitik, Berlin 1934. Furthermore: G. Haberler and M. Hill, Quantitative Trade Controls: Their Causes and Nature, League of Nations Publication, Geneva 1943.

On the conflict between the free market and collective sectors of world economy: J. Viner, Trade Relations between Free-Market and Controlled Economies, League of Nations Publication, Geneva 1943; O. Long, Les Etats-Unis et la Grande-Bretagne devant le IIIe Reich (1934–1939), un aspect du conflit des politiques commerciales avant la guerre, Geneva, 1943; W. Graf, Der Außenhandel zwischen marktwirtschaftlich organisierten und zentralgeleiteten Volkswirtschaften, Zürich, 1951.

4. (p. 163) The erratic Character of Collectivist Foreign Trade:

I have dealt exhaustively with this aspect of the disintegration of the world economy under the heading 'The erratic character of world trade' in my English book 'International Economic Disintegration' (p. 45 et seq.) and have also provided statistical proof. As regards the unreliability and uncertainty introduced into business life by collectivism by virtue of its nature, see also: F. A. Hayek, Der Weg zur Knechtschaft, Erlenbach-Zürich, no date, p. 101 et seq.

5. (p. 168) The Part played by the Small States in the World Economic System:

This subject, which has so far been much neglected, has recently been dealt with in a manner largely agreeing with my statements by K. W. ROTHSCHILD, The Small Nation and World Trade, Economic Journal, April 1944. The case of Switzerland: W. E. RAPPARD, La Suisse et le marché du monde, 'Die Schweiz als Kleinstaat in der Weltwirtschaft', St. Gallen, 1945.

II

THE FEAR OF COMPETITION

THE GENERAL FEAR OF COMPETITION

In the last chapter we found the basic cause of today's fear of a world economy to be that the days of a genuine world economy are long past, and that its chaotic condition has become a matter of habit. Fewer and fewer people can still conceive that something like a real world economy was once possible, and even fewer that anything like it could become possible once more. They shrink back from it as from an adventurous journey to a completely unknown country, and only the smallest number will take the trouble to study the detailed descriptions of this country as provided by economics. But their willingness to succumb to all sorts of *special* forms of fear of a world economy is all the greater, and this is what we now have to consider. We will begin with the type which we will call the general fear of competition.

The fear of foreign competition and the resulting wish to obtain the best possible protection against it have, of course, at all times been the real motive behind modern protectionism. But up to the time of the first World War it was as a rule more a case of fear of competition in definite branches of production than of general fear of competition which imagined a possible inferiority of the national economy as a whole vis-à-vis foreign countries. The United States of America have always been an important exception in this respect; in their case the tendency was from the beginning to base protectionism on the argument that the lower wages paid in other countries represented a danger to almost the whole of the national economy, so that every cost advantage abroad must be met by a corresponding import duty. While this principle, which derives from the general fear of competition, was designated as 'scientific' by protectionist propaganda, and finally even gained official approvement in the American Tariff Act of 1922, the leading economists in the same country had little difficulty in proving that it was scientifically untenable.

The novelty of the present day situation is that from being an exception this general fear of competition has become the rule. While it used to be limited to countries, which, like the United States, enjoyed a particularly high wage-level that had ostensibly to be protected against 'social dumping' on the part of countries with a lower wage-level, there is hardly a country left today which does not feel inferior all along the line for one reason or another to some specific or to all foreign nations. This has firmly established the conception among many people that an entire national economy could be overthrown in competition by foreign nations like a private firm, and thus driven to bankruptcy. Nobody seems to take much notice of the conspicuous fact that this fear of competition is reciprocal and is motivated by precisely contrary arguments in the individual countries. On the one hand the rich countries with a high wage-level (like the United States) fear the competition of poorer countries with their 'sweated wages', and on the other the poor countries fear the rich ones with their superior production technique. Even at best, it is obvious that only one of these two fears can be well-founded, but not both at the same time. Or are both of them unfounded, since they cancel out and only result from confused and untrained thinking? This is, in fact, the case.

Anyone who is acquainted with the theory of foreign trade will understand at once what we are driving at when we refer to the so-called 'Law of Comparative Costs', which was mentioned earlier on (p. 145) [1]. It does in fact follow from this law that even a nation which is inferior in production all along the line can not only participate profitably in free international trade, but actually depends on it in order to improve its position in life, and conversely that a nation of superior productivity all along the line will deprive itself of the advantages of its position if it does not enter into free trade relations with the inferior countries. The division of labour between these two types of countries takes place in such a way that the inferior ones specialize in those branches of production where their inferiority is least, while the superior ones specialize in the branches of production where their superiority is greatest. The inferior country must, admittedly, resign itself to the fact that it must compensate for the disadvantages of its production conditions by lower wages, while the superior country enjoys the advantages of production in the shape of a higher wage-level. Were both countries not to specialize in the relatively most favourable branches of production, the wages would have to be lower in both cases.

178

The following conclusion may be drawn from this: The higher wages paid in the superior country are a consequence of its superiority in production *and* of the advantage deriving from dovetailing into the international division of labour, while the lower wages paid by the inferior country are a consequence of its inferiority in production, which would, however, be lower still if division of labour with the superior country were to cease.

So if the superior nations fear the difference in wages as compared with the inferior nations, their fear is directed at the result of their own superiority. Conversely, if the inferior nations fear the superior production of the other, their fear is directed at a fact which they could use to excellent profit by mitigating the consequences of their inferiority by free trade with the superior country. The high wages in superior countries are in no way imperilled by imports from countries with a lower wage-level, but are promoted, since this import permits of specialization in the relatively most advantageous branches of production. In the inferior countries it is conversely the imports from countries with a higher wage-level (i.e. more favourable production conditions) which support the wage-level, since they also permit of specialization in the relatively most advantageous (i.e. in this case the least unprofitable) ways of production. To put it differently: In the superior countries productive superiority and a high wage-level, and in inferior countries productive inferiority and a lower wage-level form two aspects of one and the same thing. *While the unfavourable effect of the high wage-level on the ability to compete internationally is compensated in the first case by a general superiority in production, the unfavourable effect of general inferiority in production is compensated in the second case by the lower wage-level.*

The answer might, of course, be: but in this case what is to prevent the superior countries, say, at present the United States, from producing goods – without asking the economists – in the manufacture of which their superiority is not so great? Why not include goods, such as china ware or high-class watches, which are relatively labour-intensive? Well, they are not prevented by knowledge of the law of comparative costs, which one can hardly expect, but by a very compelling objective fact, namely, the higher wage-level of their country. Industrialists who do not see to it that the general level of wages corresponds to the productivity in those branches where the country's superiority of production is most pronounced, and who manufacture goods which it would be better not to produce in this country in view of the law of comparative costs, will immediately discover its efficacy in practice. They will complain that the wages in this country are too high for production of this kind, and they cannot, therefore, compete with other countries where the wages are lower. In good or bad faith they will present the matter as though it were a particularly spiteful action on the part of nations with a lower wage-level and a menace to the interests of their own people, and will talk of 'sweated wages', 'social dumping', or, in the case of agriculture, of 'black grease', and guileless people will believe them. But we now know the facts of the case: whoever complains of wage competition from abroad, and talks of 'nigger wages', rightly or wrongly – depending on whether the complaint is justified – accuses himself as a producer acting contrary to the common interest, because he for his part does not make the relatively best use of the productive resources of the country, and thus reduces the national rate of productivity. He can only choose between molesting us with his unfounded complaints or else branding his own production as parasitic upon the nation's economy.

Anybody taking the trouble to understand the theory of international trade, must admit that the 'sweated wages' argument of economic nationalism in its generalization is unworthy of thoughtful people. In reality 'nigger wages' are the remuneration of people whose only hope it is that such modesty in their demands will suffice to balance their disadvantageous production conditions to the point where they can sell us something, the production of which would entail for us a surrender of the advantages of international division of labour.

Now we understand that wages in the Unites States are high not because of, but despite American protectionism, since the aggregate productivity of the country is so great that the existence of individual parasitic productions does not impair it very much. This certainly means that the wages of certain categories of workers can be raised by protectionism, but only at the cost of the aggregate wage level. This becomes quite obvious when we envisage the 'sweated wages' argument being applied with unswerving consistency, and all imports being barred. In this case nobody could doubt any longer that the tremendous decrease in the country's aggregate productivity would make a serious decrease in real wages unavoidable.

We thus see that a rich country (i.e. one which can produce to advantage and therefore pay high wages) need not fear competition with a poor

180

country, and that on the contrary a certain pattern of an advantageous division of labour, corresponding to the law of comparative costs, will develop between the two countries. We even realized that it cannot take all the consequences resulting from this unfounded fear of competition without committing an act of economic self-mutilation. The United States of America have certainly gone a frighteningly long way in order to deprive by their protectionism themselves and the rest of the world of the mutual advantages of an international division of labour and to develop industries behind tariff walls which would otherwise have been prevented by high wages, but in the end they had of necessity to permit the continued existence of a substantial part of the foreign trade. It follows from this conversely that Europe's fear of the superior competition of the United States is fundamentally unjustified. For if the American wage-level alone makes certain branches of production incapable of competition on the American domestic market without high protective tariffs against countries with a lower level of wages, how can the United States be capable of ruining by their competition every imaginable branch of production in our own country, including those which they can preserve in face of our competition even on the American home-market only by high protective tariffs?

This also puts paid to a contemporary pseudo-theory, the wide acceptance of which far into the ranks of economic experts only goes to prove that knowledge of even the most elementary tenets of economics has been lost to a frightening degree in our days. We mean the idea of a *'dollar shortage'*, not from the aspect to be dealt with later on, namely that of a disequilibrium in the dollar balance of many countries, which is due to monetary policy and can in every case be remedied by monetary measures, but in the sense of a permanent state of affairs, explained by the superior position of the United States in production and in world trade, which condemns the other countries for all eternity to get the worst of it in their economic relations with this wonderland. What I mean is the idea that the dollar balance must forever show a gap which can only be closed by severe import restrictions or American grants.

The amount of ingenuity which has been expended to render so foolish an idea credible is almost unbelievable. It was alleged that American productivity was simply so much greater than that of Europe, or at least than that of the countries suffering from the peculiar disease known as 'dollar shortage'. Or, as even the British 'Economist' put it in an unguarded moment in 1943, a country which 'needs' so little of what the other countries have to offer, while they 'need' so much from it, makes it impossible to achieve an equilibrium in the balance of payments on a basis of freedom. It can be stated that the mission of economics since two centuries has been nothing less than to render such conceptions impossible once and for all. As though this 'need' made any sense – unless it were with regard to definite price relations and in connection with a definite rate of exchange, and as though there were not the theory of comparative costs – this basic law of international trade which can withstand all attacks – to explain the accomplishment of an equilibrium in international trade even under such unusual circumstances! It is naturally understood that if a country's productivity is lower all along the line than that of another country, its level of income must be correspondingly lower and that the rate of exchange must not falsify this relationship, if the equilibrium of the balance of payments is not to be disturbed. But this also means that if the equilibrium is disturbed and the currency of the more productive country becomes 'tight', it is due to the fact that the less productive country is insisting on an income and a rate of exchange which are unduly 'pretentious', i.e. they do not correspond to the true relation of productivities. This is exactly what has happened in most European countries after the war.

Anyone who still has difficulty in accepting as convincing our train of thought – in which we only give expression at the same time to common sense and to communis opinio doctorum – should seek elucidation of the case in another way. Ever since the beginnings of economics in the 18th century external trade has been compared to a machine, which permits us to reduce the cost of our supply of goods, thus promoting the ultimate purpose of economy. This comparison is still most useful in correcting distorted views. For it is a fact that the machine and foreign trade have the common property of enabling us to achieve a better production result with a given expenditure of productive resources. Thus obstruction of foreign trade has exactly the same effect as the destruction of a machine: it lowers the aggregate economic productivity. Or, as an old economist (the anonymous author of the publication 'Consideration on the East India Trade', which appeared in 1701) put it: 'It (i.e. the ban on imports) has the same result as if we were to destroy a machine or a ship-route, so that the work which is done by a few, must now be done by many'. Protective tariffs have for the same reason also been called 'negative railways'. But if foreign trade, like technical progress, is such an instrument which reduces the cost of our supplies, it is only because certain articles can be manufactured abroad more cheaply than at home for the most varied reasons, and conversely because other articles can be made more cheaply at home than abroad. But it is quite incomprehensible why it should make any difference for what reason foreign countries can produce more cheaply – to put it more precisely, whether they can do so by reason of technical (or natural) superiority or by reason of lower wages. Can the difference perhaps lie in the fact that the reference to lower wages appears to offer protectionists the advantage of being able to impart a solicitous social undertone to their propaganda, and to secure them the alliance of the workers? [2])

It is, however, true, that there is hardly any erroneous judgment in economics which does not after all, contain a grain of truth. The same applies here. There is no getting round the fact that a division of labour beneficial to all is developing between countries with different wage-levels and different productivity, it is the basis of a substantial part of both world trade and the existence of the nations. And yet we are faced with a problem here, which we must not only admit, but must acutally stress. This problem arises out of the fact that the competitive conditions of the nations, – whether based on technical and natural conditions of production or on differences in the wage-level – constantly undergo *changes* which necessitate the formation of a new pattern of international division of labour. The transition from the old to the new pattern of division of labour is, however, coupled with friction, losses, and disturbances of equilibrium, and adaptation to the new situation is not always easy. The actual problem we are faced with here is therefore a dynamic one, and will be the graver the more sudden and frequent are the changes in competitive conditions, and the more vigorous the resistance offered to adaptation with in the individual national economies.

FEAR OF FOREIGN AGRARIAN COMPETITION

The idea that the entire national economy could be reduced to bankruptcy like a private firm by the competition of foreign countries – which we have proved to be erroneous – is frequently encountered in the form of a more specific fear that the agriculture of a country might be ruined if exposed to the superior competition of foreign countries. Is such fear of competition

183

at least reasonably well-founded when it is thus limited to the agricultural production?

The evidence that all branches of production of a country cannot be ruined simultaneously is logical and conclusive, and any attempt to refute it would be ridiculous. The fear of possible ruin in an individual branch of production even if it is as large and important as agriculture, cannot be refuted with the same conclusiveness. It would be theoretically conceivable that a country might be so superior in industrial production and so inferior in agricultural production that the high wages paid by the superior industry would force it in a world of free trade to reduce and extensify agricultural production to a degree which would entitle us to speak of the 'ruin' of agriculture. But it can be demonstrated that such a case is most improbable and would presuppose conditions which would hardly ever coincide.

Anybody who believes it to be possible or even probable that, say, Swiss agriculture would fall a victim to foreign competition given free foreign trade, must in fact assume that it would fare like a special industry for which Switzerland is simply not suited, and which, should it exist, could be preserved only by far-reaching protective measures. It is not at all easy to think of an example for such an industry, but perhaps the manufacture of motor-cars in Switzerland would be a suitable example for our purpose. If such production existed today, it is obvious that it would fall a victim to competition with the American car-industry, or would have to be preserved by an almost complete ban on the import of motor-cars. But this in no way implies that the entire Swiss industry dealing with vehicles, lorries, assembly or car accessories would succumb to American competition together with the manufacture of motor-cars, not to speak of Swiss industry as a whole. On the contrary, the pressure of foreign competition would result in a shift to those branches of industry in which the absolute or relative productive advantages of Swiss industry could develop most easily. Why should this not apply to agriculture as well? There are of course branches of agricultural production for which Switzerland is so ill-suited that they could not exist in free competition with superior foreign countries. But why should there not be the same possibilities of changing over within agriculture as there are in industry, yes, and even within a single branch of industry as in the motor-car industry?

It would indeed be a completely new doctrine that agriculture is tied to a definite form and kind of production and must stand or fall with it. It would not be easy to defend this revolutionary theory against the evident fact that agriculture is the very type of economy encountered on all latitudes and longitudes in the most varied forms and with a universality not to be found in industry, and against the absolutely elementary agricultural theory of location established by J. H. v. Thünen a hundred years ago, which explains this diversity of agricultural forms of production and their geographic distribution. It can be demonstrated in a hardly refutable manner – and which has not so far been refuted – what conclusions may be drawn from this theory of location for international division of labour in agriculture and for the determination of that farming pattern which is so appropriate to a country, say, like Switzerland, that it can be preserved without a policy of protection and subsidies imposing an undue burden on the remainder of the economy [3]).

I have tried to explain details of the nature of this farming pattern in my earlier books 'Die Gesellschaftskrisis der Gegenwart' and 'International Economic Disintegration', so that I need not repeat myself here. It is the farming pattern of Thünen's 'inner ring', which is characterized by specialization in so-called high-grade farm production, but at the same time takes into account the special demands of agriculture as a complicated organic production, by copying Danish agriculture, which is the model of an agriculture thus adapted to world economy, and avoiding any one-sidedness, and striving for a mixture of animal husbandry and tillage, which imparts to family farming a high degree of stability and self-sufficiency in times of crisis, and is indispensable also for reasons of agricultural technique. This is the best structure for agriculture in the industrialized countries, which makes it possible to attain the high aim of a farming policy which maintains and strengthens intensive family farming with a minimum of protective measures and subsidies and thus a minimum burden for the remainder of the national economy. For the reasons I stated earlier on it is an unprecedented stroke of good luck that this form of agriculture, which is economically suitable for the industrialized countries, is at the same time the most desirable one for sociological reasons, as it is an intensive type of family farming, demanding maximum intelligence and energy, occupying a comparatively large number of people, and producing high-quality goods.

Were agriculture in these industrialized European countries to compete

– in direct contradiction to rational distribution of locations in the world economy – with the mechanized wheat-production of the European or extra-European fringe zones, or with the production of vegetable fats in tropical regions, which is favoured by the climate, it will indeed be seen that it cannot do so, since such disregard to economic common sense would have to be paid for by a multiple of the production costs. It is then placed in the curious position of speaking with the same indignation of 'dollar wheat' and 'black grease', and is faced with the contradictory necessity of demanding prohibitive protection both against countries with high and with low agricultural wages. But in this case it is, in fact, not a question of whether such a country must chose between agricultural ruin and the most far-reaching protection of agriculture, but whether it should give preference to a form and kind of agriculture appropriate to the economic position or to one which is not appropriate. This is, however, a decision which must be taken not only as regards agriculture, but also for every other branch of economy, and is tantamount to the question whether a country should make the most rational use of its meagre productive resources or not. This involves at the same time a decision between prosperity and poverty and high and low wages, for it is obvious that a reduction in the aggregate productivity of the country due to exclusion from the advantages of international division of labour must lead to a decrease of the level of real wages. Moreover, this will take place by the painful détour – linked with the gravest social and political struggles – via unemployment in the export industry, a rise in the cost of living and oppressive taxation of the masses.

It is no irrefutable axiom that a country must make the most economic use of its meagre resources of production. On the contrary, one may well be of the opinion that there are aims which justify some loss of economic efficiency if there is no other means of achieving them. If we had no other choice left but that of abandoning farming as we know and love it, or far-reaching protection of agriculture with all its consequences, it might very well be recommended to pursue the latter as far as consideration of the non-agricultural population would altogether permit. It would be an exceedingly difficult decision, the more so in a country where the population is crowded together in a narrow space and on poor soil, and depends for mere existence on foreign trade, but one could not reproach those who recommend it, thoroughly as it would have to be considered. The salient

186

point is, however, that on the average we are not faced with such a decision. For this reason we should also refuse to have such a decision thrust on us [4]) by an unfounded fear of foreign agricultural competition.

FEAR OF INDUSTRIAL COMPETITION FROM THE AGRARIAN STATES

Industry, like agriculture in highly developed countries, also has its specific fears of competition, and this too, has in common with all kinds of fear that it exaggerates a certain danger immoderately. In so far as it concerns the fear of having great difficulty later on in competing with mass-manufacture which a highly productive country like the United States developed to an enormous degree during the war, all that needs to be said has been stated already in the first section of this chapter. But industry has another worry as regards competition: It is not likely that the progressive industrialization (which received an additional and tremendous impetus through the war) of the agrarian and primary producing countries will steadily reduce the sales prospects of the old industrialized countries? We now intend to prove as convincingly as possible that this fear is also only partly justified and then only under certain conditions. We shall do this, not by setting a vague optimism against an equally vague pessimism, but by confronting confused ideas with some logical considerations and indisputable experiences [5]).

Reflection and experience show that the industrialization of a country must go through a certain *series of stages*. It begins with the simplest consumer goods industries, for which the domestic market suffices in the initial stage, and for which the available labour training will do; only then does it proceed slowly to other kinds of production to the degree in which in industrial experience and the domestic market expand. This classical curriculum of industrialization – in which, as proven by economic history, the coarser textile goods industry has consistently formed the starting point – will naturally deviate in individual cases, in consequence of the special conditions in a country (traditions of trade, existence of raw materials, size of the domestic market, etc.), but the example of the Soviet Union during the two last decades has shown that it cannot be reversed even in extreme cases.

It is therefore an indisputable fact that the capital goods production of the old industrialized countries will profit directly by the industrialization of new countries. In fact, it can ask for nothing better. The answer of the pessimists in the old industrialized countries to this has always been that it is a very shortsighted way of making profits, and that it amounted to economic suicide since it meant nurturing one's own competitors. This argument was used in vain and quite wrongly already at the beginning of the 19th century in England, in an attempt to prevent the export of machinery to the Continent.

But even these incorrigible pessimists do not thereby contest the exceedingly favourable effects of industrialization on the capital goods industries of the old industrialized countries. So here we have a first and obvious compensation for the decrease in imports of those goods, which the new country is now manufacturing itself. But what happens next?

As a rule the following happens:

1. *Imports of capital goods* have the tendency of not only remaining constant, but of actually rising with increasing industrialization, even if the latter has already reached the stage where certain cruder machines and other capital goods are manufactured at home. The explanation of this phenomenon is that the diminishing import of simpler machinery which is due to rising industrialization is outstripped by rising imports of higher-grade machinery.

2. While the import of those consumer goods which are now produced at home is decreasing, the import of other *consumer goods* shows a rising trend. If industrialization is not pursued in such an absurd way that it leads to impoverishment of the country rather than to its economic prosperity, it involves development of the economic resources, modernization, refinement of requirements, *enhancement of the aggregate purchasing power of the population* and with all this a *rise in the turnover of foreign trade.* Certain simple things are, admittedly, now manufactured at home, but the quality products of the consumer goods industry are all the more in demand, and in the production of such goods the old industrialized countries have a double advantage: that of their long experience in production, which is based on a mature scientific and technical civilization, and on the economies of scale, which the size of the available national and international market permits them.

3. As a rule industrialization means growing imports (or diminishing exports) of industrial raw materials and foodstuffs and thus an *increase in sales* of the remaining *agrarian and primary producing countries,* which in

188

turn acquire greater purchasing power in respect of industrial products, and thus indirectly offer compensation to the old industrialized countries. This process can be observed particularly well in the case of the United States, the industrialization of which in the 19th and 20th century imparted an ever-growing importance to the agricultural exports of Canada and Argentina, thus making them increasingly important as buyers for European industry.

All these are the effects of industrialization, rendered probable by consideration and confirmed by experience. In so far as a statistical picture can be obtained already today, developments between the two World Wars have also followed this line throughout, and that despite the fact that the industrialization in many countries took place at this time with a haste and artificiality contrary to economic common sense.

This comparatively favourable judgment must, of course, be correctly understood. It naturally does not mean that industrialization is a painless process. It must even be stated most emphatically that it involves a shift which will hit certain industries in the old industrialized countries – which participate in this process only in a negative way by the drop in imports in the new industrialized countries – very hard and may annihilate them. Decisive results will in each case depend on the skill and energy with which each country manages to change over by adaptation and increased efficiency from hopeless industrial positions to new and more promising ones. The more the industrial tradition of a country is characterized by quality and versatility the more rapidly and more smoothly will it come into the enjoyment of the compensations, which – as has been demonstrated – is offered by the industrialization of new countries.

Our analysis shows above all that the adaptation of the old industrialized countries will move in *two main directions: on the one hand* in the direction of growing importance of the export of high-class consumer goods (for instance fine and superfinished textiles) or new consumer goods, and *on the other* in the direction of a rise in the share of capital goods in aggregate export, which also shows a tendency for low-grade quality to be superseded by highgrade quality. The foreign trade statistics of the leading industrialized nations do in fact show that the actual developments are completely in line with our analysis. This applies in particular to the consistent rise in the share of capital goods and the consistent drop in the share of consumer goods in the overall exports of these countries.

Occasionally we hear the remark that present day industrialization of the agrarian countries is particularly dangerous to the old countries because the progress of industrial technology now more or less permits every country to develop to perfection any desired industry and to produce whatever it wants. No less a man than Lord Keynes, who had a tendency towards dogmatic simplification, once expressed so pessimistic a view. We know now what an immeasurable exaggeration this is. Even today there are limits to industrialization, and the classical series of stages in which it of necessity takes place have not undergone any substantial changes despite all the progress of industrial technology. Locomotives cannot be produced in Turkey, nor electric turbines in Brazil, nor motor-cars in South Africa, and though it is easier than it used to be to set up a certain production of consumer goods somewhere by means of machines which are simple to operate and which work automatically, it is in turn far more difficult than it used to be to produce such machines oneself. A fact which is, moreover, consistently forgotten, is that such machines pay for themselves only if a certain minimum in the way of sales is achieved, which is naturally difficult to achieve in the newly industrialized countries.

The present tendency of many countries to promote and accelerate industrialization by all the means of a *mercantilist trade policy* far beyond what appears to be economically justified, is admittedly all the more dubious. It is true that industrialization always took place also in the past under the protecting hand of the state, but the degree of promotion and protection nowadays transcends by far all the history examples of the 19th century, above all ever since the old industrialized countries themselves enriched the instrumentarium of protectionism by the unfortunate inventions of import quotas and currency control. This will be referred to later on.

NOTES

1. (p. 178) The General Fear of Competition:

I have tried to explain the principal features of the law of comparative costs, on which the analysis of the text rests, but which is often misunderstood even in scientific circles, in my books 'Die Lehre von der Wirtschaft', 7th edition, Erlenbach-Zürich, 1954, p. 214 et seq. and p. 223 et seq., and 'Weltwirtschaft und Außenhandelspolitik', Berlin and Vienna, 1931, p. 30 et seq. With regard to the conclusions to be drawn therefrom in respect of refutation of the general fear of competition, compare also: G. HABERLER, Der Internationale Handel, Berlin, 1933, p. 103 and 183 et seq.; F. W. TAUSSIG, Principles of Economics, 3rd edition, New York, 1932, Vol. 1, p. 493 et seq; F. W. TAUSSIG, Free Trade, the Tariff, and Reciprocity, New York, 1924, p. 48 et seq., 70 et seq., and 134 et seq. The theory of comparative costs is one of those quite obvious truths of economics which can, admittedly, be subtilized but cannot be refuted. Now as ever it is one of the main keys to understanding of international trade, and it must be understood in order to avoid the dangerous fallacies and the dreadful going astray of politics.

2. (p. 183) 'Social Dumping':

It is mainly *Japan* which is known for this as its exports caused a stir and apprehension everywhere before the last war, since that country's very low level of wages, which corresponded to the poverty of the nation on the one hand and to the increase in population on the other – the latter led to a doubling of the number of inhabitants between 1875 and 1935 – and its peculiar system of industrial production, based largely on family enterprises, and other circumstances, enabled it to offer a number of general consumer goods on the world markets at sensationally low prices. It is undeniable that the remaining industrialized countries were thereby faced with a very serious problem of the dynamic kind they are now once more faced with, as has been explained in the text. It must not, however, be forgotten, that this Japanese competition in the first place involved goods of lesser quality, which largely corresponded to the low purchasing-power demand of the population of the tropical colonies. Since this population would in any case have hardly been in a position to buy the better and more expensive goods of the other industrialized countries, the danger of Japanese competition was often exaggerated. It would probably have been in line with a sensible international division of labour to permit unrestricted Japanese exports to the colonies, thus serving the purpose of all parties: that of the Japanese from whom this export represented – and will in future represent – a necessity in view of the over-population of their country, that of the natives in the European colonies – remember Indochina – and finally that of the other industrialized nations, which would have been able to export all the more other goods to Japan and the colonial territories. A triangular trade increasing the prosperity of all would thus have developed, and nobody can tell whether Japan would then have trodden the path to conquest. The omissions of the past should be remedied after this war. The same suggestion is made by: N. F. HALL, Enquête préliminaire sur les mesures d'ordre national et international visant à relever le niveau d'existence, League of Nations Publication, Geneva, 1938, p. 74 et seq.

This is the juncture where reference must emphatically be made to the mistake of viewing the lower wages paid in overseas countries like Japan or India as an 'unfair' competitive advantage, which must be compensated both in the interests of the standard of living in these countries and in that of the workers in the western industrialized countries by a rise in wages and adaptation to western working conditions. A large part of the activities of

191

the International Labour Office is based on this mistake, and the eagerness to set up a trade union monopoly according to the western example in these countries is also inspired by it. Anybody who calls to mind the law of comparative costs, knows what the trouble is: it ignores the fact that these countries must compensate for their lower productivity of labour by these low wages, if they wish to enjoy the advantages of a balanced foreign trade and raise their standard of living by it. Thus an international social policy of levelling the wages and working conditions would have the thoroughly unsocial result of rendering the workers in these countries unable to compete, and, since they cannot emigrate, they would be condemned to unemployment and even greater poverty. The case of the Middle East oil refineries offers an example of this, as does the recent statement by a British commission of experts that India is no longer a lucrative field for investments, since labour is nowadays more expensive there than in Europe. Cf. with the article by J. V. VAN SICKLE, The International Labour Office; An Appraisal, The Southern Economic Journal, April, 1946.

3. (p. 185) The Optimal Structure of Agriculture in the Industrialized Countries:

There are two misunderstandings regarding the optimal structure of agriculture characterized by intensive 'production on farms which concentrate on meat and dairy produce'. Though these have been plainly stressed already in both of my books mentioned in the text I will elucidate them here once more. First of all it is quite wrong to say that such agriculture implies, neglect of tillage. Tillage is, on the contrary, within certain limits valuable for the biological and economic balance within the farming enterprise and also in view of a higher degree of self-sufficiency which diversity of production lends to the farming family. Secondly it is wrong to think that such an agrarian structure would unduly imperil an assured supply of food in times of war. On the contrary, it specifically permits of a particularly rational provision – i.e. one at the minimum cost to the national economy – in case of war, since owing to a lucky chance those foodstuffs which are under these circumstances preferably left to foreign production (specially grain, oil and sugar) are particularly suitable for long-term storage, while live-stock and the enhanced fertility of the soil resulting from such agricultural reform represent further valuable reserves in case of war.

4. (p. 187) Protectorates in Agriculture:

The cautious formulation of the text provides a possibility of finding justification for a policy of deliberately sacrificing economic efficiency on behalf of specially endangered regions, which are at the same time specially worth preserving. There just happen to be pronounced 'distressed areas' in agriculture as there are in industry – stagnating members of the economy as a whole, which have difficulties in maintaining themselves even during periods of the most lively general economic activity, and which are threatened by depopulation. Switzerland is constantly worried about its hill-farmers, France has been suffering so severely and persistently from a trend of concentration towards the capital which is laying fallow the provinces, that J. F. GRAVIER, geographer of the Sorbonne, has been able to write a book entitled 'Paris et le désert français', which has almost become a classic already; Great Britain had to struggle for decades with the problem of the so-called 'distressed areas'. These 'distressed areas' afford a responsible economic policy only two possibilities. Either we resign ourselves to the migration of enterprises and people, in which case the economic losses of, and hardships imposed on, the people by such a displacement should be mitigated as much as possible, or else the extra-economic reasons for staying such 'social erosion' are so momentous, that it is felt that the remainder of the economy can be expected to bear the cost of constant direct or indirect subsidies. The case of the Swiss hill-farmers, who can be maintained only by permanent subsidies of all kinds in view of the overall economic development of the plains which cannot be attained in the mountains is a specially impressive example of this, but the Swiss people has rightly decided to pay this price to maintain them.

5. (p. 187) Industrialization of the Agricultural States:

I have made a detailed statement, provided with statistical evidence, in my book 'International Economic Disintegration'.

193

III

THE FEAR OF AN ADVERSE BALANCE OF PAYMENTS

THE NATURE OF THE PROBLEM

There is hardly another conception which has accompanied the economists of my own generation throughout their professional lives in so persistent and tormenting a manner as the conception of an 'adverse balance of payments'[1]). A major part of the struggle between economic common sense and unreason, clarity and obscurity, untrammeled relations with all the world and national segregation has centred round this conception since the first World War. It is, of course, precisely in this field that the strictly conclusive truth of science is more removed from lay thinking than almost anywhere else, and nowhere is such lay thinking more disastrous and tenacious than it is here. Lamentations about the 'adverse balance of payments', the 'scarcity of foreign exchange', and the 'dollar gap' are heard at the bar of every pub, in hairdressers' salons and in the railway compartments throughout the world, as though this were some kind of an epidemic sent by heaven or due to the evil curcumstances of the times – a plague which one must somehow or other reconcile oneself to, and for which the only remedy is that of 'saving', 'distributing' and 'controlling' foreign exchange, so that the State sees to it that the account tallies. In the worst case, i.e. that of a so-called 'structural' deficit, it is considered justifiable to claim international poor relief under the most varied designations (European Recovery Programme, Financial aid for 'developing countries', credits from the European Payments Union, etc.).

The idea of an 'adverse balance of payments', which can be cured only by exchange control and by American subsidies, has until quite recently been the most popular conception in Europe and in the world, and many people have difficulty in setting it aside even today. At the same time, however, there can hardly be a conception which would be more disastrous to economic policy.

Just think of the lamentable part played by the idea of a 'fated adverse balance of payments' – as we called it sarcastically at the time – during the

194

period of the great German inflation after the first World War, as a theory excusing this inflation and paralyzing stabilization. Just bear in mind to what an extent this very fear of an 'adverse balance of payments' became a cardinal point of modern neo-mercantilist planned economy and of self-sufficient socialism under National Socialism in Germany, and then after the second World War in so many other European countries.

It must not be forgotten that this same basically wrong economic thinking then led to one of the cardinal errors in the *Marshall Aid Programme,* namely, that the deficit in the balance of payments of the individual countries was regarded as the indicator of indigence, and the degree to which it was reduced even at the price of uneconomic domestic investments were regarded as the criterium for the success of financial aid. A fraction of this aid would have sufficed, and a more permanent success been achieved as compared with the programme actually carried out, if it had been applied to the actual cause of the adverse balance of payments and used for internal financial and currency reform.

It should be borne in mind how greatly this very fear of an adverse balance of payments has contributed towards spreading the plague of currency control throughout the world and the extent to which it still causes delay in the final abrogation of this system, though nobody who is even half-way acquainted with the facts would dare to dispute its ruinous harmfulness any longer. The fear of an adverse balance of payments, the belief that currency control is indispensable and that it is impossible to restore free convertibility forms the most serious obstacle to restoration of this con-vertibility. Currency control would surely have been far less long-lived had not the few hundred people on whom decisions depend been spell-bound by the wrong conceptions of an 'adverse balance of payments', which apparently economists of every generation must struggle to correct. These wrong conceptions are probably basically due to the view that should the misfortune of an adverse balance of payments befall a country – i.e. a surplus in the import of goods and services over exports – this deficit must be met afterwards by raising capital, subsidies and the like. Anybody who habitually reads even serious professional papers with an eye to this mistake or merely to a treacherously obscure style can acquire a handsome collection of frightening examples. It says, for instance, that Germany never achieved a 'normal equilibrium' in its trade balance between the two World Wars, or that Austria had had difficulties in meeting the deficit in its trade balance by a surplus on tourism, or that Switzerland's large adverse balance on trade account had fortunately been met 'by surpluses on other accounts of the balance of payments', or that the deficit of Israel's foreign trade had in the first place been 'financed' by foreign credits, and the like.

What is wrong about these statements?

It is the idea that it is luck or chance if a 'balance' is achieved, as the deficit of the trade balance would otherwise so-to-say hang in the air 'without anything around' like Christian Morgenstern's famous lattice fence. The truth is, of course, that imports are either paid for by exports or, if this is not the case, and imports are nevertheless procured, these must be paid for by some other means or else be as gift. That is to say: the adverse balance on current account must be matched by some influx of means of another kind, irrespective of the source. What must be corrected is the idea that imports are first of all made at random, and that loans are then raised abroad in wild alarm to cover the balance. This would about amount to saying that Austria's liqueur balance was unfortunately adverse this year but that it had luckily been possible to compensate it by a favourable 'leather shorts' balance.

As a rule things are in reality (that is, apart from direct credits in foreign currency) the other way round; the balance on current account is adverse because the capital balance is favourable and vice-versa. Whether this is a good or bad thing depends on the way in which such capital is raised or disposed of. The obstinately adverse trade balance of Ottoman Turkey – and no less a personage than Böhm-Bawerk drew attention to this in a famous article – was merely the reflection of the extravagant financial policy of the Sultan, who obtained foreign credits year after year in order to cover the deficits of his budget. The case of Germany after the first World War was somewhat different; she received capital from abroad for productive, though not always unobjectionable purposes. It was logical in this case as well that the credit balance of net capital movements should find expression in a corresponding debit balance on trade-account, and nonsensical to imagine that Germany was borrowing abroad, in order to close the awful gap that had appeared in the trade balance. When the capital balance of Germany took a turn around 1930, and more credits had suddenly to be repaid than came in, the deficit on capital account was of necessity matched by a surplus in the trade balance – a surplus which was in no way

196

a preliminary condition enabling Germany to undertake repayment, but represented the precise extent to which repayments were actually taking place. Lastly, Switzerland should be cited as the opposite example of a mature creditor country, whose deficit on transactions in goods and services is balanced by a surplus in capital movements which is due to income or investments from abroad. The deficit in this case means that the country is able to import goods to with the extent of income from capital without having to pay for this with exports, and any lamenting or surprise about such a deficit is therefore quite foolish.

Upon thorough deliberation it will be found that a country's balance of payments in the sense so far considered must of necessity always be in equilibrium, just like a commercial balance-sheet, whatever the nature of the balance-items may be. This leaves no room, therefore, for a 'dollar gap' or for any item which has no foundation in fact. So long as Tito received no dollars there was no room in the Yugoslav balance of payments for an item called 'dollar gap' for which the contra-item was missing. Tito simply had to cut his coat according to the cloth and manage without dollars, a fact which the pitiable inhabitants of this granary ruined by socialism came to experience in the form of undernourishment. The Yugoslav balance of payments was in equilibrium. It is only since Tito has been receiving subsidies from America that the Yugoslav balance of payments contains a 'dollar gap' on the liability side which is balanced on the assets side by the corresponding dollar amount. The balance sheet shows an additional item both among the assets and the liabilities. To put it challengingly: A 'dollar gap' has only existed in Yugoslavia since it was filled. Prior to this it existed merely as a wish and a programme [2]).

So everything is fine? Certainly not. For so far we have only spoken of the balance of payments in the sense that it must always and of necessity be in equilibrium, that is to say, in a bookkeeping-statistical, i.e. an actual balance-sheet sense. So if some sort of calamity is meant by the term 'adverse balance of payments' this cannot occur here. But we have already indicated that this may very well occur in another sense, namely in the sense of a wish or a programme.

Let us take another example, that of West Berlin. The balance of payments of this unfortunate city will, admittedly, always be in equilibrium in the sense so far considered, even if no support is extended by the West. But we need hardly say that this would be a tragedy with unimaginable conse-

197

quences, against which Berlin, together with the West, successfully defended itself at the time of the unforgotten air-lift. We could at most speak of a structural deficit in the balance of payments, if the problem were not *au fond* a totally different one. For it is not a case of whether Berlin's balance of payments will be in equilibrium or not – we know it always will be – but on what *level* this balancing will take place. In referring to the 'structural' deficit in the balance of payments a confusion occurs – as is so often the case – between a problem of equilibrium and a problem of the level. The problem is not that of the balance of payments, but the poverty of such a region.

We can certainly talk of 'dollar shortage' in the sense that a politico-social catastrophe might occur if no help is given in a certain case. This was undoubtedly the case in many European countries after 1945. But the more remote this dramatic situation becomes, the more subjective and ultimately the more beggarly does this need for help become, with the exception of such special areas as Berlin. After all, nobody forced the European countries to live beyond their means under the slogan of thoroughly untimely 'full employment', of nationalization, of 'cheap money', of an unlimited welfare state, to set up programmes of investment and consumption which could be implemented only by American help – and then to insert this aid as a 'dollar deficit' in their estimated balance of payments and 'national budgets'. Why did France have to put into practice the Monnet Plan just at a time when capital had become exceedingly tight, well knowing that it could be put into effect only by inflation and American subsidies, in view of the lack of sufficient savings? What is the sense of talking of a 'structural' deficit in the balance of payments here? This attempt to impart to the conception of an 'adverse balance of payments' the meaning of a real concern cannot – despite the best of intentions – lead very far. Programmes and wishes are unable to impart a sound meaning to the conception, and even should it involve the very existence of the nation in question, it will be found that the object of this worry fundamentally concerns not the deficit in the balance of payments but the poverty of the country. An 'adverse balance of payments' can present a serious problem in a truly objective, logical and legitimate sense only when we consider a third conception of the balance of payments. We previously discussed first of all the balance of payments in the sense of a 'balance sheet', and found that it must of necessity be in equilibrium. After that we came to balance of payments programme, in which a deficit together with the expected cover by subsidies is budgetted for, and we will now discuss the so-called *balance of payments in the sense of the market* which means the relation of supply and demand on the foreign currency market, where all the items of the balance of payments are reflected. Here at last we find the sought-after meaning of the term 'deficit' in the balance of payments, which will occur when demand exceeds supply (and of a 'surplus', which will result when supply exceeds demand).

But if we call to mind the elementary tenets of the general theory of prices, it will immediately become clear that it is only when the price is prevented from exercising its function of constantly balancing supply and demand that there is any sense in talking of such an excess in demand. Such a deficit in the balance of payments in the sense of the market thus presupposes that the price on this particular market, namely, the rate of exchange, is kept – in contrast to the prices of the usual free market – below the equilibrium price to which it would have to rise to in order to balance supply and demand. The term 'deficit' makes sense only in respect of a given rate of exchange, which the foreign exchange authorities wish to keep unchanged.

This comparison of the exchange market with any other market – say, the butter market – at the same time permits of eliminating the difficulty of reconciling two apparently contradictory statements, one being that the balance of payments must in the one sense logically always be in equilibrium, and the other that it can show a deficit in a sense differing therefrom. If the price of butter is kept low by the authorities, it is prevented from balancing supply and demand, so that there is an excess in demand, a 'shortage of butter', a 'butter gap', and 'adverse butter balance', and it shows a common, but very obvious and regrettable lack of logic and insight to use this as a justification for continued 'control of butter'. It is this kind of disturbance in equilibrium which we mean when we refer to an 'adverse' balance of payments, and only when invested with this meaning is there any sense in using this term. But this disrespectful comparison with the butter market immediately demonstrates that the balance of payments in the sense of the 'balance sheet' must of necessity be in equilibrium, just as the excess demand on the butter market cannot change the fact that after the market is closed the amount of butter bought tallies to a hair with the amount of butter available and sold.

An excess of demand over supply on the exchange market – that is the problem. Nobody can deny that it must be taken seriously, but now we do at the same time understand its real nature. It is nothing absolute, but something quite relative which depends on another variable. It exists only in respect of a given rate of exchange, which means that there could be another rate of exchange which would make it disappear [3]). What is to prevent us from chosing another rate of exchange? Or have we overlooked some point?

In fact, what we have so far discovered is by no means the whole truth. The method we have just used of regarding an 'adverse balance of payments' as a market disturbance like any other and to explain it by means of the general price laws may admittedly do substantial services because it clarifies essentials, and the nightmare of an 'adverse balance of payments' is thus deprived of its demoniac appearance. But this method can be made use of without danger only if it is not forgotten that the exchange market is a very special market, and the rate of exchange a very special price. The merchandise which is traded on this market and – the rate of exchange being the price – paid for in the country's own currency, is the currency of another country. This means in the first place that there are very weighty reasons why this price, since it determines the external value of our currency, must not be left to supply and demand like a stock-exchange quotation, nor may it on the other hand be thrust into the strait-jacket of currency control. But it means something else as well, and that is the point in question here: Supply and demand on this very special market are decisively determined by the circumstances which we call *elements in economic circulation,* i.e. the amount and speed of circulation of the money, the aggregate expenditure and income, level of prices and costs, briefly, the plus or minus of the aggregate demand or aggregate supply, the regulation of which in the last analysis is in the hands of the authorities of a country – the Central Bank and the Minister of Finance – who open or close the taps releasing money and credit as the case may be.

In other words: The relationship of supply and demand on the exchange market – the balance of payments in the sense of the market – must be viewed not only as a phenomenon of the *price mechanism* but at the same time as a *monetary phenomenon*. The foreign exchange market is not merely a market like any other, where a gap between supply and demand presupposes a 'false' price, but it is at the same time the *hinge* linking the

200

national system of prices, costs, income and expenditure with the international one. An 'adverse balance of payments' thus either shows – depending on the angle from which the facts are viewed – that the price, i.e. the rate of exchange in question, does not correspond to this international relationship of circulation elements and that the 'hinge' is therefore wrong, or else that this relationship is disturbed and therefore demands a change in that the domestic money and credits tap is turned off. Whether one should view the facts from this side or from the other is of importance for the decision on the expedience of changing the 'hinge' or the 'relationship' or perhaps both.

It is of maximum importance to understand this 'dependence' of the balance of payments on domestic developments and thus to supplement the method of 'surveying the market' by the other method of 'surveying the relative sets of values'. It would perhaps be appropriate to employ an illustration for this purpose which I made use of at this point in the first German edition of this book, when I spoke of the relationship between Geneva and the rest of Switzerland, and the value of which was recently demonstrated by Lionel Robbins in his work 'The Balance of Payments' (London 1951). It consists in taking the conditions within a country as a premise, and then putting the simple question why there are no problems regarding the balance of payments between the various regions of a country, though the nature of inland trade in no way differs from international trade, and though conditions of prosperity between the individual parts of the country constantly fluctuate just as they do between nations. If a part of Switzerland experiences economic regression, its inhabitants admittedly suffer from a scarcity of money, but they have no difficulty in paying with their smaller income for the goods they can still afford to buy in other regions.

Why? The answer is a simple one: because all the regions belong to the same monetary system. But this simple answer is of a significance which most people – including the economists who consider themselves superior to such simple things – are not conscious of. For it also shows that the problem of the balance of payments is essentially of a monetary nature. It evolves from the difficulties which can only develop due to a difference in the monetary systems, and which can be eliminated if the various monetary systems are regulated in such a way that they become at least a de facto unit. This is plainly the case when the various monetary systems consist of nothing but coins of the same metal and with a fixed content of metal which is worth the full face value of the coin. The difficulty only starts when the difference in the monetary systems is intimately linked – as it is in our modern reality – with the difference in national systems of credit and finance, which can, at the direction of the central banks and ministries of finance, be put at the service of specific monetary, credit or financial policies. And now it all depends on whether this national monetary, credit and finance policy is of a kind that the national circulation factors at given parities are so co-ordinated that even the de jure difference in credit systems and public finance, does not prevent a de facto unification of the monetary systems.

In view of the difference in the monetary systems there is a possibility that the circulation elements in a country may be so inflated by a policy of sustained monetary expansion, at a given rate of exchange, that a continuous excess of demand on the exchange market, i.e. an adverse balance of payments is bound to result. If absolutely set upon it, any country can create an adverse balance of payments for itself within half an hour (D. H. Robertson) [4]. Such disturbances, among which is, of course, also the converse one of a deflationary policy, which produces a *favourable* balance of payments, can only be avoided on one condition: The national monetary and credit systems must be managed in such a way that the national circulation elements and sets of values are brought into a relationship with each other which corresponds with that which would exist under a unified monetary and credit system. The equilibrium of the balance of payments (with simultaneous stability of the rates of exchange) thus presupposes that the national monetary and credit policy be conducted in such a way *as though* an international *unified* system were in existence. To date the gold standard has been the only monetary system which fulfilled this condition, thanks to its ingenious 'thermostatic' mechanism (always presupposing the will of the governments to maintain the gold standard even if it caused inconvenience) which provided for the opening or closing of the taps in accordance with the fluctuations of the balance of payments. Despite the de jure difference in the national monetary systems, which cannot be overcome by political means, it did result in their de facto unification, i.e. in that 'quasi' international money, which we have already encountered earlier on. For this reason the gold standard was the only monetary system which was not faced with problems in respect of the balance of payments, or of 'pound' or 'dollar scarcity'. By consistently and silently complying in this way with the three demands to be made on a truly international monetary system – freedom of exchange, stability of the rate of exchange and international homogeneity of money – it has merited the honorary title of a truly international monetary system and we are still waiting for a new international monetary order to contest its title. It is to be feared that we shall wait in vain. The more obvious it becomes that all efforts to replace the gold standard by another truly international monetary system have failed, the more the prestige of the gold standard triumphs over all misunderstandings and unfair accusations.

Our considerations have thus shown that the balance of payments difficulties can only occur between territories with different monetary systems and even then only if the monetary authorities pursue divergent policies. Far from being a foolish platitude, this statement is of decisive importance, because it indicates the point from which the disturbances can always be eliminated – even if they do not always emanate from it – according to the classical principle that a deficit in the balance of payment calls for a restrictive monetary and credit policy and a surplus for an expansive monetary and credit policy, unless it is preferred to alter the rate of exchange.

We found that the main error in the popular conception of the 'adverse balance of payments' was that of regarding it as something absolute, as a given fact and as being beyond the government's responsibility. We saw that it is on the contrary something absolutely relative, which can be conceived of only in relation to a given rate of exchange. Alter the rate of exchange and it will vanish. But we must now add that it is at the same time relative in another sense, and, if the rate of exchange is given, it can be conceived of only in relation to a definite internal monetary and financial policy. Change the internal circulation factors and it will vanish.

In putting forward our formulations we have done our best to avoid the misunderstanding of appearing to say that the real *cause* of the deficit must also always be sought in these two elements – the 'false' rate of exchange or the 'false' circulation factors. Far be it from us to make such a statement, for there are as many possible causes which may produce such a deficit, as circumstances which alter supply and demand on the exchange market. It is true that if a country doubles its national income in relation to another by inflation, its balance of payments must become adverse if the rate of exchange remains unaltered, and it is obvious that in this case a purely monetary cause has become effective. But apart from such *monetary* causes the equilibrium of the balance of payments can also be disturbed by others which are not derived from money and which we therefore call *real* ones. Bad harvests, flight of capital, deterioration of the terms of trade (the average relationship of the prices of imported and exported goods), embargo measures adopted by foreign countries – these and many others can be quoted as examples.

And yet – as was done by Ricardo in his famous controversy with Malthus – it is absolutely justifiable to stress the monetary factors in the balance of payments. The above-mentioned real factors, which so easily impart to the adverse balance of payments the appearance of an affliction sent by heaven, can after all become effective only if the rate of exchange remains unaltered, or if no internal monetary counter-measures are adopted. This at the same time means that if an adverse balance of payments – whatever its cause may be – is more than merely transient, the causal share of the monetary factors becomes ever plainer and the responsibility of the authorities who control the internal monetary and credit policy becomes ever clearer. The 'dollar shortage' of the European countries after the war may have been influenced by real factors, but the time during which these could still serve as an excuse passed rapidly. To repeat it for the second and last time: Wherever a disturbance in the balance of payments may derive from, it only makes sense to talk of an adverse balance of payments in connection with a given rate of exchange or a given relationship of the internal aggregates, and there will always be a rate of exchange or an internal amount of purchasing power at which equilibrium of the balance of payments is achieved. So if equilibrium of the balance of payments is to be achieved at a stable rate of exchange, the only way left open is that of internal order and adaptation, the regulation of the taps controlling the monetary, credit and financial policy.

THE SOLUTION OF THE PROBLEM

Now that the true nature of the problem of an 'adverse balance of payments' has been recognized, a genuine possibility of a solution is also revealed. This presents itself all the more plainly if we first of all review the errors made by most countries after the war because they persistently failed to understand the true nature of the problem in their 'fear of an adverse balance of payments'. These errors delayed the restoration of an international order by nearly a decade, and the realization that a return from the wrong road to the right road must be undertaken is only now steadily gaining ground.

What can a country do when it is faced with a deficit in the balance of payments, and a fundamental disequilibrium at that, not merely a deficit due to fluctuations [5]) of the market? It must be stated here that if the country avoids any inflationary policy, powerful influences will in every case be automatically at work to restore the disturbed equilibrium, and this applies even to the present times under the rule of paper currency [6]). If we go a step further and ask what additional possibilities are available to the government and central bank of a country, a list will first of all result in which we can put down anything by means of which the relationship of supply and demand on the foreign exchange market can be altered, whether it be by increasing the supply (for instance also by successfully combatting import restrictions on the part of other countries), or by reducing the demand. But if we go to the root of the question, we realize that the possibilities of practical importance can be divided into two contrary groups of measures. For the country either attempts to balance the deficit by a policy which forcibly restrains imports and promotes exports by all available means of the same rugged kind (to put it in the words of the country which unfortunately set a postwar example of this: 'austerity' and 'export drive'), or else equilibrium is restored by eliminating the causes of disequilibrium by altering the rate of exchange and by internal monetary and financial discipline. One either contents oneself with influencing the symptoms by the stupidly mechanical means of restricting imports and pushing exports, or else the evil must be eradicated at the real source. The first is an error, the other is the true solution; the first is quackery practised on the epidermis, and the other is real treatment.

The one method is therefore that dictated by the 'fear of an adverse balance of payments': prior to 1931 it was that of increasing tariffs, and since the revolution in trade policy which took place at the time it operates mainly with import quotas, state monopoly of foreign trade, direction of imports and exports by a planned economy and exchange control. Why is it wrong? Because it nullifies any beginnings of a new international order and continues the work of disintegrating the world's economic system which has been in process since 1931. Because it sacrifices the advantages of international division of labour and an economic utilization of national productive resources to the equilibrium of the balance of payments. Because it creates powerful interests which not only resist the progressive removal of this autarkic balance of payments policy tooth and nail, but are inclined to use the 'fear of an adverse balance of payments' as grist to their mill.

And what is the good of all this? To achieve an effect which is of doubtful short-term value, but illusory from a long-term aspect. For if the deficit in the balance of payments is due to the fact that the internal purchasing power is inflated at a given rate of exchange, the policy of a direct dosage of the quantities imported and exported cannot eliminate this constant pressure on the balance of payments. Since nothing is done to change the internal economic aggregates, and nothing to relieve foreign trade from the pressure of inflationary internal demand, which continues to make an excessive call both on foreign and domestic goods and thus expands imports while compressing exports, the cause of the external disequilibrium remains unaffected. The position is, in fact, worse, since less goods are available than previously, while purchasing power remains unchanged. The government comforts itself with the idea that something decisive has been achieved by a policy of 'austerity', and in all innocence continues with an internal policy of expenditures, a light hand on the reins, excessive investment, unrestricted credit, and an inflation of mass consumption, which causes the country to continue living above its means. Since the evil is not eradicated, the government can make it clear to an unsuspecting electorate that the imperilled balance of payments makes an unlimited extension of its mandate essential to the nation. The economic post-war history of a large part of the world is contained in these few words.

It is of such exceeding importance to understand the error of this autarkic method of squaring the balance of payments, of the policy of 'austerity', that it is worth while lingering over it a little longer in order to review somewhat more thoroughly what happens as a result of it.

We cannot repeat sufficiently often that the basic error committed by most European countries after the war was that they lived beyond their means. This mixture of collectivism and inflation, which became a characteristic feature of their economic policy after the war, produced a constant excess pressure in their economic system – in the British system as well as in the Swedish, Norwegian, Dutch, Danish and French systems. The governments and central banks constantly created income in excess of the available supply of goods. In other words: then aggregate consumption and investment was consistently pushed up by government and central bank policy by all conceivable means beyond the quantity of goods available to the economic system from its own internal sources. A persistently inflated overall volume of purchasing power was let loose uninterruptedly in the most various ways and under the most diverse economic, political and social slogans on an inadequate quantity of goods, and despite realization of the foolishness of this policy which has meantime gained ground, some countries nevertheless continue to pursue it.

These are the old facts about the inflation, which our tortured generation of Europeans has become as well acquainted with as it has with bombs, air-raid shelters and forms to be filled in. Something new has, however, been added now, namely an attempt to 'repress' the inflation by economic controls and to counteract the inflationary upward pressure of prices by the policed counter-pressure of maximum prices, rationing, exchange control and control of capital[7]. For if we had to deal with the old type of 'open' inflation, a rise in the prices of the goods and an upward trend in the rates of exchange would have to set in, by means of which the equilibrium disturbed by the expansion of purchasing power would be restored, provided that further inflation were now stopped (as was the case in Italy, due to Einaudi's reform in 1947–1948). Nowadays this is prevented by controls, and the result is that the excess of purchasing power is not absorbed but constantly exerts pressure on the economic system not only at home, but also abroad. This constant inflationary pressure, which we owe the collectivist and inflationary policy of so many European countries to, thus leads to disequilibrium of the economic system not only internally but also externally. The unavoidable result – which is not even yet generally understood – is the dreaded 'adverse balance of payments', the 'dollar shortage'. In the same way that current production does not suffice to satisfy demand in view of the expanded internal purchasing power, the available amount of foreign exchange cannot do so either.

We must constantly bear in mind the nature of the basic evil, if we wish to understand post-war developments in Europe. It is the evil of a creeping inflation in the sense of a persistent overstrain imposed on the resources, of continued inability and unwillingness on the part of the governments and the central banks, which are largely subservient to the former, to limit the demands made on the national flow of goods to that which is available, an inflation in the sense of an incessant attempt to spend more than the economic reserves of the nation permit, of an obstinate tendency to draw more bills on the economic system than it can meet, of an incurable urge of wanting too much at a time – in the sense of the apparently ineradicable vice of nations of simply living beyond their means.

How can this disturbance in the debit and credit of the economic system be put in order again? There is obviously only one answer: the nation must retrench, cut its coat according to its cloth, and put a brake on all extravagances. But this reply is most ambiguous. It can mean two very different things, which are unfortunately consistently confused.

One of these possibilities is offered by that very policy which has been called 'austerity' after the British model. The state assumes the part of a despotic pater familias, who prescribes restriction of consumption with warningly uplifted finger and open threats, and is guided by his own conceptions as to what are necessities and what are luxuries, which – as we thoughtlessly call it – 'the country cannot afford'.

By compulsory restriction of imports to essentials and by control of domestic consumption the state attempts to compensate for the effects of the excess of self-created purchasing power on the debit and credit of the economic system. With the same aim in view it simultaneously tries to pass on to other countries the high-grade products and non-essentials of its own economy, which are as far as possible withheld from its own subjects, which resulted temporarily in the grotesque state of affairs that the European governments attempted to thrust the pick of their production upon each other, and people had to travel abroad in order to obtain the best goods from their own countries.

Yet this state is a slightly peculiar, not to say highly unpleasant pater familias, who exempts himself from the austerity he preaches to others. After all, it is he himself who is the cause of the extravagance, for it is the state and the central bank ruled by it, whose collectivist and inflationary policy are the causes of the excess purchasing power in the economic system. He himself turned on the tap and thus produced an inundation. He himself created the excess in income which constantly disturbs the equilibrium of the economic system and of the balance of payments, and having done so, he assumes the mien of a puritanic teacher and prescribes how many oranges and cars his subjects may buy, and how much they may spend on trips abroad. Sir Stafford Cripps, the deceased head of this economic vice-squad, once caused amusement in the House of Commons while still Chancellor of the Exchequer, by a classical formulation of this policy of regimentation, for when a question was put about the import of French cheese, he said that he could only admit 'serious cheese'. While the Socialist Government of Norway makes the luxury of bath-tubs dependent on a medical certificate, and practises the worst of chicanery on the consumers of domestic and foreign goods, it obstinately maintains the fiction by its interest and investment policy that the country is as rich in capital as Switzerland. While the Norwegian Government grudges its subjects the good things of this world, it wastes vast sums on an obviously unprofitable steel works in the Arctic Circle.

This characteristic of the policy of austerity makes all its disadvantages even plainer than in our first summary enumeration. Austerity is quite obviously tantamount to first of all providing the economic system with too much purchasing power, and then to prescribing to the individual in what way and to what extent he may make use of this income.

In the first place this is an astonishing presumption on the part of state bureaucracy, which will be rejected by anyone who has preserved a half-way normal idea of human freedom in our times. In the second place, however, it is a method of economic discipline which is not only unpleasant, but, as we have seen, in addition very ineffective, since it does not eliminate the real cause of the economic disequilibrium, namely, the persistent inflation of purchasing power. If the import of goods considered unnecessary by bureaucracy is forbidden, the economic system is left with a surplus of income which was intended for the purchase of oranges or for a trip abroad. This will be used for other goods, whether it be imported wares, or goods which absorb domestic resources, and the result is either an increase of imports on a reduction of exports. So the austerity calculation cannot work out, unless simply every expenditure were subjected to police control by the Government, or savings were increased by this policy. The former would presuppose a tyranny accompanied by unimaginable terrorism, while an increase in savings as a result of the prescribed limitation of consumption would be thoroughly unlikely. If an Englishman wants to give his wife a Swiss watch as a Christmas present but is prevented from doing so by import restrictions, he is hardly likely to offer her a savingsbook instead – on the contrary, he will probably try to find some other kind of fancy goods.

But another, and far more significant kind of harm is done in addition to that already known to us. If it is a case of balancing the aggregate expenditure within the economic system with the available resources, thus restoring the internal and external equilibrium, restriction of consumption is naturally the more tolerable and the more short-lived, the more it stimulates production. But the policy of austerity does exactly the reverse. By permitting the people to earn their income easily, but then preventing them from utilizing it freely, it deprives them of an important incentive to increase their performance. Anyone desiring the people to do their best, will consider it wise to do the opposite: make it harder for them to gain an income, but in exchange not to deprive them of the good things of life by which people feel rewarded for their efforts. But if – in accordance with this policy, which supposedly favours the masses – this deformation of luxury and semi-luxury goods is coupled with a cheapening of mass-consumer goods due to State price subsidies the incentive to do better is quite simply throttled. For while on the one hand the policy of austerity makes it extremely difficult for people to satisfy luxury wishes, price control campaigns have on the other hand the peculiarity of making it all too easy for them to obtain vital necessities. Why exert oneself when food, controlled housing, and other essential things are artificially reduced so that – particularly when wages are at the same time disproportionately high – the income necessary for a bare existence has soon been earned? And why make great efforts if we have no prospects in any case even with a higher income of owning our own home, a motor-car, and other tempting things? Both these forms of a fictitious 'social' policy are in themselves pernicious enough; but a combination of the two together is downright ruinous. It ultimately tempts people to prefer that one luxury which is still left to them, but which is precisely the very thing that such a country really cannot afford, viz., the luxury of leisure and a moderate working tempo. There is no doubt that herein lies the root cause of the low rate of productivity which some countries are still suffering from.

All this should be plain enough. But if we were to seek a reply to the question of what other solution would have been possible for the countries of Europe after the devastations of the war than that collectivist-autarchic method of austerity which, we repeat, corresponds with that of the export drive, we know the answer. It is the liberal 'policy of the opposite': the restoration of the general economic equilibrium by eliminating the 'false' rate of exchange and the return to the monetary and fiscal discipline at home which removes the pressure of inflation caused by expansive credit and budget policies. It is the way of liberal discipline instead of collectivist austerity. But these are not two mere alternative possibilities side by side; the one is the only solution to avoid a fatal mistake, and the other is a wrong road by which only one thing can be reached with certainty viz., the paralyzation and confusion of domestic economy and the lasting disintegration of international economy. The way of *liberal discipline* is the only one worthy of freedom-loving people and those who prefer truth to the fictions of a would-be social policy. It is the way successfully followed by Belgium, Italy, and Germany and later, Denmark and the Netherlands [8]). As regards the adjustment of the balance of payments by *changing the rates of exchange,* a few explanatory words would seem indicated at this juncture. This method is in no way on the same level as the domestic method of monetary and fiscal discipline. Nor can it replace it in any way. The continued adjustment of the balance of payments cannot possibly be left to freely fluctuating rates of exchange as instability of the exchange rates if it is made the rule would result in uncertainty in all international payments and credits relations and a continued dislocation in price and cost relations which are incompatible with an international order worthy of the name. It would also be a mistake to assume like many protagonists of this method that in following it one could dispense with the inconveniences of adaptation and cutting one's coat according to the cloth. A reduction of the value of a currency abroad, unless nullified by a new burst of inflation at home, brings in its train that tightening up of internal economic conditions which in turn is, after all, indispensable for the restoration of the equilibrium. Adjustment is not avoided but only pushed in another direction, and precisely owing to the fact that the devaluation of a currency has the effect, often mistakenly deplored, of increasing the prices of import goods, it contributes decisively to adjusting the balance of payments – provided the restricted consumption thus achieved is not cancelled out again by internal rises in income, and thus deprived of any effect. Even more serious is the further objection that the surrender of the stability of exchange rates can upset one of the most important prerequisites of a stable balance of payments, namely confidence in the currency, and give the hyper-nervous foreign exchange market psychological shocks which hamper the adjustment in the balance of payments.

211

These are all very grave reasons for upholding the ideal of the stability of exchange rates – an ideal which can only be outranked by that of the freedom of the foreign exchange market. But, although direct adjustment (by restrictive monetary and credit policies at home) generally deserves preference to indirect adjustment (by changing the rate of exchange), and although the latter cannot be allowed to develop into the permanent practice of the nations, it must be conceded nevertheless that there are situations in which indirect adjustment is the more expedient and milder form, or even the only feasible one, particularly if adjustment is necessary to a degree in excess of a certain maximum. For there are cases in which the exchange rates of a country are so clearly 'false' that their correction is unavoidable. However, there are two things which we must hasten to add. Firstly, such cases must only be regarded as exceptions, as a violation of an ideal that should be double emphasized when it is no longer possible to avoid the lesser evil and ultima ratio of violating it. Secondly, it must be pointed out that even such sacrifice of an ideal is pointless if it is not accompanied by the restoration of the monetary and fiscal discipline at home.

WILL-O'-THE-WISP OF 'FULL EMPLOYMENT'

The first German edition of this book was compiled at a time (1944–1945) when the points made above were a scandal and a folly in the eyes of the world. With the exception of a few countries, Switzerland where this book was written and published occupying the place of honour at the top, everyone was absolutely against adjustment, monetary discipline, freely working forces and loyalty to the old and tried principles of a good pater familias. People were paralyzed with the fear of large-scale deflation which might overtake the nations again after the war, and thus believed that they could not achieve the goal of full employment excepting by pursuing an audacious policy of expansion. It was thus that the post-war policy of collectivist and inflationary 'full employment' came about, which is only now gradually being recognized in all its noxiousness – it and the fatal false predictions on which it was based. I had to expect at that time that what I wrote would be dismissed with the terrifying mention of 'deflation'.

In the meantime things today are such that, I am happy to say, it would be like bringing coals to Newcastle if I were now to repeat my warnings of the 'deflation psychosis', although many of my remarks at that time would probably still be of some interest at present.

In referring those who are still interested in what I said from the 1945 perspective, to the first German edition of this book, I feel that a few explanatory remarks are called for by the world situation in 1953.

I have no hesitation in leaving it to the informed reader to answer the question of who was right and who was wrong then, but I nevertheless feel compelled to emphasize how carefully I at that time tried to repudiate the doctrine of a possible antinomy between a policy based on stability of production and employment and the postulates of a free international order [9]). The example I quoted then of the United States has in the interval only increased in importance in proportion to the way in which that country has become the undisputed leading power in the international economy of the West. The importance of the American economic situation for the entire world makes it impossible to evade the question of how the other countries should behave in the event of a serious depression in the United States.

But – and here I come to another observation which is important today – this question has never been asked since 1945. A continued period of prosperity has prevailed in the United States during the past eight years – with a few interruptions – and its basis is an inflationary credit and budget policy. In other words, it has always been a capital error to think that if the European countries had wanted to balance their external payments after the war they would have had to put up with a policy of deflation. As the United States had, so to speak, done them the favour of carrying through an inflation it would have been enough if they, on their part, had refrained from taking such a liberty. However, not only did they not do so, but they even outdid the American inflation in spite of the arrears in their own production potential [10]).

Finally, it should be emphasized very strongly that the idea that economic stability in a country necessitates a rigid and comprehensive control of foreign trade, is a fundamental and dangerous fallacy. True world economy is not, for instance, an element of instability, but an element of stability. It was no coincidence that until 1914 economic fluctuations remained within reasonable limits at the very time when world economic integration had reached its highest level. It should be plain that the extent of the world

213

markets comprising as they do, countries in varying phases of the business cycle has always offered possibilities of adjustment by which the fluctuations of production and employment in the individual countries could be moderated. Conversely, it is very likely that the combination of the great depression after 1929 and a disastrous collapse in world economy was mainly responsible for aggravating and prolonging that depression, and for its fatal degeneration into a 'secondary depression'. As this aggravation of the depression now drove certain countries further and further along the road to economic nationalism, a *vicious circle* developed of economic nationalism, intensification of the depression, desperate acts of national policy to raise production and employment, an intensification of economic nationalism, and so on. As regards the situation at present, the conclusion to be drawn from this is that scarcely anything is so likely to promote the economic expansion of all countries as the final liberation of world economy from those hindrances the worst of which is exchange control.

EXCHANGE CONTROL

We have emphasized exchange control in the course of these remarks because it constitutes the actual spanner in the works of international order, and because we can only expect to restore that order and achieve genuine international economic integration by removing that obstruction, i.e., by restoring the free convertibility of currencies [11]).

As regards the essence of exchange control not much more need be said. It is the classical instrument of that trade policy formerly described as 'new', i.e., collectivist and not in accordance with market economy. At the same time it has become the necessary corner-stone of the collectivist and inflationary overall system of the European countries since the war, the chief means of damming a 'repressed inflation'. It is a form of control where maximum prices are fixed and there is rationing on the exchange market, a particularly serious case of the familiar policy which destroys the adjustment mechanism of the market by forbidding the free formation of prices and fixing a price below the point of equilibrium, and then replaces the lost self-regulating device with the artificial adjustment of supply and demand by forcing reluctant suppliers on to the market and by rationing. Exchange control is an essential part of the system of fictitious and enforced values which is characteristic of 'repressed inflation'; they are fictitious in the double sense that the official value, in this case the rate of exchange, does not correspond with the real value – which is quoted on the 'black' exchange markets –, and that only one – as a rule the smaller – part of the turnovers are cleared at the official rate, whereas the other takes refuge in illegality which the State prosecutes under penal law, with its informers, policemen, prisons, and, finally its executioners, as a 'crime' so defined not by the moral code but solely through the arbitrariness of a misguided government.

Exchange control means fighting an adverse balance of payments caused by a false rate of exchange or a false monetary and credit policy, in the spirit and with the means of a commando economy, which merely tackle the symptoms and thus conserve the deficit. It is nothing but the police protection of a false rate of exchange or of an excessive price, income, and expenditure level, a police campaign applied to an exchange rate or a domestic expenditure level which, if they were right, would not require such protection. While this campaign is excused by invoking the 'shortage of foreign exchange', it is bound to perpetuate that shortage like any other economic control which causes the demand to exceed the supply by fixing the price below the point of equilibrium. It means the brutal attempt to oppose the adjustment of the balance of payments both via the exchange rate and via the internal system of values, with the executioner.

This 'monetary iron curtain' as a wide-spread and effective system is not older than twenty years just as old as the brutal police-State which was necessary to produce it. Classical economists, such as Ricardo and J.-B. Say, had taken for granted that exchange control, gold export embargos and similar interference with foreign payments were simply impossible, but then, these economists were incapable – a fact which speaks highly for them – of imagining the degree of State power and of obedience on the part of the population, the mental servility on the part of the subjects and the brutality on the part of the government without which the very idea of such a fundamental deprivation of freedom seems incomprehensible [12]). The older generation of economists to which I myself belong, still grew up in this conviction of the classical economists, and the circumstance that it was socialist Russia that after the 1917 Revolution was the first and only country to make exchange control a lasting and effective part of the totalitarian system, only served to confirm us in our opinion. To make use of this solution in critical situations during times of peace seemed to us unworthy of a civilized State. I am sure that I am not alone in still upholding this opinion today.

There is no gainsaying the fact that exchange control which the youngest generation of most nations seems to think is a normal element in nature, constitutes a staggering innovation. As such an innovation it is part of an economic system which must be described as collectivist and of a State system which must be described as despotic. It first became possible as an effective system in peace-time in conjunction with a State whose unrestricted power, whose all-embracing bureaucracy, and whose contempt of the elementary rights of freedom anywhere outside Russia, would have been inconceivable only a few decades ago; they are, moreover, in the long run incompatible with the standards of western political tradition. Exchange control, no matter how relatively innocent the immediate cause of it, has become the corner-stone of the modern collectivist State which only exist in extreme national isolation.

This corner-stone cannot be dislodged without causing the whole building to collapse. Exchange control and a planned domestic economy are as a rule interdependent today. Whoever desires the first-mentioned is bound to have to resign himself in the long run to the latter; whoever does not wish the latter will have to think of abolishing the first. And if you wish the last-mentioned you cannot dispense with the first. Those who wish to 'control' the national economy cannot leave foreign trade and its equilibrium to the free market. They must fight to the bitter end in order to continue exchange control, and Neptune would rather surrender his trident than a socialist politician his foreign exchange bureaucracy. The mere thought of abolishing these functions is bound to be considered 'criminal', just as the unheard-of action of 'imagining the King's death' was a crime under Old English law.

Collectivism, as we saw earlier, is identical with an extreme form of economic nationalism because it is forced to make of the State frontier by exchange control an impassible rampart with few draw-bridges. It must be a bitter irony for an honest socialist to have to defend exchange control – of which no mention is made in Marx – as the actual key-position in the collectivist system. For it means defending an institution which carries national isolation to an extreme and excludes the possibility of international cooperation. Apart from the absolute State monopoly of foreign trade – there are no measures of economic policy which so radically separate countries from each other as exchange control, none which sub-ordinates foreign trade so unresistingly to State bureaucracy, none which realizes to such a degree the aim of national autarchy, none which would so drastically dissolve the community of nations, political, intellectual, and economic. It is Pandora's box from which necessarily escape bilateralism, balance of payments crises, obstruction of international trade channels, paralysis of international capital transactions and 'dollar shortage'. It is the means with which the collective State justifies to the world its monop-olist control of economic life. When not even money – minted 'freedom', as Dostoyevski calls it – can freely cross the State frontiers, the highest degree of international disintegration has been reached. Nowhere is that more tragic and less tolerable than in Europe. For this reason the final abolition of exchange control must be the ceterum censeo of any truly European policy.

NOTES

1. (p. 194) The 'adverse balance of payments' as a subject of dispute:

The 'adverse balance of payments' (or 'dollar shortage') has today become an extremely sensitive spot in the collision of trends in economic policy. Any objective explanation of the logic of this term as undertaken, for instance, by F. MACHLUP in his essay, 'Three Concepts of the Balance of Payments and the so-called Dollar Shortage' (Economic Journal, March 1950), is usually received very testily by the exponents of a collectivist and inflationary avant-gardism, firstly, because they object to the proof that the balance of payments rights itself without the polypragmatism of economic planning if only the opposite of their beloved policy is pursued, and secondly because they are bitterly opposed to the proof that their own policy is responsible for the 'adverse balance of payments'. Cf. in this connection my essay entitled 'Zentralisierung und Dezentralisierung als Leitlinien der Wirtschaftspolitik' (Wirtschaftliche Entwicklung und soziale Ordnung (Festschrift Degenfeld) edited by Lagler-Messner, Vienna 1952, pp. 11-26). On the theory of the balance of payments: G. HABERLER, Der internationale Handel, Berlin 1933, pp. 8-93; FRITZ W. MEYER, Der Ausgleich der Zahlungsbilanz, Jena 1938; F. MACHLUP, as above; L. ROBBINS, The Balance of Payments, London 1951; E. KÜNG, Die Selbstregulierung der Zahlungsbilanz, eine Untersuchung über die automatischen Methoden des Zahlungsbilanzausgleichs, St. Gallen 1948; J. E. MEADE, The Balance of Payments, London 1952; ALFRED KRUSE, Die Mechanismen des Zahlungsbilanzausgleichs, Wirtschaftstheorie und Wirtschaftspolitik (Festgabe für Adolf Weber), Berlin 1951, pp. 83-98.

2. (p. 197) Tito and the 'dollar gap':

In a publication by the International Monetary Fund the assumption 'that in some way a deficit develops and financing must then be found for it' is rightly described as mistaken. 'Unless it is financed, the deficit cannot come into being' (Balance of Payments Year Book, 1938, 1946, 1947, International Monetary Fund, Washington D.C., 1949, p. 23.)

3. (p. 200) Balance of payments and exchange rate:

The exponents of an economic policy which, because it is collectivist, cannot admit the possibility of a free adjustment of the balance of payments, have gone to great trouble to dispute the logic outlined in the text, by trying to prove the impossibility of a free equilibrium by means of hypotheses concerning abnormal elasticities of demand in foreign trade. This leads to the assumption however that the foreign exchange market behaves in exactly the opposite way to any other individual market which no one disputes having an equilibrium price where supply equals demand. On the contrary, it should be emphasized that the foreign exchange market is the very one which, composed as it is of numerous individual markets, offers a unique chance for the compensation of any inverse elasticity of demand, and most particularly in the western industrial States with their enormously varied production and requirements programmes. Cf. G. HABERLER, The Market for Foreign Exchange and the Stability of the Balance of Payments, Kyklos, Vol. III., No. 3; F. A. LUTZ, Euopäische Währungsprobleme, Ordo, Vol. IV, 1951, p. 312 etc. Incidentally, we encounter here an important example of the fact that in this field of theory sharp perspicacity very often not only does not prevent a complete misjudgment of the overall situation but is actually the cause of such misjudgment. What a catastrophe can result from this, in putting monetary policies into practice was demonstrated drastically by the Swedish monetary policy after the war, in particular the unfortunate revaluation of the Swedish Krone in 1946 which can be described as a characteristic combination of shrewdness as regards detail coupled with a minimum of common sense.

4. (p. 202) Purely monetary cause of the adverse balance of payments:

The above-mentioned Swedish economic policy after the war is such a striking example of this, for the reason that in this case of an economically exceptionally strong country spared from the war, even the most obstinate person must admit that apart from the monetary and credit policy practically all other real causes are out of the question. This economic policy might even have been deliberately chosen so as to lend conviction with the forcefulness of a laboratory experiment, to the sentence by D. H. Robertson quoted in the text (taken from his essay, 'The Economic Outlook', Economic Journal, December 1947). This power of conviction is increased still further by the fact that Switzerland, a country with otherwise comparable economic conditions, at the same time demonstrated the opposite, viz., that monetary discipline can make a currency the hardest in the world. It was extremely difficult to 'soften' the Swedish krone, and that task could only be managed by a policy which did its utmost to make sure that there was an inflationary excess of demand to avoid pressing on the resources of that country.

5. (p. 205) Fluctuation and fundamental deficit:

In contrast to the fluctuating deficit which arises owing to chance shifting in supply and demand on the foreign exchange market, the fundamental deficit ('fundamental dis-equilibrium', as it is called in an important provision of the statutes of the International Monetary Fund) reflects an alteration in the causes governing the 'natural parity' of a currency. It is the expression of a genuine. serious, and more than temporary disturbance in the external equilibrium of a national economy. This distinction presents great difficulties in theory, but is of extreme importance in practice for the central banks which could safely utilize their reserves to compensate a mere fluctuating deficit, but in the event of a fundamental disequilibrium would be throwing them into a bottomless pit like the German Reichsbank in spring 1923 and the Bank of England during the few weeks of the restored convertibility of the pound in summer 1947. A fluctuating deficit, in as far as it is not met by the self-equilibrating forces of the foreign exchange market or by international interim finance, demands the use of monetary reserves to protect exchange rates stability, whereas in the case of a fundamental disequilibrium such use of reserves would be an irresponsibly applied palliative.

6. (p. 205) Self-adjustment mechanisms:

The most direct of such mechanisms, effective also with a paper currency (if it is not abolished through inflation) functions to the extent that the central bank, in the event of an import surplus, sells foreign exchange from its reserves, withdraws money from circulation to that extent, and thus exercises a restraining effect which liberates more goods for export and curtails the demand for further imports. The opposite – expansive – effect takes place in the case of an export surplus. Thus, the currency reserves of the central bank are seen to have a double function. They not only serve, as shown in the foregoing note, as a direct compensation for a fluctuating deficit, but also indirectly as a means of guiding the monetary conditions of the balance of payments. The use of the currency reserves by the central bank thus becomes a special case of 'open-market operations'.

7. (p. 207) Open and repressed inflation:

Cf.: G. RUEFF, Die soziale Ordnung, Bremen, 1952, in particular pp. 537-706; W. RÖPKE, Offene und zurückgestaute Inflation, Kyklos, I, 1947, No. 1; W. RÖPKE, Repressed Inflation, Kyklos, I, 1947, No. 3.

8. (p. 211) The 'policy of the opposite':

Cf. for further details my contribution, 'Alte und neue Ökonomie', in the collection 'Wirtschaft ohne Wunder', edited by E. A. Hunold, Erlenbach-Zürich 1953. The reader is also referred to my essay, 'Germany – Rock of Wrong Prophecies', The Freeman (New York) of 24 August 1953.

9. (p. 213) Balance of payments and market policy:

Reference is had to the following examples from the abundance of literature on this subject: G. HABERLER, Prosperität und Depression, Bern 1948, pp. 388 et seq.; HANS GESTRICH, Geldpolitik und Weltwirtschaft, Berlin 1934;H. RITTERSHAUSEN, Vollbe-schäftigung und Außenhandelspolitik, Publications of the Association for Social Policy, new series, Vol. 3, Berlin 1951; FRITZ W. MEYER, Stabile oder bewegliche Wechselkurse? Ordo, Vol. IV, 1951; H. BELSHAW, Stabilization in a Dependent Economy, The Econom-ic Record (Melbourne), April 1939, Supplement; W. RÖPKE, Crises and Cycles, London 1936, § 22; W. RÖPKE, International Economic Disintegration, London 1942, pp. 203 et seq.; W. RÖPKE, Tipo aureo e politica della congiuntura, Rivista Internazionale di Science Sociali, November 1935.

In December 1949, the Secretariat-General of the United Nations published an experts' report entitled 'National and International Measures for Full Employment' which I criticized in my article, 'The Economics of Full Employment' (New York 1952). The said report was subsequently withdrawn and replaced by a somewhat more reasonable one ('Measures for International Economic Stability', 1951).

10. (p. 213) Europe surpassing American post-war inflation:

No less a person than KEYNES in the last publication of his life (The Balance of Payments of the United States, Economic Journal, June 1946) had described a serious 'dollar shortage' after the war as unlikely, particularly because he took for granted that the United States would become 'a high-living, high-cost country beyond any previous experience'. In other words, he was expecting the pressure of inflation to continue in that country. And his prediction was right. But the mistake he made was that he, strange to say, did not foresee the simultaneous inflation in the countries of Europe, that is, he had not expected them to take his untimely doctrines so seriously.

11. (p. 214) Foreign exchange controls:

For further details see W. RÖPKE, Devisenzwangwirtschaft: das Kardinalproblem der internationalen Wirtschaft, Außenwirtschaft, March 1950.

12. (p. 215) Views of the classical economists:

In his book entitled 'The High Price of Bullion' (4th ed. 1811) RICARDO asserts plainly that if it is advantageous to export gold, no law can effectively prevent its exportation. Around the same time J.-B. SAY wrote, 'Il est impossible, même lorsqu'un citoyen n'émigre pas, d'empêcher l'extraction de sa fortune, s'il est bien décidé à la faire passer dans l'étranger'. (Traité d'Economie Politique, 2nd ed. 1814, Vol. I, Bk. I, Chap. 20).

PART FOUR

TOWARDS A NEW WORLD ECONOMY

*Ceteros pudeat si qui se litteris abdiderunt ut nihil possint
ex his neque ad communem affere
fructum neque in adspectum lucemque proferre*

Cicero, *Pro Archia oratio, VI*

I

ATTEMPTS, TENDENCIES AND PROBLEMS

Whereas in the German edition of this book (1945), in view of the world situation at that time, a most gloomy picture had to be drawn of the breakdown of world economy, the task of its reintegration being represented with extreme emphasis to all responsible persons as something the implications of which had not yet been universally grasped, still less undertaken seriously, today (at the end of 1953) we have reached a stage of development at which a somewhat different language may be used. This is certainly not the language of satisfaction at what has been achieved, nor of confident hope as regards further progress. For sentiments of this kind, we are confronted far too grimly by the unsolved problems of international order. Nevertheless it is not the language of unbounded criticism concerning the headway made since 1945, nor yet of catastrophic visions for the future. For it can not be denied that since the end of the War, and above all during the last few years, since fatal errors of the preceding period have been progressively set right, a greater measure of order, freedom and prosperity has come into the international economy of the free West than would have been considered possible – even by people who were by no means incurable pessimists. If, therefore, we attempt today to present an interim balance with regard to international reconstruction, it will, on the one hand, be impossible to deny that – particularly in Europe, the most important yet at the same time the weakest and most vulnerable point of the entire Western front – we have put behind us the melancholy period during which the countries shut themselves off from each other, through the most senseless autarchic policy, living, at the same time, on aid from the United States. On the other hand, however, various things have occurred to give cause for reflection, and which cannot fail to make us feel both humble and uneasy.

In the first place, there is not the slightest reason why the progress, so far as it has been realized, should be considered as an achievement where in those who are principally responsible for international constructive planning, could be particularly proud, when they compare it with the tempo and success of the international work for reconstruction after the first World

War. Such pride seems, indeed, not too well founded, since it would require a most faulty vision to attribute this progress, so far as it has been realized, to the great international plans and organizations for reconstruction. To do this would mean to repeat, in retrospect, one of the fundamental mistakes which may be held responsible for the disappointments and failures experienced in international reconstruction since 1945, i.e. the belief that international economic recovery is to be expected from international organizations, conferences and charters instead of from the soundness and balance of the individual national economies themselves, from, in a word, that 'false internationalism', which was discussed earlier in this book.

Neither the International Monetary Fund – which, as an international credit institution, has up to the present been of very little use, and, as an international monetary authority, has done harm rather than good[1]) – nor the International Bank for Reconstruction and Development (World Bank), the second creation of the Bretton Woods Conference of 1944, nor the Marshall Plan, however salutary it was as a political move, and bountiful as international poor relief, nor the efforts of the International Trade Organization with its one surviving live child, the General Agreement on Tariffs and Trade (GATT), nor the other institutions of one kind or another, almost too numerous to be counted, nor the Schuman Plan are the real instruments of the relative progress of the last few years, and even OEEC with its European Payments Union, which may, before most others, claim a not inconsiderable credit, can, at the best, be considered merely as an impermanent emergency structure. Rather is such progress as is actually on record to be placed predominantly to the credit of two factors: to that of the colossal vitality of modern economy, whose sturdy stomach seems capable, of eventually digesting even the big lumps of modern autarchic policies, and to the extent to which it has proved possible, within a number of the national economies, to abandon the false road which, like no other, had led to the disappointments and delays in international reconstruction since the War, and even robbed the so generously designed Marshall Plan of its full effect. It is, as we know only too well, the false road of an inflationist and collectivist economic policy, in which socialism, Keynesianism and the ideology of the Welfare State had joined together to constitute a power of fateful strength and efficacy[2]). Where the international economy today shows real and noticeable signs of a healthy growth, it is in

224

those countries which have resolutely abandoned this false road, or have never trodden it. The more important of these are easily enumerated: the United States, Switzerland, Canada, Western Germany, Belgium, Austria and – with reservations in a greater or lesser degree- countries such as the Netherlands, Italy, Denmark and perhaps Mexico.

If we weigh up the two sides of our interim balance, there can be no doubt whatever, that in the task of creating a genuine international economic order, we have, in spite of everything, not passed beyond the stage of partial successes, starts and preliminary measures, and the real decisive problems still lie unsolved before us. Among these the problem of a genuine international monetary system is of such overwhelming importance that the treatment of it is being reserved for a special last chapter. In the meantime it will be worth our while, in this chapter, to consider some of the other unsolved problems which hem in the way to a new world economy.

EUROPEAN ECONOMIC INTEGRATION

Out of the administration of the Marshall Plan and of the parallel organization of European countries (OEEC) a policy has been evolved which, impelled by the major, uncontested task of the political consolidation of Europe, is striving, under the name of 'European economic integration', to find a solution to the problem of international economic order. All that can be objected to the 'Regional Principle in World Economy' had already been set forth in the first German edition of this book, in anticipation of today's campaign for 'European economic integration', and is at present finding concrete confirmation. If, in addition to this, the reader also considers what has already been said in an earlier part of the present work (pp. 103 et seq.) concerning the muddles and the false roads of 'European economic integration', he will understand why any sober judgment, of this part of the international pattern, cannot be otherwise than highly sceptical[3]). If it is true that the term 'European economic integration', to be reasonable, can only mean a state of affairs which will permit trading relations among different national economies to be as free and mutually advantageous as those which exist within a national economy, the essential condition for such state of affairs – we repeat this, because it is so important – is that close community of markets and prices which makes an economic area a whole. This means, primarily, that within such an area every person, at any time, is at liberty to buy on the cheapest and sell on the dearest market, i.e. that he profits by a state of affairs which, in international economic relations, is known as multilateralism. This, however, is only possible if a second condition is fulfilled – the free use of money, without regional limitation, i.e. the condition which, in international economic relations, is known as currency convertibility. Only then will real economic integration be realized, as also, thanks to this community of markets, prices and payments, the possibility of an unhampered division of labour among the various areas with its extraordinary increase in productivity. An integrated international economy presupposes free multilateralism, which, in its turn, presupposes a free convertibility of currencies.

This highly desirable state of affairs, as regards the economic integration of Europe, already existed; indeed, scarcely twenty years have elapsed since it was destroyed. To a degree, which nowadays we are hardly able to imagine, or to dare to wish for, European economic integration was realized, at a time when Europe was not yet cut in pieces through systematic national exchange control and cognate measures of a collectivist trade policy, and had not yet been robbed, by the inconvertibility of currencies, of the multilateral character of economic relations. It was an integration which required no plans, no planners, no bureaucracy, no conferences, no customs' unions and no High Authorities. Certainly, this integration was impaired by protective tariffs, though these had perhaps scarcely greater significance than have the easily overlooked distances within the territory of the United States (so eagerly held up as a pattern to Europe!), with their high cost of inland transport, which has the same effect as would inter-States customs' tariffs. In contrast with this, our continent is compressed into a narrow space, most parts of which can, moreover, be easily reached by cheap sea-transport. Besides, those protective tariffs which, until a couple of decades ago, constituted the sole means of a European trade policy, differ fundamentally from the modern collectivist (quantitative) methods of trade policy, especially exchange control, in that they did not touch the convertibility of currencies and thus did not affect the multilateral character of trade relations. They were able, it is true, to impair integration (in the manner of natural obstacles to trade such as distances or mountain ranges) but they could not abolish it. Finally, let us not forget, that that genuine integration which Europe possessed until about 1932, excelled everything offered today under that high-sounding name, in that it was not confined to Europe, but was world-wide. It was an *open,* not a *closed* system. It was part of a world-wide, not the ideal of a regional order, and therefore quite free, with no subtleties attached.

This integration was destroyed by the new trade policy which began twenty years ago in the midst of the international payments crisis of that time, and developed subsequently into a gigantic world-encompassing system which was only the logical and visible conclusion of a national development along collectivist and inflationary lines. In those days, at that pre-collectivist time, when, in regard to international dealings, we had only to reckon with protective tariffs – as a rule by no means prohibitive – and, generally speaking, the conditions of freedom prevailed, the separation of peoples through distance, monetary systems, frontiers, language or customs proved no obstacle capable of preventing the formation, by the entire globe, of a cohesive economic system, a real world-wide economy.

Thus, European economic integration, as it existed a short time ago, was a liberal, open, and at the same time universal institution. It has been destroyed by trade and monetary policies which had, if not their origin, certainly their main props in a specific economic, credit and fiscal policy pursued by governments, at home, in that policy, indeed, which I have defined as collectivist and inflationary. As however, for reasons which have been discussed earlier, there can be no thought of seeking a way out of this cul-de-sac – now universally recognized as such – in an *international* system of inflationary economic planning, there only remains one possibility i.e. to cure the sickness where it originated. Since the disintegration of European economy has been brought about by the leftist course of national economic policy, which is bound to lead to planning and controls in foreign trade, and to culminate in exchange control, which is irreconcilable with an integrated international economy, it results – by strict logic and not as the expression of a vague inclination towards a liberal solution – that the more or less collectivist and inflationary system of national economic policies must now be abrogated to clear the way for the abolition of exchange control and the other measures inherent in a collectivist trade policy. Here lies the Archimedian point at which the lever for European economic integration has to be placed. The problem of European economic integration, as it presents itself today, would be practically solved if some means could be found of removing this upper stratum, composed of collectivist, *absolute,* trade restrictions, which twenty years ago was

227

superimposed on the old layer, composed of the *relative* trade restrictions of protective tariffs. This, however, is a matter for each separate European Government. Everyone who is honest with himself must acknowledge that we would thank God on our knees if we in Europe today had nothing further to worry about than the obstacle to trade caused through protective tariffs which was all we were concerned with twenty years ago.

European disintegration, like charity in the English proverb, began at home, and the reintegration of Europe's economy must likewise begin at home, i.e. within each individual nation, with a decision by the Governments and Central Banks to abandon at last, after twenty years of error, the collectivist and inflationary path of leftist economic and monetary policies. The way out is possible everywhere, provided the necessary insight and strength are to hand. Not merely is it the only way open to us, in view of the impossibility of solutions based on economic planning, but is also the only one worth striving for, since it leads, as it did formerly, to an open, and not a closed, form of European integration. Only so may we hope to integrate Europe in such a manner as not to lead to a corresponding seclusion from the rest of the world. People will become increasingly convinced of this in the United States, where, until a short time ago, under the influence of confused ideas, so much was done to cause Europe to go wrong i.e. to drive it into a collectivist and closed form of integration.

As the actual problem of European integration is traceable to the harm occasioned by the 'upper stratum' of trade restrictions, it follows that all those plans, which are continually being put forward, for a regional or continental *customs union,* rest on faulty reasoning. For either we succeed truly in getting rid of the top layer – in which case we do not need customs unions, which are in any case bound to give rise to exceedingly difficult problems of a political or administrative nature or, if we do not succeed in getting rid of that layer, the customs unions will present one more instance of what seems to have become the general rule in our time – a mere façade, an optical illusion, a 'roof without a house'. If a customs union be accepted as a solution, it means that, on the one hand we are demanding too much, and, on the other hand, too little: too much, because such a union always constitutes a task which rarely succeeds, too little, because a mere customs union leaves unsolved the actual problem i.e. the demolition of the *absolute* obstacles to trade, and merely amounts to a waste of time and energy, – to say nothing of the fundamental problems of a regional solution of this kind [4]).

Such is the compelling and inevitable logic as regards European economic integration. Only from this firm footing is it possible to judge the two schemes, which have been acclaimed as the first great steps towards European integration: the European Coal and Steel Community of the Schuman Plan, and the European Payments Union (EPU). In neither of these cases, however, have we to do with schemes for a genuine European economic integration, since they do not solve the actual problem – the demolition of the upper layer of obstacles to trade. In any case, however, they can only fulfil the functions properly assigned to them if they are supported by a genuine economic union of the kind described *ad nauseam*, and – by a species of Hegelian 'logic', perhaps prepare the way for this. Both the said actions are doomed to failure unless they are supplemented by decisive action on a national basis. Both imply the danger that, owing to them, this national action may well be delayed, whilst they foster the illusion that they are able to offer a substitute for a genuine, though uncomfortable, integration.

As regards the *European Coal and Steel Community,* any definitive judgment must, in fairness, take into consideration both the political aim, i.e. to provide a catalyst for political integration, as also the specifically economic aim of securing a system for regulating competition in the sphere of heavy industry, which inclines so strongly towards monopolies. With regard, however, to the intention of effecting, by means of such union in a single industry, a direct contribution to a genuine European economic integration, such supposition of a piecemeal ('functional') integration rests on a misunderstanding of the problem which is hard to conceive. What use would there be in solemnly proclaiming a 'common' European market for iron, steel and coal, while the production branches affected remain integral parts of separate national economies, cut off from each other by the entire system of organizing, planning and isolating economic and financial policies of a strictly national character, and primarily by monetary autonomy and change control? Such reckoning leads nowhere. In some way or another the impatient attempt is doomed to failure to achieve an international economic integration without first removing the causes – as explained – of the present disintegration, above all non-convertibility of currencies with the balance of payments trouble and false rates of exchange that go with it; once these causes are removed, the desired economic integration will automatically ensue. Once more a 'roof without a house' is obviously being built. If we try to 'integrate' any single branch of the economy, whilst, the forces, which tend again and again to disturb the balance of payments from inside continue to operate, the appearance of a 'common' market for the group of goods concerned must inevitably be bought at the price of serious disturbances and stresses, in certain cases difficult to foresee, which we finally try in vain – being impeded by the limits set to any international economic planning – to master by means of a highly complicated system of control measures.

Nothing good can be expected so long as European trade, in regard to a single type of goods, is handled *as if* there existed no disturbance in the balance of payments, no exchange control and no false rates of exchange. The results of such a *policy of fictions* are patent for all to see. So long as European countries adhere to an internal credit and budget policy, and to exchange control at the wrong rates of exchange which push first one country then another to the limits of its credit margin in EPU, and thus keep the 'see-saw of liberalization' merrily swinging, in other words, so long as they are not heading for genuine economic integration, but are retaining the quantitative regulation of imports and exports as the chief means of achieving a balance of payments equilibrium, any permanent and complete 'liberalization' of a single branch of the economy (and this is what the 'common' market of the European Coal and Steel Community amounts to) must inevitably be bought at the price of a corresponding decrease in liberalization for the rest. Somewhere the fox must come out of his hole. This effect will only be obviated in proportion as a genuine integration is effected, i.e. one which is associated with free convertibility of currencies and the abolition of quantitative trade restrictions. Once this is realized however, we shall need none of these unions, 'pools' or 'High Authorities'. In this connexion we will refrain from going once more into the question whether the international dirigisme, which is common to all these organizations, is politically feasible or not.

The idea of a so-called 'functional' integration after the pattern of the Schuman Plan – which at any rate can be defended on political grounds – is based, therefore on an inadequate appreciation of the interdependence of economic phenomena. The only solution is an 'integral' integration, which will consist in the free convertibility of currencies and the removal of other collectivist restrictions, but which, on its part, presupposes a healthy economic and monetary policy within each country.

When, in 1950, the other relevant creation by the policy of 'European integration', the *European Payments Union* was founded, common sense suggested the question what use there could be in setting up such a payments system among countries which continue to resort to exchange controls in view of the lack of equilibrium in their national economies. The Payments Union appeared like a kind of gigantic cheese plate cover placed over unchanged national economic and monetary policies and the balance of payments discrepancies that went with them. Once it was foreseen that under these circumstances the EPU would not be able to function properly and furnish a further example of the policy of fictions, the further question arose whether it might not be superfluous, once the balance of payments difficulties were removed, since it would then in any case be possible to adopt free convertibility of currencies. Was not the European Payments Union therefore, either incapable of functioning or unnecessary? To this one could reply with a certain amount of right, that the EPU could justify its existence by developing into a supra-national body which, by its well-designed mechanism and direct influence on the economic policies of the various countries would guide the Governments and Central Banks towards a sound policy of equilibrium as a re-emergence of the gold standard in the shape of a political institution. Once this work of education was completed, a system of freely convertible currencies could take the place of EPU.

The actual development of EPU undoubtedly did justice to the common sense way of thinking. In a report to the German Federal Government in Summer 1950 [5]), I made the following statements, quoting Germany as an example: that a country in Germany's position, which is a member of a regional payments union would experience all the disadvantages of a country in a natural creditor position in relation to the other members, and a corresponding natural debtor position in relation to the rest of the world; that the functioning of EPU would presuppose a perpetual readiness on the part of countries with a balanced economy to 'finance that policy of other countries which leads to the balance of payments difficulties', and that everything would depend on 'whether the mechanism of the Union would give member countries the time and incentive to undertake the necessary revision of their national economic policies, and thus to

231

make the Payments Union itself superfluous'. Events have shown that this appraisal of the situation was correct and even too favourable, since the creditor countries of EPU have found out in the meantime that the extreme debtors not only resorted to them for compulsory finance, but also passed the commercial burden of their balance of payments problems on to them by way of 'deliberalization' (the see-saw of liberalization) with all the disadvantages this implied. Moreover, I was, unfortunately, also right in viewing without optimism the chances that the EPU might have a disciplining effect and thereby render itself superfluous. If I finally added that it was doubtful whether one could count upon the unlimited patience of the creditor countries – and it is obvious that this limit has now been reached.

There is no need to belittle unduly the achievements of EPU, or its historic role, in order to become resigned to the view that this way leads no further and that the task of a genuine international integration by free convertibility of currencies still lies unconquered before us. Today the EPU lives merely on the patience of the creditor countries, and this patience cannot be prolonged indefinitely, from one 'rallonge' to another. Even if this institution had fulfilled better its purpose of educating the undisciplined countries in monetary policy, or would do so better in future, it still has an irreparable constitutional defect in that it is merely a regional payments union, which continues to produce surpluses in the balance of payments of creditor countries (notably Germany) that cannot be used to offset deficits incurred elsewhere. Liberalization, even as a total and unchangeable measure (to which end efforts are being made in vain), is no true way to convertibility; only the full settlement of EPU net balances in gold or in hard currency would accomplish this, and then there would be no further need of EPU and convertibility would, without further ado, become possible in all countries, in the simplest manner. Convertibility – the actual and decisive end – cannot therefore be achieved through a mere reform of EPU, but through its ultimate obviation, the necessity for which was clear to all at the time of its foundation.

THE FOREIGN BODY OF COLLECTIVISM IN THE WORLD ECONOMY

The free world in its search for economic integration is confronted by the colossal block of the Communist Imperium. How is any *modus vivendi* between the two, in regard to economic relations, possible, which would not work out to the serious disadvantage of the West, economically as well as politically? A few principles may be cited in this connexion.

Firstly, we shall have to reckon with the imperium of Soviet Russia and its economic block as with a powerful area of totalitarianism and economic collectivism, bent on world conquest. *Secondly,* so long as this imperium exists, the economic collectivism, inseparable from it, will necessarily imply a collectivist system of foreign trade, which will preclude any kind of automatic regulation through the powers of the market, these being substituted by arbitrary direction. *Thirdly* and lastly, this collectivist system of foreign trade is irreconcilable with the liberal system of world economy and represents a foreign body in the same, which, if not encapsulated by the rest of the world, would lead to a chronic sickness in the new world economy.

From these facts, which we have to face without any uncertainty or illusion, it follows that the essentially liberal world will, even now, after the removal of National Socialism, have to contend for a long time to come with the same difficulty which it experienced during the years 1933–1939, when it had to accustom itself to the methods of the Third Reich in regard to foreign policy. This difficulty consists in the coexistence of a sector pursuing a free market economy with one dominated by a collectivist system of international trade, a question which we discussed earlier (see pp. 163 et seq., also note 3, pp. 175 et seq.), and found disquieting. Nevertheless the world today could lighten its task to a not inconsiderable degree by a willingness to learn from the experiences which it underwent in the past, with the National Socialist economic block, and apply these lessons to the new conditions. From these experiences it should, above all, have come to realize that a world economy based on a free market, and a collectivist economic block, are two entirely different systems of foreign trade. The *collectivist State is no partner in a game for the liberal world, as it is incapable even of observing the rules of the game, and any attempt to treat it as such can only lead to severe disappointments and losses.* Besides this, the collectivist State which would be bound by no considerations of prices and costs, would, in such unilateral trading, reserve to itself the right to upset, where and when it liked, any liberal economy governed by the laws of the free market.

In order to counter this danger to the free world, represented by the foreign body of Collectivism, it will be necessary to maintain the same distrustful

233

watchfulness as is also rendered necessary in the *political* interplay of the world forces, by the existence of a collectivist State which is bound by no unbreakable rules. If the liberal world does not wish to be duped, it will have to make up its mind to meet the collectivist 'economic block' with similar weapons, applying to it the methods of an enforced bilateralism, so that the sector of the free market economy may remain free from disturbances, yet without itself succumbing to collectivist infection. The liberal world will have to get used to the idea that its relations with the collectivist 'economic block' take the form of short-time makeshifts, thus bearing the stamp characteristic of collectivist foreign trade. In face of the powerful economic weight which the collectivist sector is able to throw into the scale, the task of effectually encapsulating this foreign body, for the protection of liberal world economy, can only succeed if the *liberal countries,* faced by the monopoly position of the collectivist State show a *minimum of solidarity* in matters of foreign trade, instead of letting the other side play up one bidder against the other. This appears to be one of the most important tasks of the free world, a task which presupposes, as a primary condition, a clear grasp of the significance of collectivism in world politics and the world economy. We have to confess that before this is achieved we have a terribly long way to go!

UNDERDEVELOPED COUNTRIES

We had occasion earlier on (p. 190) to draw attention to the fact that one of the most serious problems in the reintroduction of an international order is that process of economic and social fermentation which is taking place in the so-called 'underdeveloped countries' [6]). What is going on here is something far beyond what is usually understood by the expression 'industrialization of agrarian States'. The slogan 'Development of the underdeveloped countries' means ultimately that we witness what has never taken place before in the whole course of history: the apparently irresistible spread of a now world-dominant culture, that of the West, at the cost of an inexorable disintegration and dissolution of all others. Whether this will result finally in a 100-percent Westernization of the earth, is doubtful. One thing however is certain – the *negative* result i.e., the shattering, wilting, disintegration and final destruction of the non-Western forms of culture, life and society, and at least the tension and fermentation arising among the most distant

234

peoples and races as a result of the continued contact, becoming ever closer and more tightly gripping, with the Western, 'modern' world. This refers above all to western technology, to the allurements and grip of which these nations, although showing varying grades of inner resistance, succumb in the end with the same inevitability as ourselves.

Now this process is, as far as the West is concerned, further complicated, in that it has become identical with the end of Western colonial rule. This end, which is inevitable, in view both of the character of such rule and of the entire world-political constellation, and which can only be delayed at isolated points, occurs with all the crises incidental to such transition, unfortunately just at the moment when – in view of world Communism and its Socio-psychological strategy, the free world is least able to afford the emancipation of the colonial peoples and even the most impatient critics of the colonial system, if they are intelligent, must be found on the side of the forces seeking to delay, rather than to hasten, such end. The West is therefore faced with the task of effecting, with the utmost tact and human understanding, two things simultaneously, which are not easy to combine i.e. extending an active sympathy in regard to the economic and political condition of these countries and meeting the errors of their leaders with a vigorous resistance and undisguised criticism.

The most essential condition for this is that the West should become clearer in its own views as to the conditions and limits of the 'development' of these countries. Every development programme must inevitably end in disappointment if it is not guided by the understanding that most of the essential pre-conditions, intellectual, political and sociological, on which a western industrial economy ultimately rests, are not, as a rule, fulfilled in the 'underdeveloped countries', even though the programme may be based on the illusion that such conditions can be imported or speedily created. This leads us to the second point to be realized i.e. that such 'development' is a process which demands an unending patience, a deep human understanding, a flexible adaptibility to existing conditions the ability to allow for slow growth – which demands, in short precisely the opposite of what has become almost second nature to the ambitious planner, the well-intentioned rather than clear-sighted social reformer the economist working with theoretical formulae and doctrines, the western engineer with his visions.

All of these – and with them the intellectuals of the countries concerned who are fascinated by these western materialist concepts and alienated from their own cultural and social traditions – will have to learn that the ultimate secret of 'rich' lands is to be sought, not in 'capital', machine models, technical or organizational recipes or natural wealth, but in a spirit of order, foresight, combination, calculation, enterprise, human leadership and the freedom to shape life and things, also in citizenship, a sense of responsibility, loyalty to work, reliability, thrift and the urge to create, and in a civil middle-class, providing the humus for all this, – things, in short, which can neither be conjured up from the soil, nor imported. The idea that it merely needs the artificial manure of 'capital' and 'technical assistance' from the West, in order to induce the dormant economic powers of these countries to spring up into growth, must be given up as a fundamental error. In this connexion we need not revert to a problem, without the solution of which all efforts are doomed to frustration which seek to help those countries of Asia and Africa, now cruelly cursed with a genuine over-population, towards an existence more worthy of human beings for the masses of their people, i.e. the problem of birth control, which is rendered all the more serious by the triumph of western medicine and hygiene over the thousand forms of death and disablement, which lie in wait for the millions in those latitudes.

Any development programme will prove to be more surely on right and sensible lines the less it does violence to natural conditions and to the circumstances already existing. This means, on the other hand, that it becomes the more questionable in proportion as it requires, for its carrying out, a protective isolation and the compulsion of a planned economy, those expedients that are rated highly – fatal though this may be – by all concerned, i.e. by the leaders of the underdeveloped countries as also by their Western helpers and advisers. The sensible course would be to continue with that which has already been done in those countries, but to do it better, more sensibly and more profitably, not, however, to indulge in a pretentious imitation of the West, nor emulate that national and socialist fashion in the West, to which so many economists succumb. Wherever, hitherto, this fundamental rule has been disregarded under the spell of socialist and industrial obsession, catastrophic consequences have always followed, agriculture becoming the obvious sacrifice to such economic power-policy. In how short a time flourishing agrarian lands can in this manner – contrary to all probability – be transformed into regular famine areas, is shown by Yugoslavia and Argentina, to say nothing of the countries on the other side of the iron curtain.

Thus, if it seems indicated that the development of the countries under consideration be sought in the improvement of primary production rather than in industrialization, this certainly does not mean that they are thereby condemned to play a Cinderella role. The popular idea that the world's primary production provides less possibilities for a profitable expansion and with it a steady rise in the national income, than industrial production, is shown to be a dogma which needs revision. This is becoming apparent in view of the increasing population of the world, rising mass incomes in industrial countries, higher and more diversified requirements, the expansion of industry and the disquieting signs of an incipient exhaustion of natural reserves (in particular – owing to erosion – of the fertility of the soil), there is a danger that the industrial superstructure of the world might in the not too distant future grow out of proportion to a too narrow foundation in the production of foodstuffs and raw materials.

Another more far-reaching and highly important consideration must be mentioned here. The development of those countries could indeed become a veritable curse, if an attempt were made to erect on that social, economic and political morass with which we usually have to do in countries with a feudal agricultural society, an urban, industrial superstructure, or to extend one which is there already and which is questionable enough. That would amount to nothing less than transforming the present rural semi-proletariat, whose livelihood has not yet been torn adrift from all its anchors, into a complete industrial proletariat, of a most wretched type, and without roots. By this very means a soil is being prepared for Communism, more fruitful than can be imagined, more especially if at the same time an intellectual mass-proletariat is bred. It is a cause for the most serious apprehension that this sort of thing has been going on for a long time and is still making headway. This is, moreover, an example of the prevalent blindness towards those highly delicate problems of an intellectual and sociological order, with which we have to do here. Even now people lack a sufficiently clear understanding of the catastrophe which they are calling down, if, in the name of a 'higher standard of living' and everything appertaining thereto, they interfere with living and social conditions, some of which seem to belong to the Stone Age, and if, through misguided zeal, people are isolated from the social organism in which they were hitherto embedded, even if in poverty and illiteracy. Dissolution, proletarianization of the worst kind, demoralization, tensions of a highly dangerous nature and the mass-fabrication of an unhappy and discontented population – such are the inevitable results; and only Moscow stands to gain from a programme which was actually meant to steal the Communist's thunder.

Now all inflated and abortive development programmes are sooner or later forced back to the sphere of reality in so far as their implementation presupposes the help of foreign capital. Here we are faced with a situation which is tragically paradoxical that very emancipation of the colonial peoples of yesterday, which expressed itself, economically in the urge towards 'development', is now assuming forms calculated to shatter the legal, political and monetary conditions which could alone attract Western capital and yet it is on this capital that the desired development depends. In place of these conditions there is too often something else: dependence on obscure and unstable internal political conditions, submission to a legal system alien to the West, and which is not by any means always reputed for impartiality and incorruptibility, distrust and even hatred towards everything Western, the continuous threat of expropriation, open or concealed, obstinate resistance to any demand, however understandable, on the part of the investor for special security, possibilities for control, influence commensurate with the capital risk undertaken, and for the appointment of reliable, trained Western personnel. The most paralysing effects, however, result from the arbitrariness of a collectivist and inflationary economic policy, which is not rendered more attractive by the fact that it was inspired by Western models, an extravagant labour policy, which often does not even permit the maintainance of the wage advantage these countries originally enjoyed, a system of taxation which threatens capital yields with unpredictable levies, and finally an exchange control which deprives the Western investor and entrepreneur of that which remains.

An 'Underdeveloped Country' that is not – as the Belgian Congo – one of the few remaining colonial territories, whose credit standing is raised to a Western level by the backing of the motherland, does not offer the conditions necessary for the inflow of private foreign capital. If, however, the source of free and commercial capital cannot be induced to flow, a well of political finance is sunk. What will not flow freely must now be pumped to the surface by the pressure of conferences, propaganda and more or less veiled threats, even at the risk of diminishing or evaporating it in the same heat of passions which has already caused the source to dry up. If it is no longer possible to turn to a private investor of capital, attempts are made to mobilize the Governments of the West, and through them their tax-payers. Not even the World Bank is able to do much about this state of affairs, since it cannot afford to extend its loans too far beyong the limits set to purely commercial transactions, nor can it risk, in regard either to amounts involved or to the choice of projects to display considerably less caution than would a private investor. It is thus clear that the margin between capital assistance on a purely commercial basis – i.e. for a consideration – and purely political capital assistance which does not necessarily involve costs – is extremely narrow.

That is how matters stand. So long as there is no radical change in the whole policy and mentality of the 'underdeveloped countries', it is not to be expect-ed that development will be fructified to any appreciable extent by capital assistance on a commercial, i.e., free and non-gratuitous basis, and no hybrid arrangements, though they may conceal this state of affairs, can abolish it. Moreover, as the possibilities of capital assistance on a political basis ('compulsory formation of international capital') are very limited, this means, practically, that the development programmes will have to adapt themselves, in regard to their volume, direction and implementation, to the amount of capital available, and to the conditions under which it may be expected to be increased by private capital assistance from the West. There should be no doubt in the mind of any well-informed or thoughtful person, but that, even in the case of underdeveloped countries, an economic order based on the functions of a free market, competition and a free price mechanism, is superior to one based on a socialist system, and this notwithstanding any concessions which may be made to the prevailing lower grade of development and the different psychological and sociolo-gical conditions regarding governmental planning and controls.

INTERNATIONAL CAPITAL MOVEMENTS

The problem of the 'underdeveloped countries' has led us to the further, more general problem of international capital transactions, the importance of which calls for a few special remarks. The problem arises from the fact that international capital transactions have, since the last two decades, practically come to a standstill, in so far as they concern normal and voluntary investments abroad, which are guided, like those in the interior of any country, by considerations of private advantage. The knowledge has become general that here in the paralysis of international capital transactions, lies the crucial point at which the forces of economic progress get stuck more than anywhere else. Here is the bottleneck which has resisted all efforts to push through. Moreover, it is more and more generally agreed that the stoppage at this decisive point is fraught with consequences of so serious a nature, that to overcome the bottleneck is one of the principal conditions for decisive progress in the reconstruction of Western economy. Without it a new world economy can scarcely be contemplated.

But why this chronic stoppage in the international capital transactions of our time? The answer is given by the following argumentation which will bring us once more, by way of conclusion, to the basic problems of the international order.

In times when economy and society are profoundly shaken, as we have experienced in so unprecedented a manner during the last quarter of a century, it becomes apparent, for fairly obvious reasons, that international economy is the most sensitive part of the entire economic system. If money begins to fail, if standards of right, property and confidence break down, and the arbitrariness of Governments gains the upperhand, in a word, if the water level of civilization sinks by a hand's breadth it is the international economic relations which are the first to be left dry. Further, – they constitute that part of the entire world-wide economic process of our time, which will be the first to suffer from a revolutionary economic policy on the domestic scene i.e. inflationism and collectivism. International disintegration, as we know full well, is the inevitable consequence of the rigid organization, by national Governments, of the economic life in the interior of a country. Nevertheless, there is, in the domestic organism also a particularly sensitive part of the economy, a highly delicate nerve plexus which reacts before all else, and most strongly, to anything which unsettles the circumstances that determine peoples' confidence in law, government, money, the honesty of others, and in the future. This highly sensitive nerve plexus is the supply and investment of capital, because here decisions are taken for an always uncertain future. Such decisions are always entered into at some risk, which people only take when it bears some reasonable relationship to a possible gain. Let this relationship be disturbed by all sorts of measures which render gain so much more doubtful than loss, and capital investment will be discouraged and shrink.

Now we understand what has taken place in the sphere of international capital transactions of our time. The paralysis thereof will be seen to be the most natural thing in the world when we reflect on the fact that here we have the meeting-point of the two most sensitive, delicate and defenceless sectors of our modern economic system. If everything which has to do with investments is, in itself, already the most sensitive part of the whole system, this sensitivity will be augmented to an extreme degree if it is a question of investments effected in the tension-ridden field of international economy. International investments constitute the most sensitive spot in an already highly sensitive field. This spot is where the complex business of investment and that of international economic relations converge. Even if *international* traffic in goods and services is, in general, sufficiently robust – as we see it today – to assert itself more or less readily in an epoch of shocks and crises, the delicate plant of capital transactions cannot survive in this deadly climate. Even if *national* investment activity is, in general, sufficiently resilient to acclimatize itself, in a certain measure, within the borders of States, such international activity cannot survive. Either of these two risks, the one of international business and the other of capital investment, is already terrifying enough. Both combined exceed the measure of what people can be expected to face [7]).

Those are the stark facts which we have already met with peculiar clarity in our contemplation of the 'underdeveloped countries'. We saw how these countries have to choose between foreign capital and a policy which frightens away such capital. This is no less true, however, of the countries in Europe which are in dire need of capital. Whilst here conditions are, in other respects, far more favourable than in the case of the 'underdeveloped countries', the factor actually hindering international capital movements sticks out all the more plainly: *exchange control.*

NOTES

1. (p. 224) The International Monetary Fund:

General review: F. A. LUTZ, International Monetary Mechanisms, Princeton 1943; R. F. MIKESELL, The International Monetary Fund 1944-1949, International Conciliation (Carnegie Endowment) November 1949.

2. (p. 224) The wrong way, as represented by a collectivist and inflationary economic policy.

Detailed treatment: W. RÖPKE, Alte und neue Ökonomie, Sammelband 'Wirtschaft ohne Wunder' ed. by A. Hunold, Erlenbach-Zürich 1953.

3. (p. 225) European Economic Integration:

Detailed treatment: W. RÖPKE, Europäische Wirtschaftsgemeinschaft, Der Monat (Berlin), June, 1952 (also in an enlarged and revised French version: La communauté économique européenne, Bulletin d'Information et de Documentation de la Banque Nationale de Belgique, November 1952).

4. (p. 229) Problems concerning Customs Unions:

Principal works for reference: J. VINER, The Customs Union Issue, New York 1950, (a slightly different opinion: J. E. MEADE, The Removal of Trade Barriers: The Regional versus the Universal Approach, Economica, May 1951). The experiences of the Benelux Countries: J. VAN DER MEUSBRUGGHE, Les unions économiques, Brussels 1950; M. WEISGLAS, Benelux, Amsterdam 1949.

5. (p. 231):

Reference is made here to the report published originally under the title 'Ist die deutsche Wirtschaftspolitik richtig?' (Stuttgart 1950) together with an appreciative foreword by the Federal Chancellor, Dr. Adenauer.

6. (p. 234) Underdeveloped Countries:

Detailed treatment, including further indication of works on the subject: W. RÖPKE, Underdeveloped Countries, Ordo, Yearbook for economic and social order, Düsseldorf and Munich, 1953. Cf. also J. VINER, International Trade and Economic Development, Oxford 1953; HERBERT GROSS, Neue Märkte, Chancen in Übersee, Düsseldorf, 1953.

7. (p. 241) Paralysis and revival of international capital transactions:

The question has long been asked, whether, by means of binding agreements under international law – through an 'International Investment Code' – the hindrances referred to, in the way of a free flow of capital to countries in urgent need of funds, could be eliminated. Such a code would certainly not be without its uses, since it would set up standards against which it would be inconvenient and dangerous to transgress. This places us, however, in a known dilemma. Such agreements will, indeed only promise a genuine solution of the problem, if we may presuppose, not only a modicum of good will, but also a reasonable prospect that the Government of tomorrow will stand by the promises of the Government of today, being supported therein by public opinion in the country. Should this condition be fulfilled however, the Investment Code would not be needed, any more than it was needed in the by-gone days of a free world economy. And how are we going to enforce these standards? By submitting the dispute to the United Nations, or to the Hague Court? Already it is scarcely possible to ask such questions without sarcasm! The extreme maximum which might perhaps be gained thereby seems to me to have been anticipated by a proposal made recently by F. A. HAYEK in the New York periodical 'The Freeman'.

II

INTERNATIONAL MONETARY ORDER

WAYS TO CONVERTIBILITY

The words at which our last chapter closed, bring us once again to the cardinal problem, by the solution of which any genuine international order – extending far beyond the narrower, purely economic sphere, stands or falls. Compulsory exchange control has, indeed, revealed itself repeatedly as the final and most important cause of the disintegration of international economic relations. To overcome it, and to restore the free convertibility of currencies is therefore the goal on the attainment of which all else depends.[1])

In this matter, as in no other, the moment has come when an end must be made to all irresolution, through a courageous decision – prepared to go the whole way. Any further hesitation would, for various reasons, be undesirable, indeed dangerous. In the *first* place, there is practically nothing so demoralizing as a perpetually protracted discussion which is followed by no action. As, however, the abolition of exchange control is, in the last resort, a question of political morals this danger of demoralization is one to which the highest significance should be attached. *Secondly,* the circumstances, economic, political and psychological are more favourable today for the abolition of exchange control than they have been at any time since 1945, and we can by no means be certain that they will not once more deteriorate. *Thirdly,* it has been shown that now that the return to normal in economic matters has, in general made considerable progress, the shackling and distortions in international payments have become the point where further economic progress in the Western world is most seriously impeded. The importance can scarcely be disregarded which a final bursting of this bottleneck of international payments – which, as we have seen, is also a bottleneck in the international flow of capital – will have in deciding whether the development of economic forces is giving way to stagnation and retrogression, or whether an immense new field of expansion has been won.

With this is connected a *fourth* reason for the urgency of determined action. If, through the restoration of the convertibility of currencies the chief barrier to the international flow of capital in the Western world is not very soon eliminated, the danger will arise that those countries which are unable to maintain their investment activity by genuine savings at the rate which is required to secure progress and employment, will once more have recourse to inflationary investment financing, whereby the efforts for restoring convertibility would suffer a severe setback. A *fifth* reason lies in the fact that so long as exchange control continues to operate as the main cause of European economic disintegration, the efforts towards economic integration of Europe will be channelled in the direction of a continental autarchy and economic planning. It is right and necessary continually to expound – as in this book – to those romantic dreamers where European integration is concerned, the truth that as soon as the elimination of exchange control has reduced trade barriers in Europe to customs duties at reasonable rates, the problem of European economic integration will practically be solved, and in such a manner as to include the economic integration of countries outside Europe. If it is already difficult to find people able to grasp this, the cause of reason must inevitably become more hopeless the longer people in Europe are kept waiting for genuine, open integration through convertibility .Whoever holds the fictitious and closed integration of the romantic dreamers to be fraught with dangers, has all the stronger reason to create as soon as possible by the abolition of exchange control, the preliminary conditions for a Europe maintaining a free market economy and open to the whole world.

A *sixth* and last reason: – the more quickly and thoroughly an entirely new situation is created through the abolition of exchange control, the less will be the danger that through a change of Government the course of economic policy might once more become uncertain; for this course will be fixed decisively by convertibility, seeing that a return to exchange control would, for any government today, represent an extremely serious step. Once this is abolished and the abolition has moreover become – as we must earnestly desire – part of an international monetary system, it would be exceedingly difficult for any subsequent Government to destroy what has already been achieved, by a return to a 'leftist' course of economic policy. From this it follows not only that the basic assurance of a free market economy constitutes a sure foundation for convertibility, but that

245

the contrary also is true, i.e. that a transition to convertibility constitutes the surest anchor for a free-market economy. Whilst the opponents of a free-market economy are by no means uncertain of this, which explains their resistance, open or concealed, against convertibility, it is open to doubt whether, on the other hand, the adherents of a free-market economy understand equally clearly that a transition to convertibility is the essential step which has now to be taken in order to secure a free-market economy.

We said just now, that a return to convertibility is, in its essence, *a question of political morals*. The abolition of exchange control has that much in common with the gold standard, which, in this connexion, must be taken seriously once more, since the restoration of convertibility can only be viewed in its right setting if, over and above it, the necessity is perceived of reconstructing a real international monetary system, – for which, after much painful experience, the gold standard remains the only possible pattern. The strongest barrier in the way of a restoration of the gold standard is not objective, but subjective in nature; it is a belief – quite recent but which has already stiffened into a dogma – that the gold standard is something that has been finally done away with and which one is now ashamed to own up to. The discussion on both convertibility and the gold standard, which should be the ulterior aim, is still characterized by an inclination to treat the status quo, in spite of its entirely recent origin, as something hallowed by usage. It is in accordance with the law of mental inertia, that that which is customary is easily allowed to prolong itself into the future, as the philosophical insight is lacking which would cause people to remember that what is customary today represented a clean break with what was customary yesterday. However, that which, in the case of the gold standard is at least highly probable, may, in the case of convertibility, be considered practically as certain, i.e. that the inner readiness of conditions for such a step has gone far beyond any outer expression thereof. Thus, merely a strong push is necessary in order to bring to this hitherto hesitant desire for a change-over to an almost explosive reality.

Convertibility means the abolition of exchange control, and with this, the overcoming of the European Payments Union, which is built thereon. The unequivocal nature of this aim does not, of course preclude the possibility that it may be expedient to arrive at it through stages of an increasingly perfect convertibility, e.g. if the situation in any one country were not considered sufficiently ripe to permit that country to follow the example of Canada, where, at the end of 1951, exchange control was abolished without reservation, with one stroke of the pen. Most proposals with any claim to realism, practically envisage such an approach by progressive stages.

Among the manifold varieties which may be contrived, one must be ruled out as undesirable, namely the one which may be termed 'non-genuine' convertibility, the reason being that it constitutes a species of 'convertibility' which achieves the freedom of payments transactions from exchange control at the cost a corresponding stiffening of import restrictions, and thus sacrifices substance to appearance. Such a *pseudo-convertibility* – sometimes termed merely 'monetary', – is dishonest, and unsuitable for attaining the object for which the abolition of exchange control is intended, namely the restoration of a free multilateral world-trade which, freed from bureaucratic arbitrariness and discriminatory practices will generally – i.e. limited only by customs tariffs which cannot so readily be removed – re-establish free prices and competition as a regulating and stimulating device also in international economic relations. The restoration of convertibility must inevitably imply the immovable principle that quantitative (collectivist) foreign-trade controls must cease to be the chief means of controlling the balance of payments. The responsible authorities in every country must be enjoined to produce a natural balance of payments equilibrium instead of an artificial one, and this by the time-honoured instruments proper to a balance of payments policy: for the equalization of short-term fluctuations, through an 'open market policy' on the exchange market (playing on the reserves by the purchase and sale of gold and foreign currency) and, for the equalization of fundamental fluctuations, through the regulation (restrictive or expansive as occasion demands) of the national economic aggregates (credit policy, supplemented by an appropriate budget). A further instrument which they will have to be permitted to use, in exceptional circumstances, but during a period of transition, and within certain limits, is the adjustment of the rate of exchange.

Whatever technique may be selected for the transition to convertibility, the result will depend on *two basic preliminary conditions* which correspond to the two instruments mentioned as pertaining to a classical balance of payments policy. One of these preliminary conditions is indicated by the simple truth, never sufficiently emphasized, that the way to convertibility leads inevitably through *a change in the economic policy of each individual country*. Convertibility begins at home, so that what happens within each country is of decisive importance in regard to the restoration of an external equilibrium, through a non-inflationary freemarket economy. There would be no sense, after the experiences encountered, in reverting once more to the EPU principle of the 'cheese-plate cover' and attempting to squeeze as many countries as possible into some international apparatus, whilst the causes of disturbance to the external equilibrium – which actually lie in national economic policies – continue to operate. We must begin at the bottom, i.e. with the individual nation, just as exchange control was introduced independently by each nation, although there was a mutual influence in both the world of ideas and the world of economic facts. This does not mean to deny that the step to convertibility becomes easier for each individual country in proportion as more countries decide simultaneously to take it, thus giving one another mutual support. Only by such means is it possible to create once more an international monetary system worthy of the name. National economic rehabilitation and international cooperation must be complementary the one to the other, and only through such a combination is success to be expected.

The other root-problem, on the solution of which a general return to convertibility depends, is the *restoration of general liquidity,* so as to allow each country sufficient manoeuvering space to parry any blows against equilibrium, promptly and effectually. In so far as single countries, in key positions, have not yet been able, through an increase in their reserve funds, to reach the amount necessary for their international liquidity, it will be necessary and expedient to obtain assistance for them from countries owning a sufficiency of gold, notably from the United States of America, in the form of exchange loans or the creation of an international convertibility fund. Meanwhile it should however be noted that the most important step to a restoration of international liquidity, is the *revival of the international flow of credit*. The more this can be reactivated, the smaller need be the size of national reserves, and *vice versa,* which provides the main explanation of the fact noted in many quarters, that at the time of the gold standard countries managed to exist with remarkably small reserves, also the other fact that the movement of gold among EPU countries is much more considerable than it ever was at the time of a gold standard because it must to a great extent substitute for international credit transactions, which the policy of exchange control has immobilized. That is one of the main reasons why a return to convertibility must not be limited to transactions on current account, but must include, as an essential condition, the freedom of international credit and capital transactions [2]).

This demand is opposed by the fact that the main difficulty, as regards a return to convertibility is thought by many to lie in the danger of an incalculable export of capital, which is termed – with a frown, and, assuming a slightly demagogic air – the *flight* of capital. Thus, it is thought in many quarters that the abolition of exchange control should be limited, for the present, to transactions on current account, and that a more or less strict control of capital transactions should be retained. The idea appears to be clear enough, and its carrying out to be simple. And yet neither is the case.

In the first place it is by no means easy to prove whether this danger of a capital 'flight' is not very much overrated specifically in the event of an abolition of exchange-control, and in the climate created by the then prevailing economic policies which alone would allow such a move. Where would this 'fugitive' capital come from? What would be the motives? How large would the amounts be, at most? Whither would it be fleeing? Who would have an interest in liquidating his assets, which are probably invested in business of some kind, and transferring them abroad, unless it was somebody who would follow his money abroad? Secondly, it is an error to consider 'capital flight' as merely the manifestation of an incalculable psychological factor. Incentive and possibility depend much more decisively on internal economic policy, particulary on credit policy, the brakes of which need only to be drastically applied in order, should occasion arise, not only to check any 'capital flight' but even to compel 'fugitive' capital to return home, as happened in Italy in 1947, through Einaudi's currency reform, and recently in Austria. As, indeed, a drastic credit policy constitutes, in any event, the primary condition for the equilibrium of its balance of payments, any country which, by taking such action, has shown itself ready for the abolition of exchange control, should *ipso facto* be reckoned as one in which the possibilities of capital flight are very limited.

This brings us to a third point. The idea that a bolt must be pushed in order to prevent 'capital flight' is rooted usually in the desperate notion that, when everything has been done to ruin the international credit of a country, the best one can do is to hold tightly on to what one has, transforming it by this very policy of control, into a 'capital-trap'. A more courageous economic policy, and one giving better hope for the future, would be to put the question quite differently, starting with the assumption that everything depends on getting rid of the defeatist concept of a 'one-way street' where capital transactions are concerned (in the sense of a possible 'capital flight'), and to develop traffic 'in the other direction'. The greatest hindrance to this is, however, the exchange control itself. It amounts to the 'moral devaluation' of a currency, a stigma which must result in capital gravitating towards foreign countries as naturally as water flows by its gravity. It gives rise to a 'mousetrap' currency with the well-known consequences thereof; it corresponds to an economy of compulsion in the interior of a country, which always seeks to 'make a fair distribution' of available goods, instead of unleashing the forces that will increase production. It surely belongs to the world of totalitarian and collectivist concepts, to treat those persons as criminals who refuse tamely to expose their savings, financial assets and investments to the fate, which a collectivist and inflationary economic policy in their country is preparing, or threatens to prepare for them. One might, with equal right, attempt to prohibit skilled workers from emigrating to avoid such fate, – alleging their action to be a wicked 'labour flight', and arguing that this does as much harm to the national economy as does 'capital flight'. In both cases this constitutes the melancholy privilege of totalitarian States. It is more civilized and at the same time more intelligent, to suit economic policy to people, and not people to economic policy.

This leads to the conclusion, which is anything but frivolous, that an abolition of exchange control in otherwise favourable circumstances (presupposing, in particular an appropriate discipline in monetary and financial policy, also the 'right' rate of exchange) will actually eliminate that 'flight' of capital, on account of which it is thought that exchange control cannot be given up. Here too the elimination of controls will create its own prerequisites; it will break a vicious circle in which we have been moving for the last decade. A currency, too, has its 'goodwill', which is just as important for the welfare of the country as is the quality of its products, and the prosperity of Switzerland rests as much on the one as on the other. One of the essential props of her balance of payments is the 'goodwill' of the Swiss franc. To regain this prop should be the main objective for each country, which has lost it. The most essential condition for this is, next to stability, a free currency, i.e. convertibility. That in itself is reason enough for the utmost wariness in the application of such controls on the flow of capital as shall, after the restoration of convertibility, still be deemed necessary. The door which is closed from the inside against those without, is also secured on the outside, against those within. That which, in virtue of a purely static calculation, we think to gain for the balance of payments, may be lost many times over in the dynamic reality.

A NEW INTERNATIONAL MONETARY ORDER

The abolition of exchange control by an individual country is, for that country itself, of tremendous significance if it wishes to restore an essential portion of its overall social order on the basis of freedom, and enjoy the fruits offered by the 'goodwill' of a healthy currency. There is sufficient reason, therefore, to restore free convertibility for one's own country, even if this cannot be made part of a joint international action. We must repeat, however, that nothing short of such international action will constitute a return to convertibility in its full sense, because more important than the advantage to an individual country, pursuing this course independently, is the reconstruction of a genuine *international* monetary order, without which any international order, as a whole, would lack an essential part. After the failure of the Bretton Woods system, this was the vital purpose at the founding of EPU, and even if, – with all due respect to its merits –, the functioning of the latter did not, in this broader sense, come up to expectations, there is no reason why, today, this same objective shall not be attained by a better method.

For the attainment of this purpose, one must acquire a right historical perspective, by realizing fully that the present objective is to build up, after more than twenty years, from the chaos of national exchange controls, a new monetary system for the West, capable of functioning, in place of the international monetary system, which collapsed at that time, and which was imperfect and, above all, wrongly guided by the United States, resting as it did on a gold standard which had become meaningless. This consideration brings our thoughts inevitably back to the gold standard itself, since this constituted the international monetary order of the old economy and appears actually to be indispensible for the new economy also, after all attempts to find even a half-way substitute for it have failed.

The substance of these attempts was to combine money and gold by means of a simple but ingenious coupling mechanism, so that – at any rate for international payments – money could be exchanged for gold, and gold for money, at a fixed rate. The deeper significance of this currency order for international economic relations lay in the fact that it created an actual international monetary system, which not only united the national currencies, one with another, in a fixed relationship, but at the same time guaranteed the free exchange of national monetary units at this fixed rate, so that all countries on the gold standard were united, for practical purposes, in an international payments community. The three principal postulates for an international monetary system, namely those of *unity, stability* and *freedom,* were fulfilled to perfection by the gold standard, and none of the systems, which have been proposed as substitutes, are in any way equal to it.

Such an international payments community of free and stable currencies is, indeed, an essential sign both of a genuine world economy and of international economic relations along free-market lines. From this the following may be deduced: – The gold standard, which is practically the only possible form for such a payments community, was, in actual fact, an essential component of the old world-economy; it may well be described as the (liberal and economic) international monetary order which conforms to the free market economy, in contrast to the collectivist (political) order of national paper-currencies patched together by planned controls. It will therefore become an essential and, it appears, an indispensible ingredient of a new world-economy, in so far as no fundamentally different form can be found for an international monetary system which conforms to a free-market economy, i.e. any fundamentally different possibility of a genuine international payments community of free and stable currencies, suitable for a human society not bound together in a single world State. It must be understood, however, that experience and reflection both testify to the absence of any prospect of finding a substitute for the gold standard of even approximately the same value. It follows therefore that the question 'A gold standard or not'? amounts to such questions as 'A free-market or a collectivist monetary system?' 'Non-political selfregulation or political control'? and finally 'A free-market economy or collectivism'? In the recognition of these facts one should not, under any circumstances allow oneself to be confused by muddled thinking or vague sentiments,

252

although gold has unfortunately become of late – and in a considerable measure – the object of a real 'complex', which prevents many people from logical and sober thinking, and makes them incapable of following up any objective analysis of the actual interrelation of facts. What has to be said about the unassailable position of gold in human society in general, has been set forth in my earlier book *Die Gesellschaftskrisis der Gegenwart* (5th ed, p. 403 et seq.).

Such concepts would, even a short time ago, have brought on one the gloomy reputation of a rather limited mental capacity and a hopelessly antiquated outlook. That collectivists of all shades of opinion reject a gold standard and even, on certain occasions speak of gold, in its general function as the commodity with the highest liquidity, as being worthless, is entirely understandable and corresponds to their idea – which is perfectly correct – that gold and a gold standard belong, in fact, to the liberal (free-market economy), and not to the collectivist, world. When, however, as has been happening for a long time even in quarters where adherence was expressed to the basic principles of a free-market and a world economy, gold and a gold standard, have been relegated to the sphere of outworn things, this has always been a sign of intellectual confusion, and would seem to be more and more recognized as such. This confusion had its origin in the fact that people did not understand the vital functions of gold in the machinery of world economy, and they thought that while maintaining a fundamental loyalty to the free-market economy they could nevertheless dally with the ideas of collectivism. The gold standard was criticized on the ground that gold was no stable measure of values, – as if the national paper-currencies had given proof of a greater stability, and as if much could not be done to increase the relative stability of the value of gold – the intrinsic worth of which is already high and makes it so universally sought after in disturbed times. Jokes were made to the effect that in South Africa gold was dug out of the earth with much toil, only to be buried once more in the vaults of Central Banks, – and in the meantime we have learnt that it is much more senseless and costly to expend much toil in bringing people into the world, and educating them, only to bury them once more, in an unproductive fashion, in the foreign exchange offices, among mountains of forms, if not actually in the prisons of a collectivist enforced economy. The gold standard was held responsible for the extraordinary unevenness in the international distribution of gold – which is very much like the views of a layman in medical science, who might try to make the water in a person's body responsible for dropsy, instead of tracing it to deep disturbances in the circulation. It was deplored that the gold standard did not leave to a Government full autonomy with regard to its national economic policy – as if there ever could be such autonomy if there are close international economic interrelations [3]).

If the general attitude towards gold and a gold standard seems recently to have become more favourable, this is probably bound up with another change of view which we have observed in the sphere of *ideas on the theory of money*. A contempt for gold was recently accompanied by a boundless overestimation of the possibilities of monetary management which resulted from a rather mechanical over-simplification of the quantity theory of money – however indispensable such simplification may be to grasp the essential interrelations. It seems that dangerous tendencies, only too near at hand in monetary thought prevailed, tendencies of mathematization, of thinking in terms of unreal aggregate values (e.g. 'quantity of goods', 'price-level', 'volume of investments', 'volume of savings', 'value of money', 'purchasing power parity', etc.), of expressing qualitative and functional things in terms of quantities, and of inadmissible simplification. This over-simplification of the quantity theory of money made its subscribers feel that the esoteric monetary doctrine in their possession was far superior to the barbarous imperfection of the gold standard, and that they were sufficiently equipped with a few intricate equation systems to look down contemptuously on those who preferred to trust themselves to the well-tried efficacy of a monetary system on a metal basis. Nevertheless it has in the meantime come to be increasingly realized how questionable this monetary variety of technocracy is, since it has become obvious what a world which is ruled by systems of equations instead of by a gold standard really looks like, and that gold, driven out by the proverbial pitchfork, always returns by the backdoor.

Anyone who, notwithstanding, still hesitates to acknowledge the basic principles of the gold standard, should contemplate that a decision in favour of a world economy includes, for all practical purposes, a decision in favour of this international monetary order. As matters stand today, therefore, a world economy presupposes a gold standard. The contrary is equally true, – that a gold standard presupposes a world economy. Just as a fundamentally free multilateral world economy cannot function without

254

a gold standard, the gold standard is also unable to function without a fundamentally free multilateral world economy, i.e. one which allows all the national economies that are part of it to adjust to an external disequilibrium by means of appropriate movements of prices and quantities, which would be free to move in all directions. Such a world economy must be fundamentally free from 'non-conforming' commercial and monetary measures (those of economic planning, such as exchange control, quotas, foreign trade monopolies and barter agreements), and any 'conforming' interference with trade (in particular, import tariffs) should, as a general rule, not reach prohibitive proportions, least of all in countries like the United States, which, by reason of their wealth, importance and position as international creditors are mainly responsible for the functioning of the world economy.

Such freedom and mobility in the economic process which constitute the basic conditions both of the gold standard, and of a world economy, rest, on their part on two final and ultimate principles. *On the one hand,* the necessary minimum of economic freedom both within the national economies and in international economic relations, is incompatible with *market rigidity, group anarchy* and *the paralyzation of production by monopolies,* all of which have dominated the economy to an ever-increasing degree during the last two decades, and have made it a battle-field for embittered and narrow-minded contending interests. How, finally, this portentous question is to be effectually met, and an irreducible minimum of mobility restored, has become, indeed, the fateful question of our time. An answer to this question can, however, only be found if it is realized that the ultimate causes of the paralysis of the economic process, through the tenacious defence of each individual and group interest, are identical with the ultimate causes of the general social crisis of the present time; the emergence of the masses, proletarianization, and the infinite uncertainty of modern existence. The detailed conclusion from such a situation for a reform of our society and economy, have been stated in an earlier book by the author. We are still convinced that this is the only way of salvation, and are entirely sceptical concerning every attempt to solve the problem by some well-contrived mechanical method.

On the other hand a world economy (including a gold standard) positively requires, as does the free market economy as such, a stable frame-work of *political, moral and legal standards,* such as will secure to international economic relations in general, and, in particular to the gold standard, which depends so essentially on honesty, consideration and loyalty to principles, the indispensable climate of confidence, reliability, continuity and peaceful disposition. The gold standard is therefore not merely a matter of monetary technique, but is the final outcome of a deep-reaching ramification of economic political and sociological conditions, and attainable only at this price, at the same price at which, alone, a general international order, grounded on peace, justice and consideration, may be purchased. This means that a gold standard and a world economy are only possible among national economies, which are constituted as free-market economies, and which have retained that minimum of elasticity in regard to prices and costs which is presupposed in a free-market economy. Whoever holds a world economy, and with it a gold standard, to be worthy objectives, because, for him, peace, prosperity, security, justice and universality are also worth striving for, will immediately recognize in the conditions essential for a world economy and for a gold standard signposts for the orientation of his country's internal economic policy. Thus, it is shown once more that all the urgent reform problems of our time, constitute an inseparable unity and that, without a glance at society as a whole, they cannot be rightly formulated, let alone solved.

But can we go back to the past? Has not something collapsed, which seems to mock any attempt to restore it? And are we then reduced, for lack of any other alternative, to accept this extremity and make the best of it?

Such questions, implying resignation, are entirely understandable, but they are also highly dangerous. For they are indeed the favourite refuge of all whose views are unclear or undecided, also of the extra-ordinarily large number of time-servers and of persons with interests in the present-day state of affairs. Everywhere in the social life of today, where programmes and ideas have gone bankrupt, their domination is artificially prolonged by the concept, deliberately spread, that we must stick to them, otherwise chaos will ensue. We have transported to an island, the dreaming palm-beaches of which promised an island of the blessed. And now that it has proved to be a devils' island, attempts are being made to argue us out of the truth of our situation, or to frighten us into accepting it, by assuring us that our ships are rotten and that the idea of building new ships would only occur to weak-minded folk or to visionaries. It is our fate, they say, to end our lives on this island of serpents.

Is this really our fate? Or shall we not rather examine our ships as to their seaworthiness, repair them and, if necessary, build new ones?

One last thought. May we not ask ourselves – rightly – whether it may not be that, just as at the end of the Thirty Years War, all the energies which had given life to the wars of religion, were spent, so we, today, have already passed the climax of the mighty tide of revolutionary ideologies and are heading towards a new age, which looks for quiet, order, work and inner reflection, an age which is heartily tired of high-sounding words programmes, ideologies and myths, of material and intellectual mass-existence, of slogans, demagogues and watchwords, and is turning once more to the consideration of the things which are of lasting value to an impartial and honest person? This is nothing more than a question, which, however, we venture to submit – not without some hope, although without any self-deception. Neither in good fortune nor ill, neither in hope nor fear, must we let ourselves be troubled by the supposed dictates of any 'spirit of the age', nor be turned either from a decision which rests with ourselves or from the duty incumbent on each one of us to see to his own spiritual enlightenment, when such issues are at stake as the social crisis of the present time and its overcoming in a *civitas humana* and an international order.

NOTES

1. (p. 244) Convertibility:

I have treated in further detail this problem, which is exceedingly complicated, in my study entitled 'Wege zur Konvertibilität', which appears in the compendium 'Konvertibilität' edited by A. Hunold (Erlenbach-Zürich, 1954).

2. (p. 249) The role of gold:

The question arises here – and is much discussed today – whether the most effectual and promptest help which the United States could offer to restore international liquidity, would not be a noticeable rise in the American price for the purchase of gold (today $ 35 per ounce of fine gold). One can, with perfect right, refer to the fact that the rigid adherence to an unchanged goldprice, after the first World War, was one of the mistakes of that time which was fraught with the direst consequences, because, by reason of the world inflation since 1914, it came into a dangerously wrong relationship to the international level of prices. This led partly to heavy deflation, partly, however, to a gold standard bent on gold saving methods (Gold Exchange Standard) also to a colossal edifice built-up of intertwined international credit relations, which collapsed in the international liquidity crisis of 1931, burying world economy beneath it right up to the present time. Thus, the conviction is beginning rightly, if slowly, to dawn, that, with the official purchasing price of gold as it is today, the international value of all the gold available has become far too low to bear the strain of free international payments transactions. Should such a rise actually be effected, most of the problems of international liquidity would probably solve themselves, and against this the disadvantages, so often cited, would weigh lightly. It would be a measure calculated to put an end to a state of affairs which, anyhow, cannot be maintained permanently entirely abnormal, – a measure without which the reintroduction of a gold standard is unthinkable. It would of course, be dangerous to present this tension-reducing measure to a world determined to use it for the continuation of its undisciplined economic and monetary policies, instead of for a transition, through internal economic stabilization, to an external monetary freedom. It remains, however, to be seen, whether it might still not be possible to induce the United States to change their rigid attitude in this matter, if a sufficiently large block of countries were to submit to them a serious and well-founded plan for a return to convertibility, pointing out that a final adaptation of the price of gold to the international level of prices would constitute the most effectual, and the promptest help. For further details cf. the statements in the first German edition of this book, pp. 315-332 and 336.

3. (p. 254) International integration and national policies of stimulating economic activity:

A more detailed treatment will be found in the first German edition, pp. 324 et seq.; ALLAN G. B. FISHER, International Implications of Full Employment in Great Britain, London, 1946; W. RÖPKE, The Economics of Full Employment, An analysis of the U. N. Report on National and International Measures for Full Employment, New York 1952.

EUROPEAN FREE TRADE – THE GREAT DIVIDE*

The common market and the free trade area are the latest methods by which the goal of European economic integration is being sought. One or the other of them has captured the support of most of the champions of a European economic order because it has become widely believed that the possibilities for integration offered by the Organization for European Economic Co-operation and the European Payments Union are now exhausted.

The belief in new devices for integration extends also, of course, to Euratom, which was set up with the common market. Euratom has attracted much less attention than it should have done, which is perhaps to its advantage. For it is doubtful whether it could survive any searching analysis. Weighty evidence that it is necessary has neither been asked for nor given. It has been launched behind a cloud of vague ideas of a 'new industrial revolution', reminiscent of the technocracy of the 1930s, and if there is a core of fact within these ideas it is largely inaccessible. Here it is not proposed to give Euratom the examination which it merits. We shall merely note that it shares the principle of a supra-national organization with the common market and the European Coal and Steel Community. While the common market is already under way the career of the plan for a free trade area has been chequered. Those who from the beginning have spied danger in the new approach to European unity are seeing their fears confirmed. For the frightening prospect now looms forth that if the common market is not capped by the free trade area it will disintegrate Europe. What was meant to be mortar may prove to be dynamite.

If Europe now faces a crisis it is because confusion surrounds the concept of economic integration. In its ten fruitful years the OEEC has gone far to unify Europe, and the common market is envisaged as a great new stride along the same route. It is not. Its path, which was opened up by the Coal and Steel Community, is very different from that of the OEEC, and the two cannot for long be followed together [1]).

* Originally published in *The Banker*, September 1958. See preface.

The true task of integration is in fact re-integration. It is to restore the Europe of free exchanges and multilateralism, in which the only obstacles to trade were customs duties, and these of moderate proportions. Such duties, albeit artificially produced, were comparable to the costs of transport between countries, and did not seriously hinder the free interchange of goods and money which is the mark of integration. It was only in the minds of those who did not see that the market was the great economic integrator and who thought that economic units must be co-terminous with political units, that this was not an integrated Europe. The market was not thought of as a specifically European economic integrator, since it integrated the European countries with the rest of the world also; but European integration does not require European exclusiveness.

THE COLLECTIVIST CONTRADICTION

The European economy was fragmented, mainly after 1931, by exchange controls and quantitative trading restrictions; and these devices, which became so popular and seemed so new, were the result of the spread of the belief in policies of inflation and economic planning, which in turn they strengthened. As national collectivism was thus the cause of disintegration, the task of re-integration was to remove it. But this could not be easy or pleasant; first, because it required widespread, and now deep-rooted, notions to be abandoned, and secondly, because a tempting alternative to the removal of the original cause of disintegration has appeared to be available. This is the policy of supra-national collectivism.

However, a scheme for a European collectivist order must have grave disadvantages. First, if it were practicable, it would create a closed bloc, different only in size from its former national blocs. External controls, internal planning, and inflation, which go hand in hand under collectivism, would continue to do so, though on a larger stage; and thus integration would proceed without performing the task of liberation for which it is needed. Secondly, it would not in fact be practicable. For European economic planning requires a strong centralized European government; and even the most fervent planners of the new Europe seek no more, and know that no more is feasible, than a loose political federation.

Hence every step along the path of European collectivism or *dirigisme* subjects our continent to rising political stresses and strains. It has not been possible to extend the Coal-Steel Community beyond the Six, and the chances are faint that the common market will show any greater power to spread. Here is the dilemma of the Coal-Steel/common market method of integrating Europe. It requires a supra-national political order which, if it is combined with economic planning, most of Europe will not submit to. As economic planning is of its essence, it therefore cannot integrate the whole of Europe.

We must now, however, come to a dilemma of the opposite, or liberal, method of integration. If the European economy was disintegrated by national collectivism, it was as part of the disintegration of the world economy. Why then is anything necessary beyond the abandonment by the individual European nations of their collectivist practices? What need is there for, and what relevance is there in, a specifically European movement towards freedom? Why not leave it to GATT, the General Agreement on Tariffs and Trade? Or, if GATT is insufficiently effective, why not strengthen it? Clearly there is a conflict between liberal principles and regionalism, for regionalism does not make sense unless it creates some kind of preferential arrangement.

This conflict arises from the needs of the strategy of economic liberation. Unfortunately the attempt to dislodge the hold of collectivism from within each country has in general not succeeded. Economic planning, the welfare state, full employment, cheap money, and the like are fountains of extraordinarily seductive slogans, and the frontal attack on them, in favour of the liberation of external trade and exchange, is heavily handicapped. As liberation can plausibly be made to appear to be a way of doing the foreigner a favour, few people will be enthusiastic about it without international agreements and institutions that will produce, or promise, reciprocity. Hence regionalism, at least as a first step, is unavoidable. In fact we know that regionalism, in the form of the OEEC and the EPU, has been successful. It has loosened the grip of economic nationalism in Europe as probably nothing else could have done; and in the process it has done no harm, and much good, to the rest of the world.

OPEN CLUB OR RESTRICTIVE BLOC?

The test of regionalism as a means of integration by liberation is whether it is of the 'open' or 'closed' character. A regional arrangement of an open kind starts in a limited area but is capable of, and indeed naturally tends to produce, extension to the rest of the world. A closed arrangement is one which is, at least in practice if not in theory, incapable of extension, and naturally tends to raise barriers between its region and the rest of the world. The OEEC and the EPU clearly pass this test. They can move, when it is desired, from a preferential to a general non-discriminatory system. Thus there is no reason why they should not be gradually extended to the dollar area, and in practice, through the mechanism of the exchange markets and commodity markets, dollar transactions have been coming within their ambit for some time. And the EPU could be gradually transformed into a system of free convertibility by, for example, increasing the amount of debit balances payable in gold. These are not mere theoretical possibilities. They comprise part of a practical policy, and if achieved they would make the strategy of European integration conform once again to the requirements of true internationalism.

Contrast this with the pattern of the 'closed bloc'. The Coal-Steel Community may be taken as the best-tried modern example. In theory it does leave the door open for further countries to join, but in practice, as we have already suggested, the principle of supra-national controlling power was bound to keep the door closed. And furthermore, the closer the integration achieved by the Community, with its highly complicated structure, the more difficult and unpleasant would be the adjustments required for any extension of membership. It is for these reasons that the OEEC has been able to comprehend the whole of non-communist Europe while the Coal-Steel Community has had to limit itself to six countries. But the fundamental character of the difference between the open and the closed system has not yet been fully appreciated – as may be seen from the fact that the architects of the common market seem to have assumed that they can continue to make use of EPU and enjoy its benefits. Only recently, and to their surprise, has the possibility presented itself to them that their project may destroy both OEEC and EPU.

A major reason why it has been possible to push these contradictions of policy out of the field of debate is the expectation that at least within the common market the benefits of free trade will be reaped. Here the champion of the common market seems to borrow the liberal's clothes. In fact the expectation is hardly well-founded. First, there are the hazards of the long transitional period. Secondly, and more important, the final result in terms of economic benefits will depend far less upon the freedom of trade within the Six than upon the degree of inflation, *dirigisme*, and external protectionism practised by them. Thirdly, freedom of trade within a large bloc that is under the pressure of uniformity has a feature that is too seldom mistrusted. Here free trade is confused with the ideal of mass-production, which is too often lauded without qualification as the source of American success. In fact the case of Switzerland, among others, shows that high prosperity and the giant firm or plant are not necessarily inter-linked. Of course free trade among nations must produce some geographical concentration of production, but that is not the same thing as the concentration of enterprises [2]). Free trade will tend to weed out inefficient enterprises, large or small.

This last point enables us to place in perspective some of the complaints that are being made about France. The spirit with which France approaches the common market differs from that of the others, apart from Italy, because it is a spirit of anxious defence rather than cheerful confidence in the expansionist forces of unrestricted international competition. This arises from the fear that France may fall victim to a process of European concentration which would destroy the still un-American character of the French economy without conspicuously raising productivity. The French are not so wrong about this as their critics believe. Where the French are really wrong is in joining the common market despite these anxieties, without relieving their economy from its dangerous and long-established inflationary pressures, and indeed hoping that the common market will free them from the need to do so. In joining in this spirit they unavoidably become hostile to the free trade area.

This brings us to the nub of the problem facing the common market. There is a line running right across Europe which divides it into two groups of countries, and this line splits the common market itself. On the one side are the few countries that, by the exercise of monetary controls and by reliance on market forces, have achieved equilibrium with the rest of the world and thus a *de facto* convertible currency; on the other side are those suffering chronic difficulties in their external payments. If the second group followed the example of the first, the problem of European economic integration would be largely solved. But for this we do not need a common market; and without it the common market will leave Europe disintegrated.

But will not the association of countries from the two groups have a beneficial influence? Unfortunately the trend will be the other way. Market forces and monetary discipline are much harder to make popular than 'welfare' policies and inflation, and the countries pursuing the latter will infect those of the former. We may realize too late that, where they exist, the market economy and monetary discipline should not have been sacrificed on the altar of 'Europe'.

'HARMONIZATION' TO INFLATION

Thus integration will tend to settle at the lowest degree within the Six of economic freedom, monetary discipline and restraint in social policies. This tendency expresses itself in the demand for 'harmonization' of labour costs, characteristically put forward by the country with the weakest balance of payments. Of course, 'harmonization' means the levelling upwards, not downwards, of costs, and is as grotesquely incompatible with the requirements of free trade as the familiar demand by American protectionists for duties to balance the difference between the standards of living of America and the countries supplying her. Trade does not require equality of the costs of factors of production; in some countries labour cost may be high, in others capital cost, or some other cost. In fact it is free trade that tends to reduce the differences between factor costs, but the trade must come first. If factor costs are first 'harmonized' the trade cannot take place.

Now the high French labour costs (at current rates of exchange) are not an expression of high productivity. They have been pushed up by political pressure so far beyond the rise in productivity that they have become the mainspring of inflation. And the crises in the balance of payments and losses of reserves of gold and foreign exchange have not been stemmed even by new import restrictions, export subsidies or the devaluation of the franc. Thus the demand for 'harmonization' becomes a demand that the French economy should be restored to equilibrium not by monetary discipline and the proper adjustment of rates of exchange, but by inducing other countries to fall into line with French costs. The 'harmonization of social costs' comes to mean the 'harmonization of inflationary pressure'.

What must be understood is that, both in the common market and the free trade area, it is impossible to combine more than two of the following three things: free trade, fixed rates of exchange, and uncoordinated monetary policies. One of them must be sacrificed.

First, the sacrifice might be free trade, a member country falling out one line being allowed to defend its balance of payments by what the Rome Treaty euphemistically calls '*mesures de sauvegarde nécessaires*'. It is interesting that for the first time in the history of customs unions the possibility of restricting trade in order to regulate the balance of payments is not regarded as a '*dolus eventualis*' but is solemnly incorporated in the treaty of union. But it must be presumed that trade restrictions cannot be the primary instrument of adjustment to external fluctuations.

RATHER A MONARCHY . . .

Secondly, the sacrifice might be fixed rates of exchange. Now no doubt some current rates are wrong and need adjustment; and no doubt also there is something to be said for floating rates. Still this is hardly a practicable solution. I have elsewhere claimed that Switzerland would rather become a monarchy than renounce the stability of its franc exchange rate; and this is only an extreme formulation of a point of view dominant in all Europe. We have recently seen that when devaluation is necessary in France it is extremely difficult to get because it threatens the prestige of the Government; while when revaluation is desirable in Germany it is met by fierce and successful opposition from industrial and trading interests.

Thus the only reasonable choice is the sacrifice of entirely independent and unharmonized monetary policies. Co-ordination of monetary discipline must be agreed upon. But this immediately raises the question of the degree of discipline that it is desirable and possible to reach. We can easily say what is desirable. It is such a degree of discipline for all as has already been achieved in Switzerland and Germany; it can be defined as the measure of monetary control that would produce equilibrium with the freely convertible currencies of the world and thus make European currencies fully convertible. But what hope is there of achieving this? We have already suggested that the countries of 'full employment before all else', of inflation, and of advanced 'welfare' policies are much more likely to draw the others their way than to be drawn away from it by them. Thus would the sick contaminate the sound. This is a problem for both the free trade area and the common market. But the free trade area has this advantage: if a member country has the will to resist, it is much less likely to be dragged down to the lowest common level of monetary discipline than a country in the common market.

Now let us consider the rift between the Six and the rest of the world that will be caused by the adoption of the common outside tariff. There are three main reasons why the rift will become wide and deep. First, although the Rome Treaty requires the common tariff to be the arithmetic average of the four levels of France, Germany, Italy and Benelux, there will in fact be strong pressure, as interests ensconce themselves behind the new tariff wall, to raise it ultimately above the average. In any case, averaging hardly helps outsiders, even where it brings down, say, the French or Italian tariff; for they will have to compete with duty-free goods of Germany and Benelux.

HOW PROTECTION MAY EXTEND

Secondly, the greater the diversity of the productive structures of the countries forming the union, the more likely is it that the total protectionist pressure will rise. For producer interests which now exist solely in one of the Six will demand protection in all of the Six. In this way, the extension of the tariff area may have perverse effects [3]). The economies of the Six may not be judged to be conspicuously heterogeneous, it is true, but they have been made artificially more heterogeneous by the inclusion of the overseas territories, so that even tropical products must enter into the account. Thus revenue duties such as those on coffee and bananas, which exist in a country like Germany, will now become protective duties for all. In the case of some important raw materials most of the Six will find that they have erected barriers, and hence cost-burdens, that are new; and this immediately makes the common market an awkward bedfellow for the free trade area. For the countries of the rest of the free trade area can hardly be expected to burden themselves with the common market level of tariffs on raw materials [4]). Thus the price of the integration of the Six becomes less integration *vis-à-vis* the rest of the world.

Thirdly, there will be the effect of the period of transition. The line of least resistance will almost certainly be to tackle those duties first which affect producers outside the union; those which affect competition within it will be low on the list for change. It will be an easy concession to 'Europe' to reduce the partners' mutual duty on oranges. The Italian producers could not want anything better than that the common market should remove the duty on their oranges and maintain the duty for competitors outside the union. But the Italian car industry, which is now protected to a degree which almost gives it a domestic monopoly, is likely to be given the benefit of maximum permissible delay at each stage of tariff reduction. These tendencies would mean not only that the 'distorting' tariff reductions will take precedence over those that on balance may liberate trade and increase competition, but also that the processes of the transitional period may be particularly provocative and disturbing to the world economy.

The common market and the free trade area alike can improve the use of resources and raise productivity only to the extent that the removal of tariffs hurts producers inside, not outside, the union. To this extent, the discrimination inherent in the reductions in intra-regional tariffs will be less provocative to the outsiders. The longer is the transition during which careful consideration is given to producers within the union, the more will the de-merits outweigh the merits. But a gradual process in the reduction of tariffs is inevitable in any regional scheme; the road to union must pass through a swampy belt of half-measures, delayed action, exemptions, hardship clauses and distorting preferences.

Here again is the dilemma of any form of regionalism compared with either a universal or a unilateral reduction of tariffs. Ideally a regional system requires speedy, energetic and drastic steps, but in practice it cannot get them. In contrast a reduction of tariffs generally applied can proceed gradually without producing trade dislocations and distortions. However, for reasons set out above, the distortions of the common market are likely to be much more enduring or harmful than those of the free trade area: for they will be aggravated by the effects of its supra-national economic planning. Thus, for example, if the European Investment Bank really performs the task of controlling investment in the Six that is allotted to it, the common market will see to it that errors in the planning of capital uses will not become exposed to view and to test by free competition from abroad.

We see now that in taking the name 'Europe', the common market and its institutions (the European Economic Community, European Investment Bank, etc) usurp the name. Their discriminatory and disintegrating effect is now becoming more and more clear. At first the area of integration was to become that of the whole OEEC. But when the Outer Six took the Inner Six at their word and proposed the free trade area, the Inner Six became shy. More and more is heard about the difficulties of the free trade area. If these difficulties are as great as they are said to be, they confirm the rashness with which the common market has been rushed into being. Now we are told that if the 'outside countries' cannot join the common market, they must adjust themselves to the disintegration of Europe.

All this has happened because the architects of the common market were in such a hurry that they failed to realize that the Treaty of Rome would be a provocation to the other OEEC countries and would shake the structure of the Europe which had been pieced together by OEEC. If so thoughtful a statesman as M. Petitpierre, who directs the foreign policy of a country so prudent as Switzerland, has thought fit to declare in the Swiss Parliament that the discrimination of the common market would threaten the foundations of the EPU, the true friends of Europe must sit up and take notice. As M. Petitpierre went on to say, a country like Switzerland, with which the Six may have a negative balance of payments, cannot be expected to continue to extend credits, in lieu of payments in gold, in order to cushion countries that discriminate against Swiss exports while they enjoy the free opportunities offered by Switzerland for their exports. Such discrimination not only would be contrary to the spirit of OEEC and EPU, but also is forbidden by the treaties relating to them. The Austrian Government has sounded a similar warning, and, of course, the British position is known to be on similar lines.

If Europe has to choose between the common market without the free trade area and the state of affairs existing before either was mooted, there can be little doubt that the latter is to be preferred. If there can be no free trade area then let it be recognized that the path chosen by the Rome Treaty has been a mistake. We could then press forward with greater energy for the integration of Europe along the OEEC path. Such a renunciation would have to be called for in the name of European integration, of which the most vocal supporters have been the architects of the common market. This would offer the finest proof of their 'Europeanship'. On the other hand, it is too early to write off the free trade area, and it is still possible for the common market countries to show their true 'Europeanship' by making sure that the common market is capped by the free trade area. But the free trade area must genuinely befit its name. The temptation to bridge the gap by compromises on fundamentals may be just as dangerous as the complete rejection of the project. In this connection the proposals by the industrial federations of the Outer Six countries are well conceived and reasonable. They ought not to be the subject of compromise.

Obviously we cannot close our eyes to the danger that the common market Six will continue on their course regardless of the effect on Europe. But even if we make the most favourable assumption and proceed on the basis that the immensely difficult task is achieved of fusing the common market into a free trade area worthy of the name, problems will still face us. The list is headed by the problem of monetary equilibrium and the national balances of payments, in short the problem to which a solution was found before such words as 'integration', 'harmonization', 'European this and that' became common currency.

NOTES

1. (p. 259) Economic Integration:

See the author's *'Integration und Desintegration der internationalen Wirtschaft'* (Wirtschaftsfragen der freien Welt, Frankfurt a. M., 1957).

2. (p. 263) Concentration of production:

'There are few industries, even where large-scale production is common, in which there are not plants of moderate size which are as efficient, or nearly as efficient, measured in unit-costs, as the giant plants; and there are few giant firms which do not maintain some of their plants, presumably at a profit, on a moderate scale'. – J. VINER, 'The Customs Union Issue', New York, 1950, p. 46.

3. (p. 266) The tariff area:

The theory of customs unions, in its modern form, demonstrates that the less alike are the economies of the member-countries, and hence the less is the competition between them, the less will be the amount of trade freed by a union, and the greater the danger of diversion of trade from lower-cost producers outside the union. It is true that the greater the geographical extent of the customs union, the more will trade within it be freed; but if this extent increases heterogeneity it will tend to raise the ring-fence, and the net effect on trade may be harmful.

4. (p. 266) Tariffs:

It is such a privilege to have low tariffs! The advice given on February 12, 1958, to the French Government by the *Conseil Economique* (intended as the *coup de grâce* of the free trade area) was: 'The absence of a common external tariff, and the inequality of terms of supply of war materials, especially of certain overseas products, set up a risk that there will be a diversion of trade to the benefit of those foreign countries having a weak customs protection'.

270

REGISTER OF PERSONS

272

SUBJECT INDEX

274